TUSCANY FOR THE SHAMELESS HEDONIST

ARIELA BANKIER

2014

Front Cover Photo: JeniFoto/shutterstock.com

Back Cover Photo: TomaB/shutterstock.com

Series Manager: Ariela Bankier

Editor: Emma Tracey

Technical Editor: Lisa Smith

Graphic design: Jim Gaffney

Map: Julie Witmer

General note: Travel information tends to change quickly. In addition, the recent economic crisis has influenced many businesses and attractions, including restaurants and hotels. Shops may close without notice, and some sites may change, or reduce, their opening hours unexpectedly. For this reason, we recommend confirming the details in this guide before your departure, just to be on the safe side.

Disclaimer: Although the author of this guide has made every effort to provide readers with the most accurate and up-to-date information (as of the date of publication), she accepts no responsibility for any damages, loss, injury, or inconvenience sustained by readers of this guide. The author makes no warranties or representations of any kind regarding the accuracy of the information (text or maps) listed in this guide, including the completeness, suitability or availability of the products and services listed, and does not endorse, operate, or control any of the products or services listed in this guide. The author is in no event liable for any sort of direct or indirect or consequential damages that arise from the information found in this guide. If you have come across any errors in this guide, please let us know so we can correct our future editions. If you have any comments or concerns, please write to this address: info@travel-italy.guru

Thank you!

Tuscany *for the* Shameless Hedonist

The difference between a good trip, and an incredible one

ARIELA BANKIER

Contents

Contents

There is a difference between a good trip, and an incredible one.

And while planning a reasonably enjoyable vacation in Tuscany isn't too much of a challenge, designing a unique and memorable journey is an entirely different story.

Tuscany for the Shameless Hedonist was written for travelers who, much like us, want more. For those who aren't interested in settling for the usual round of restaurants, standard hotels, and touristy shops and sites that are listed in most guides. Rather, it was written for fellow travelers who seek to discover and experience the very best that Tuscany has to offer—from a dinner in a real, active jail to exclusive boutique shops, from tiny delicious restaurants only the locals know about to fantastic wine tours, from beautiful night spas to thousand year old castles and moonlit horseback treks across the Chianti hills.

This guide is the result of years of research, and includes several suggestions and ideas that will speak to different travelers. It was composed with passion and, naturally, reflects our taste. But we have taken into account the opinions of many others. We have trusted the experiences of friends, family, and local connoisseurs, too, in the hope of offering a comprehensive and balanced list. For this reason, we recommend using this guide as a reference book. Read through it, pick the suggestions that interest you most, and incorporate them into your trip. Even if you use no more than five to ten of our recommendations, we are confident those will be some of the most memorable moments of your vacation.

There is something for everyone in the guide. **Foodies and wine lovers** will discover dozens of recommendations to help them navigate Tuscany's myriad restaurants, wine cellars, specialty food shops, and eateries. We make suggestions on where to buy sumptuous olive oils, moist ricciarelli biscuits, flawless focaccias, artisanal pecorino, and glorious truffles. We list the restaurants where you can enjoy fresh, perfectly prepared seafood, tender steaks and *cinta sense* cold cuts, delicious pasta, ribollita, and antipasti. We bring you to the best gelato in Florence, the most delectable chocolatier in Lucca, and to the finest Michelin-starred restaurants. And of course we explain the regional wine tradition; where to buy the best bottles of Chianti, Brunello, and the Super-Tuscans, which monastery prepares the most delicious tonics, how to traverse the *enoteche* of Montepulciano and San Gimignano, and which wine tours and tastings should not be missed.

Shopping enthusiasts and those looking to get up close and personal with the best of Italian fashion will enjoy our tips. For bargain-hunters, we know all about discount Dolce & Gabbana, Prada, or Roberto Cavalli in Tuscany's leading outlet stores. We also explore prestigious antique and décor shops in Lucca, small family-run boutiques stocking handmade leather goods in Florence, as well as some of the most fashionable boutiques in the region. Those looking for unique souvenirs will enjoy our tips on where to find traditional, artisanal alabaster artifacts in Volterra and hand-made fashionable Italian jewelery in Pisa.

Nature buffs and experience seekers will appreciate our tips about guided hikes and excursions, including incredible jeep-led tours of the marble quarries in Carrara and hikes across the stunning Orcia Valley. We also offer lists of the best panoramic spots in Tuscany, hidden corners for a memorable picnic, and secret little areas of natural beauty that will take your breath away. **History and art lovers** will revel in our suggestions of colorful and century old medieval parades and jousting matches, little known museums and Renaissance-era villas that once belonged to the Medici family, and tours of historical gardens which are still owned by noble families.

We make a point of recommending activities that are suitable for various budgets. And while we do propose a number of high-end resorts and pricey award-winning restaurants, we also believe that a shameless hedonist doesn't necessarily have to be a big spender. Years of traveling in Tuscany have proven to us that price is not always a reflection of quality; in fact, many of the most delicious and unique discoveries we've made in this region are surprisingly affordable.

Lastly, we do our best to make our readers' traveling experience as easy and hassle-free as possible, leaving them time and energy to focus on authentic Tuscany at its best. For this reason, we have included valuable information in our detailed introduction that will help you bypass the most common tourist pitfalls. We have also included a detailed index at the end of the book, listing the featured attractions and recommendations by category. To read more of our reviews and updates, visit us at: www.travel-italy.guru

We hope you have a wonderful Tuscan adventure, and discover the charms of this region just as we have been doing for the past decade.

Buon Viaggio!

Ariela Bankier

Map of Tuscany

How Long Will It Take to Get There?

Florence to Pisa, 1.2 hours

Florence to Radda in Chianti, 1 hour

Florence to Montepulciano, 1.2 hours

Florence to Lucca, 1 hour

Florence to Siena, 1 hour

Florence to Arezzo, 1 hour

Siena to Pienza and Montalcino, 1 hour

Siena to San Gimignano, 40 minutes

Siena to Porto Ercole, 1.5 hours

San Gimignano to Volterra, 40 minutes

Lucca to Carrara, 45 minutes

Lucca to Forte dei Marmi, 30 minutes

Pisa to Bolgheri, 1 hour

Montepulciano to Cortona, 40 minutes

Planning Your Trip

Choosing When to Travel

Tuscany changes from season to season and each season has its advantages and disadvantages. Most tourists visit Tuscany during the summer months, with July being Florence's busiest period. There are pros and cons to summer travel in Tuscany. On the one hand, most of the cultural events and festivities take place in the summer and the days are longer, which means you can get more done. The fine weather permits you to explore the countryside, to hike or laze on the beach, and hours of operation for attractions are longer, as they are adapted for the influx of tourists. On the other hand, everything is crowded and there are lines for every major attraction. Italians are on vacation, too, so the beaches and major tourist attractions are absolutely packed. Hotel prices are also higher, and a well-located apartment, room, or villa can cost 35–40% more during the high season.

The loveliest time of the year to visit Tuscany, in our opinion, is in September and October, just before the *Vendemia*, the vintage or fall grape harvest, when the air cools down but the days are still long and the majority of places are still open. After November, rain tends to spoil most of the fun, and several places—including restaurants, museums, and attractions—close down or drastically reduce their hours until the season begins again in April or May. Spring is also very pleasant, and in May and June you will enjoy, for the most part, great weather, although some rain is still possible.

Documents You'll Need before Leaving

If you are an EU citizen, you will just need your ID card. We also recommend bringing your national health certificate with you, which allows you to receive free emergency medical treatment if needed. If you are from outside of the EU, you will need to bring a passport. Passports must be valid for at least six more months from the date of your entry into Italy. We also recommend making photocopies and virtual copies of all your important documents in case anything gets lost or stolen. Scan the documents and e-mail them to yourself, or save them onto a USB, or both.

If you plan on renting a car, you will need a driver's license and a credit card. Most companies require at least two years' of driving experience and the credit card must be under the same name as the driver's license.

You may also want to print out driving directions to your hotels or at least the hotel where you'll be staying your first night.

If you've booked your ticket or rented your car online, print out the confirmation letter and the e-tickets. Some companies require just the code you were sent; others require the actual printed ticket/voucher, especially if there is a barcode on it.

If flying with low-cost companies, like Ryanair or EasyJet for example, carefully read about their check-in process and luggage limitations, which can be very strict.

Local Money

Like the rest of the EU, prices in Italy are in Euro. As of May 2014, 1 euro was worth about $1.36 or £0.83, though you should check the rates yourself before traveling. You can change money in the airport and in most city centers, though it is much easier to find a place to change money in Florence than in Pisa, Lucca, or Siena, let alone the smaller hill towns. When changing money, either in Italy or in your home country, ask for bills no higher than 50 euro. 100 euro bills are hard to break and 500 euro bills, which are very rare, will arouse suspicion.

If you have an international credit card (A very useful item; contact your bank for more information.) you can also simply withdraw money, in the local currency, from ATMs across Italy. Though these cards do save a great deal of hassle, they are also notorious for the high commissions the banks charge, both for the withdrawals and for the conversion from Dollars/Pounds to Euro, so do check in advance what those might be. We also recommend notifying your bank before you leave the country that you will be using your card abroad. Several travelers have forgotten to do so, and their card was blocked, because it was assumed that their card was stolen and was being used fraudulently. Lastly, note that American credit cards and European credit cards have different security systems. While the new standard in Europe is a card with a microchip (and a PIN code), many cards in the US still rely on magnetic strips. Though most machines in Italy will be able to read both types of cards, some machines, especially automatic machines (such as ticket selling machines in train stations, gas machines in gas stations, etc.), might not be able to read your card. If that happens, either use cash instead of your card, or go to the ticket office, where they usually have more sophisticated machines that should be able to charge whichever card you have.

Fraud

Two of the most common frauds involve false bills/coins and identity theft. The probability that you will be given a false 20 euro, or even 100 euro, bill is extremely low. This trick is mostly used in stores when trying to scam the owner. False coins, however, are a popular trick in markets; check the 2 euro coin you're given as change to make sure it really is a 2 euro coin and not an old 500-lire coin. The two look very similar but the lire is obviously now worth nothing. Identity theft happens when thieves attach a small camera to ATMs to steal PIN numbers. Simply cover your hand with your other hand, your wallet, or a scarf while entering the PIN code to avoid any problems.

Crime

Tuscany is a very calm area, and even though there is, naturally, some criminal activity, as there is in any other country in the world, it is rare for tourists to feel unsafe. The biggest hassle is pickpockets, especially in Florence. The city's main train station, *Santa Maria Novella*, is particularly notorious, as are the bus stops, especially the number 7 bus stop, leading to Fiesole. A little common sense will go a long way to avoid unpleasant events. Don't carry all of your money in one purse so that, even if you do get targeted, you won't lose $600. If your hotel has a reliable safe, leave some of your money there. Don't put your wallet in your pocket or in the outer or side pockets of your backpack or purse, where it can be pulled out without you even noticing. We promise you that the pickpockets in Florence could teach Oliver Twist and his crew a trick or two.

Don't put your documents and your cash in the same wallet, that way if your wallet does happen to be stolen, you will still have your passports and tickets, and your vacation won't be ruined. Keep a piece of paper with the emergency number of your credit card company so you can call immediately if your credit card is stolen, and always take extra care when in touristy, crowded spaces, or on packed transport. If you do get robbed, you will need to file a complaint at the police station, so they can help you get new documents and for insurance purposes. Try do this as quickly as possible as some banks and insurance companies insist that you lodge a complaint within the first twenty-four hours of the robbery.

Insurance

Consider taking out some sort of travel and luggage insurance. There are several options available, and a quick search online will yield affordable results. If you plan on partaking in any physical activities while on vacation, from horseback riding to Vespa rides, good travel insurance becomes an even better idea.

Emergency Numbers and Medical Emergencies

Call 113 or 112 from any phone to reach the police.

Call 118 for an ambulance.

If you need a pharmacy or a hospital or any other shop or service, call 1254. This number will put you in touch with a sort of information service, where an operator will help you find whatever you are looking for. Alternatively, use the Italian yellow pages website: www.paginegialle.it

Doctors in Florence

A standard visit to the doctor costs between 80–100 euro; a higher fee may be charged if you show up without an appointment. If there is an emergency, go directly to the hospital. You won't be turned away, even if you don't have insurance, and it may very well cost less than a private doctor.

Dr. Stephen Kerr is a general practitioner/family physician trained in Britain. Office hours: weekday mornings and afternoons (by appointment); weekday afternoons, 3:00 p.m. to 5:00 p.m. (without appointments). His clinic is in Piazza Mercato Nuovo 1, Florence. Tel and Fax: 055.288055, Cell: 335.8361682, www.dr-kerr.com

Dr. Giovanni Fazi is a dentist, trained in the US. Office hours: Monday–Friday, 9:30 a.m.–1:00 p.m., 2:30 p.m.–7:30 p.m. His office is in Via A. La Marmora 22, Florence. Tel: 055.583258

To find a full list of doctors in all of Tuscany, consult the American or British embassy websites—both offer an updated list of English-speaking physicians.

Regardless, we highly recommend packing some basic medicine with you, especially if you suffer from any medical conditions. Ear and eye drops, analgesic medicine, anti-acid medicine, vitamins, and, of course, whatever prescription drugs you require. (Bring extra, just in case.) There are numerous pharmacies in Tuscany, but they won't necessarily carry the specific medicine you are used to, and trying to translate the name, or finding out the local equivalent of the medicine you need when you are ill can be quite a hassle.

Calling Home and Using the Internet while in Italy

Aside from the well-known apps and programs you can use on your computer or smart-phone to call home, such as Skype or WhatsApp, you can also buy a local SIM card to use during your travels. This is a good idea if you plan on staying for a week or more in Italy. Keep the SIM after you go back home, and use it for your next trip to Italy. It should remain functional for two to five years.

A local SIM card will work with your phone as long as you have a GSM-compatible, unlocked phone—which means it will work in Europe—and your phone allows the use of SIM cards other than the original one. If you don't have such a phone, you can get one in Italy for as little as 40 euro for a basic phone and slightly more for a phone with Internet. An Italian SIM card costs 5 euro to 10 euro and is already charged with that amount of money. You can add more money to it and activate an Internet service that will allow you to use your phone and the internet for a very low fee during your entire trip in Italy. You will need an ID or passport to buy a SIM card, as the shop must make a photocopy for legal reasons. Normally, within 24 hours or less, your phone will be activated. You can buy a SIM card at any of the main cell phone operators' shops, which can be found on the main street of the larger towns; we personally recommend TIM and VODAFON.

Ask for a *ricaricabile*, which means pay as you go, and ask the shop to activate the cheapest Internet offer they have, which usually works out at around 9 euro per month. Make sure to remember to deactivate the offer when you leave Italy.

If you are using your own phone, make sure you deactivate international data roaming, which can be very costly.

Getting Into Italian Mode

Hours of operation

As time goes by, more shops and museums are adopting what is known as *orario continuato*, which means they are open all day long, but this is not yet the norm for Italian businesses. Many places, especially in smaller towns, still operate according to traditional business hours.

Shops: Monday–Saturday: 9:30/10:00 a.m.–1:00 p.m. and 3:30/4:00/5:00 p.m.–7:00/7:30 p.m. Sunday: Most shops are either closed or open during the morning hours only. Several shops are also closed on Monday mornings. In smaller towns, it is common to find that all shops are closed for no apparent reason on a specific weekday, and that weekday changes from town to town (though it is usually either Monday, Tuesday, or Wednesday).

Banks: Monday–Friday: 8:30 a.m.–12:30/1:00/1:30 p.m. and 2:00/2:30 p.m.–3:30/4:00/4:30 p.m.

Trains: There are very few trains after 10:00 p.m. and virtually no trains between midnight and 5:00 a.m., except for a few night trains, which cross the region and make a number of stops.

Museums: It depends on the specific museum, but several museums are closed on Mondays. The museums in Florence are particularly known for their tricky opening days and hours. Luckily, you can pick up a printed sheet with the updated opening times of all the Florentine museums from the local tourist office, which is located in front of the Santa Maria Novella train starion in Florence.

National Holidays

Everything, including museums, attractions, and most shops and restaurants, will be closed on:

January 1st	(New Year's Day)
January 6th	(Epiphany)
Monday after Easter	(Easter Monday)
April 25th	(Liberation Day)
May 1st	(International Workers' Day)
June 2nd	(Republic Day)
August 15th	(Assumption Day)
November 1st	(All Saints' Day)
December 8th	(Immaculate Conception Day)
December 25th	(Christmas)
December 26th	(St. Stephen's Day)

Traveling Off-Season and In August

August, though part of the high season, is a month when many Italians go on vacation. Although they often don't bother to make any mention of it on their websites, many restaurants and shops may close for a week or two, for what is known as *ferie*, or holiday. This is most common during the second and third weeks of August. If you are traveling during that period, it might be a good idea to double-check if a place is open before driving specifically to visit it. You should also know that a lot of markets will be closed, too, and since the Italians themselves are on vacation, it might be more difficult to find an available room in popular resorts, especially on the beach. For these reasons, July is a better month to travel in Tuscany.

When traveling off-season, from December to April, you run the risk of finding quite a few places, such as various attractions, restaurants, shops, and even some museums closed or with reduced hours of operation. While most, though not all, restaurants in the main cities, such as Florence, Siena and Lucca, do remain open, many restaurants in the countryside and in small towns will shut down completely during the winter, especially if their clientele usually consists of tourists rather than local patrons. In addition, many restaurants, including those in the main cities, will shut down for the winter break, which lasts from the third week of December until January 7th. Certain tourist attractions may also close down in January and February and reopen in March. Double check everything to be on the safe side. This is yet another advantage of having a local SIM; you can always call before driving somewhere, avoiding the disappointment of finding a closed gate.

Understanding Italian Addresses and Phone Numbers

Home and office telephone numbers have an area code, followed by the number. Rome's area code, for example, is 06. Milan's is 02. Most towns in Tuscany have an area code that begins with 05. Florence's code, for example, is 055. Pisa's is 050. Whether you call a number from within Italy or from abroad, you will have to dial the full area code, including the zero at the beginning, unlike area codes in other countries, where you remove the zero when calling from abroad.

Cell phone numbers begin with 3. For example: 338.2222222 or 329.4444444, etc.

Addresses in Italy will always include the name of the province in which a town is located. For example: Via Dante 4, Altopascio (Lucca). In this case, Lucca is the province. The reason the province is added to the address is that you will find several towns by the same name in all of Italy, and without specifying the province, there will be confusion. This is also helpful to remember when you are setting your GPS.

Note that in some cases, especially when looking for hotels, *agriturismi*, and restaurants that are located in the countryside, you will encounter this type of address:

Agriturismo Buongiorno, Via Puccini 14, Loc. San Giuliano Terme, Pisa

Loc. stands for *località*, and it simply means a suburb, or a small village, that technically is part of the town but is physically located outside the town itself. If you don't have a car, you will have a very difficult time reaching these places. Another type of address you may encounter is:

Agriturismo Ciao Bella, Pod. Marche, Volterra (PI)

Pod. stands for *podere*, which means a farm. In this example, the farm is located near Volterra (but not actually in Volterra), which is within the province of Pisa (PI). A *podere* will always be in the countryside. Typically this address will belong to a horseback riding farm, a rural *agriturismo*, or even a remote restaurant. If you book an *agriturismo* or dinner in such a place, see if they can give you their GPS coordinates, which will make navigation much easier.

Transportation

Arriving in Tuscany by Plane

The main airport in Tuscany isn't the one in Florence, as many would expect, but the Galileo Galilei Airport in Pisa. Thanks to several low-cost companies that have diverted their flights to Pisa in recent years, the airport has significantly grown and improved. It is small but modern and efficient, very close to town, and close to the highway. All of the major car rental companies have offices on the premises. If you are arriving from Europe, you will find the best deals with low-cost companies like Ryanair and EasyJet, who both fly to Pisa. If you are flying from the USA, there are daily direct Delta flights from New York to Pisa. Alitalia and several other companies also offer direct flights to Pisa, as well as connecting flights to various Italian cities. Find out more here: www.pisa-airport.com.

If you have landed in Pisa, and plan to rent a car, we recommend renting one at Pisa's airport, and not in Florence, for two reasons. Firstly, Pisa offers more convenient offices, with all the leading companies gathered in one space, connected to the airport, instead of scattered around town. Second, and more importantly, many rental companies in Florence are located inside the city center, not in a ZTL area, but near to one. See the explanation below about what a ZTL is and why it should be avoided. This means that, once you get your car, while trying to drive out of the city center and get on the highway, you might find yourself accidentally entering a ZTL area. The rental car offices in Pisa, on the other hand, are just a few meters from the main highway.

Moving Around in Tuscany

A common dilemma for many visitors to Tuscany is whether they should rent a car or not. The short answer to that question is yes, you should rent a car. Without a car, it will be very difficult to visit anything off the beaten path, including hill towns, wineries and vineyards, and special little restaurants and resorts. You won't be able to book a stay in a charming little *agriturismo* or B&B either, as those are not serviced by public transport. Without a car, you stand to waste a great deal of your time by having to depend on the sometimes erratic bus schedules, which are especially difficult on Sundays and holidays.

The only case in which you don't need to rent a car is when traveling in Florence, Pisa, Lucca, and Siena. If you plan on visiting only these four destinations, and nothing in the countryside, then you can do very well using only public transportation. In fact, if your visit is limited to Florence, Pisa, Lucca, and Siena, then driving a car is not only unnecessary, it's actually a bad idea. These are all towns whose historical centers, or *centro storico*, are marked as a ZTL, *Zona Traffico Limitato* or limited traffic zone. This means they are closed for non-residential traffic. Drive into a ZTL area without a permit and a hefty fine of around 100 euro will arrive by mail. Since all four major towns are easily accessible by train, and their historical centers are small enough to be visited by foot, a car really isn't necessary.

Driving, Parking, and Renting a Car in Italy

Driving in Italy

If you are an EU citizen, your driving license is valid in Italy, and you need no other documentation. If you are traveling from outside the EU, you need to obtain an international driving permit before leaving for Italy. Driving in Italy is just like driving in any other country. Don't be intimidated by stories of horrifying and insane Italian drivers; for the most part, they are not true.

There are two kinds of highways in Italy: free and toll. Those with a toll are called *autostrada*, and they are marked with green road signs. The free roads have different names but are always marked with blue road signs. From Pisa to Florence, for example, you can take the free, blue-marked Fi-Pi-Li, or the Autostrada A11, which is a motorway with a toll, marked with green signs. The advantages of the tolled *autostrada* are that it takes less time to reach your destination and the maximum speed limit is higher. It can be up as high as 130 kph (kilometers per hour).

The maximum amount of alcohol permitted in your blood while driving is 0.5 mg/ml. This is especially relevant if you plan on doing any wine tasting in the many delightful little vineyards scattered throughout Tuscany during your trip.

The ZTL is an issue that many tourists aren't aware of. They should be, however, as it is the main reason tourists are fined when traveling in Italy. Most towns in Italy protect their historical center, which is where most of the attractions are, by defining it as a ZTL, a limited traffic area, where only residents can drive and/or park. There are security cameras at the entrance to any ZTL area that register your vehicle number and send you, or your rental company, a fine, which, together with handling fees charged by the rental company, will be about 100 euro.

Stories about tourists getting confused and entering the same ZTL area three times in less than 10 minutes and being fined each time are more common than you'd think. Our best advice is to simply avoid driving in the city, especially in Florence. Most town centers in Tuscany are so small you don't really need a car anyway. If arriving with a car, park in a car park outside the *centro storico* and walk or take a bus to the center. You will usually find very accessible car parks, especially in touristy towns.

What does a ZTL sign look like? A white circle surrounded by a red ring and next to it another sign saying ZTL (or *zona traffico limitato*).

Parking in Italy

Parking spaces marked with white lines, or no lines at all, mean parking is free. That is, of course, unless there is a sign prohibiting parking in that area. Blue lines mean you have to pay for parking: look for the parking meters around the parking lot, decide how long you will stay, and put the appropriate amount of change in the machine. Take the receipt the machine prints out, and put it, facing out, on the dashboard of your car, near the steering wheel. Yellow parking lines mean you can't park there; such spaces are reserved for those with a permit.

Renting a Car in Italy

The major rental companies in Italy are Avis, Europcar, Sixt, and Hertz. We suggest looking into all four before booking a car. You can rent a car in Italy if you are over 21 and have had a license for more than two years. Some companies require only one year of experience. When renting a car, you have to present a personal identification document, a passport or ID card for EU citizens, and a credit card, though not a debit card. Both must belong to the person who is renting the car. For example, you can't rent a car with Mr. Smith's license and pay with Mrs. Smith's credit card; the names on both the document and the card must be the same. There are a number of insurance options, but we recommend taking the most comprehensive one. Regardless of the type of insurance you have, mark every scratch and bump on the car. Some insurance deals declare themselves as all-inclusive, but the small print can reveal that damage to mirrors, for example, or lower parts of the car or wheels, is not covered.

You should know that most cars in Italy have a hand gear, or stick. If you don't feel comfortable driving such a car, make sure you specifically order a model you are comfortable with. Cars that run on diesel will save you money.

Always fill up the gas tank when returning the car; you will be charged extra if the company has to fill it up for you. You may also be charged extra for returning the car very dirty. You don't have to take it to the car wash; just make sure it's acceptably clean. Charges can also be incurred for returning the car at a different office than the one where you picked it up, for handling any fines or tickets you received, and for renting accessories such as a GPS, snow chains, baby seats, etc.

GPS units are very useful and we highly recommend using them with this guide for a number of reasons. First, they are far more comfortable to use than maps (phone apps like Waze are excellent, but will consume your battery very quickly, leaving you lost with a lifeless phone). Second, signs in Italy are often hard to understand or follow. It is not unusual to find a tiny sign indicating the exit to the town you need just a few meters before the exit itself. Often signs on regular country roads (i.e., not *autostrada*) are quite small and can't be easily seen from afar. On rural roads, which are also very poorly illuminated, it is highly unlikely that you will see any of the signs at all if driving after dark. A GPS will save you the hassle of having to play detective, and indicate when and where to turn. If you plan on renting a car with a GPS for a week or more, it's probably cheaper to buy your own GPS, as long as it has recently updated European maps on it. You can walk into any of the three largest chain stores for electronics in

Italy, Mediaworld, Euronics or Unieuro, and buy a GPS for less than 100 euro, inclusive of all world maps, and then take it back home with you.

Snow chains are obligatory by law if traveling between mid-November and mid-April in Tuscany. Rental companies never seem to mention this fact, but if you are stopped by the police, and don't have either snow chains or winter tires, it is you who will have to pay a hefty fine, not the rental company.

One last thing, try not to fill your car with gas on Sundays. There usually is no one manning gas stations on Sundays, so you will have to use the automatic machine, which isn't complicated at all, but may be a problem if you don't have the exact change.

Moving Around in Tuscany on Public Transport

Trains

Trains are a great way to move around and reach the main towns (Florence, Siena, Pisa, Lucca, Grosseto, Livorno, etc.). The central station will often be called *Stazione Centrale*, pronounced "statsione chentrale" and marked like this: FS. Alternatively, it may simply be based on the city's name: Pisa Centrale, Siena Centrale, Lucca Centrale, etc. There are a few exceptions to this rule. Florence's main train station, for example, is called Firenze SMN (*Firenze Santa Maria Novella*).

There are a number of train companies in the country, but in Tuscany there is just one, Trenitalia, which is also the largest company in Italy. While other companies cover only parts of the Italy, Trenitalia covers every nook and cranny. Find out more here: www.trenitalia.com.

Buying a Ticket

The Trenitalia trains can be divided into two categories: regular trains, known as regional or IC trains, and high-speed trains, known as *freccia* trains. When traveling inside Tuscany, you will mostly be using the regional trains. The high-speed *freccia* trains connect major cities—like Rome and Milan or Florence and Venice—but not small towns like the ones in Tuscany. *Freccia* tickets are more expensive and they have a specific time and place for booking. Regional trains, on the other hand, have no specific booking restrictions. When purchasing a ticket from the self-service machines, you will be given the option to purchase first class tickets on the regional trains. However, on regional trains, unlike *Freccia* trains, first class looks no different to second class, and sometimes is even unmarked. So, on regional trains, it makes sense to choose the second class option and save the money!

To buy a ticket in the train station, either go to the ticket office (*Biglietteria*, in Italian), or use the self-service machines. The self-service machines are easy to use, and you can select a menu in English, too. Though before you start take a look at the illustrations on top of the machine; some only have an illustration of a credit card, which means they don't accept cash.

A useful tip is that if you are traveling a short distance, usually under 80 km, from Pisa to Florence, for example, you can buy a generic "up to X km" ticket at a newspaper stand, instead of waiting in line at the ticket office. Just make sure this ticket covers the right distance. Ask the vendor, "*Va bene per X?*" meaning, "Is this ticket okay for reaching X?"

Always validate your ticket before getting on the train in one of the little yellow, or more modern white and green, machines near the tracks. A ticket is valid for six hours from the moment it is validated. A non-validated ticket can lead to a hefty fine.

Finding Your Way in the Train Station

With the exception of Florence, most train stations in Tuscany are rather small. Tracks are called *binari* (or *binario* in singular). In every station you will find screens or electronic boards listing the departing trains—*partenze* in Italian.

It can happen that when you go to look for your train on the departures board, the board may list a different destination than what is on your ticket. Let's say, for example, that you've just bought a ticket to go to Pisa from the Florence train station. Your ticket says "Pisa" and you were told at the ticket office that the train will leave at 4:00 p.m. Yet, when you check the departures (*partenze*) board to find out from which track (*binario*) your train is leaving, you can't see a train leaving to Pisa at 4:00, only a train to Livorno. Don't be alarmed. The station that appears on the departures board is the final destination and most regional trains (and some high speed trains) make several stops along the way. It is very likely that the stop you need to reach isn't the final destination of the train, which is why it doesn't appear on the board. Simply walk to the track and check the more detailed board on the track itself. It will list all the stops along the route. If you are still unsure simply ask one of the personnel at the station.

Urban Buses

Every town and city has its own bus system. This means that a bus ticket you bought in Florence won't be valid in Siena and the bus ticket you bought in Pisa is useless in Lucca. Small towns in the same area, on the other hand, are usually serviced by the same company.

The easiest way to buy a bus ticket is at a newspaper stand, or at the *Tabaccaio* (cigarette shop). There is always a newspaper stand in medium-sized and large train stations. Ask for a bus ticket, "*Un biglietto per l'autobus per favore,*" (pronounced, "oon bilieto per l'aootobus, per favore"). If there is no place to buy a ticket, try buying one on board, though it will be more expensive and the driver will ask for the exact amount. It is unlikely he will be able to break any bills.

Like the train, you must validate your bus ticket once you get on the bus. While the validating machines for trains are outside the train, on the platform, the validating machines for buses are inside the bus itself. These are usually little machines at the front and back of the bus. Depending on the city, bus tickets are usually valid for about an hour from the moment you validate them.

Extra-Urban Buses

Most towns can be reached by train or by bus. Several towns, specifically hill towns (such as San Gimignano, Volterra, Cortona, Monteriggioni, Radda, Greve and many others), can only be reached by bus as the trains can't climb such high paths. These buses are called extra-urban buses, and they usually leave from the train station or a block or two away. Extra-urban buses from Florence, for example, leave from an area located just two minutes away from the station. With your back to Santa Maria Novella, turn right, and walk along the street until you see the buses.

Eating and Drinking in Tuscany

Food is one of the greatest perks Italy has to offer, and this guide goes to great lengths to introduce visitors in Tuscany to the many gastronomic delights available in the region.

Italian food served outside of Italy can be quite different from the original version. Italian restaurants in the USA, for example, tend to prepare heavier, creamier versions of traditional Italian food, so it might take a few tries to get used to the new flavors. In this guide we chose to focus on the most authentic places. Among the recommendations listed you will find, side by side, high class bistros and street food vendors, Michelin-starred restaurants and tiny shops selling the freshest ricotta cheese, chic *osterie* run by promising chefs and award-winning olive oil mills, recommendations for luxurious hotel bars offering the best views, and an exhaustive list of farms in the valley selling pecorino cheeses and truffles. We feel that the mix of high and low is an important part of the uniqueness of Tuscany; you can find subtle brilliance in the most unexpected places and those that choose to focus solely on the well-known spots are surely missing out.

The Origins of Tuscan Cuisine

Tuscan kitchen is known as a "poor man's kitchen", and indeed, many dishes on the menu were originally born out of necessity. To understand the way these dishes came about and the basics of Tuscan cuisine, it is important to remember the peasant tradition from which modern Tuscan cuisine grew. While vast parts of Tuscany now seem like places of luxury, not that long ago, this was a relatively poor land.

Locals would use everything they had to survive, and nothing was ever thrown away. Three- to four-day old bread, for example, was transformed into a tasty and nourishing soup with beans, black cabbage, and other winter vegetables—

the famous *ribollita*. In the summer, it could be mixed with creamy tomato sauce to make the mushy but delicious *papa al pomodoro*. Alternatively, the most basic ingredients—vinegar, some vegetables from the family vegetable garden and olive oil—were tossed together with day-old bread to make the tarty and fresh *panzanella*. Bread wasn't the only ingredient that was never thrown away. To this day, there is a saying in Tuscany – *"del maiale non si butta niente"* meaning "you don't throw away any part of the pig." Indeed, it isn't rare to see older men and women buying traditional sausages made with certain parts of the pig that would make most tourists shudder away... But don't be put off by the humble origins of the Tuscan kitchen. With time and, as the region grew richer and more developed, the traditional dishes that were born out of necessity became more refined and, today, most of these have developed into delicious and popular delicacies that you will surely enjoy.

Nowadays, Tuscan cuisine is varied and each area of the region prides itself on its own typical specialties, in addition to the well-known pasta and meat dishes that you can find all over Tuscany. In Siena, you will find the *pici pasta*, a handmade, chubby *maccheroni*. In Livorno, the restaurants compete over who makes the best *cacciucco*, a typical fish and seafood stew. Lucca is famous for its *tortelloni*, filled with ricotta cheese and spinach and served with a meaty sauce which is similar to *ragu*. In Florence, they are proud not only of their steaks (the famous *Bistecca alla Fiorentina*, naturally), but also of their *lampredotto*, a dish made of the cow's fourth stomach, today a popular street food, served in a bun. The *maremma* region, in southern Tuscany, is famous for its meat, while the hilly towns in the Garfagnana, in northern Tuscany, are known for chestnut flour-based dishes, as well as their rich stews and their potato *focaccia*.

Eating Like a True Italian

The three main meals are *colazione, pranzo,* and *cena. Colazione*, or breakfast, is usually eaten at the bar. A bar in Italy isn't a place that serves alcohol but a place that serves coffee and snacks in the morning. Italian breakfast is very limited, which can be a big surprise for guests expecting a large ordeal involving eggs and bacon at their B&B. Instead, it usually consists of nothing more than cappuccino, brioche, and some marmalade or Nutella to spread over a piece of toast. *Pranzo*, or lunch, is usually served between 12:30 and 2:30 p.m. You will find very few, if any restaurants that serve lunch later than 2:30/3:00. *Cena*, or dinner, is served between 7:30 and 9:30 p.m. With the exception of pizzerias, most places won't seat you at a table after 9:30–10:00 p.m.

Unless you buy a sandwich to go or sit down for a light lunch in a bar, you will usually eat in either a *ristorante* or a *trattoria*, or an *osteria*. A *ristorante* is the more high-end, serious dining option; stylish and reserved with prices that match. *Osterie* and *trattorie* are more homely places; they cost less and have a more casual atmosphere, but they can also be huge discoveries, as they often offer excellent, authentic Tuscan food. *Trattoria Mario*, in Florence, is a perfect example. Here you'll find no-frills service, tiny tables, and waiters that yell the order right into your eardrum, but the food is delicious and as Florentine as you can get, and the prices are modest. *Il Campano* in Pisa and *Taverna San Giuseppe* in Siena are other examples of excellent places that combine an easy-going rustic feel with refreshing prices and, more importantly, quality dining. To discover the best Tuscany has to offer, we suggest mixing and matching, trying out both homestyle places and upscale, sophisticated restaurants.

Whichever restaurant you choose, whether it is a neighborhood diner or a 3-star extravaganza, remember that most restaurants have a day off in the week, even in high season. Whenever possible we have inserted the relevant info in the guide, but for other places not mentioned in this guide check the restaurant's website or call to see when they are closed.

What should we order?

Breakfast

If you ask for *un caffe*, you'll get an espresso. Alternatively, ask for a *cappuccino*, or for a *caffe latte*, which is closer to the Starbucks version of coffee, with a lot of milk. Note that if you ask for a *latte* (the popular American term), you will simply get a glass of milk and a perplexed look. You can also try a *macchiato*, which is an espresso with a touch of milk foam. Our personal recommendation for the hot summer months is to ask for a *shakerato*. This is a cold coffee, shaken with ice cubes. If you want it sweetened, make sure you ask for it *con zucchero*. Accompany that with a brioche or croissant; there are plenty to choose from, and they will all be on display, together with a small selection of savory sandwiches. If you eat standing up by the bar, as most Italians do, you will be charged less than if you sit down at the table and order. If it's been a long day of sightseeing, and you need an afternoon pick-me-up, you can always ask for *un caffe corretto*, which is an espresso "corrected" with a shot of grapa, sambuca or some other liqueur.

Lunch/Dinnertime

Traditionally, a meal starts with an *antipasto*, which is a selection of meats, cheeses, and other little bites that will awaken your appetite. The *primo*, or first dish, usually follows and is most typically pasta or soup, or a *risotto*. Next is the *secondo*, or main dish, which usually consists of meat or fish. The *secondo* can be served with a *contorno*, or side dish—usually of vegetables, roasted potatoes or French fries—and is followed by a *dolce*, or dessert and a coffee (*espresso* or a *macchiato*, an Italian will never order a *cappuccino* after his meal). At dinnertime, this is occasionally followed by an *ammazzacaffe*, also known as *digestivo*. This is a liqueur, like *limoncello*, (or, often, some local concoction made by the owner's grandmother) to help you digest. Of course the entire meal is accompanied by wine, whether that is the house wine or your choice of bottle, and water.

Clearly, you won't be able to order this much food every time you sit down to eat. What most Italians do is choose either a *primo* or a *secondo* and add to that something small that can be shared, like an *antipasto*, a *contorno*, or even just a dessert. Whatever your order, bread and water will be brought to the table. Bread is free, included in the price of the *coperto* (see below), while water is charged separately. You can ask for still water, called *naturale*, or fizzy water, called *frizzante*. We have yet to see an Italian restaurant that will serve tap water. Your bread basket will usually contain a few slices of Tuscan bread (which is unsalted), regular salted bread, and sometimes *focaccia* and *grissini* (though not always).

Naturally, when eating in a *trattoria* or *osteria*, you will be asked if you want the house wine to go with your food. Though the house wine is often perfectly tasty, in recent years we've started ordering a bottle from the menu. The reason is simple: if you are planning to drink more than a glass each, it is worth it to pay a little extra and get a bottle of something better to complement your meal, rather than settling for whatever the restaurant has on hand at the moment.

Antipasto

For the *antipasto*, you will often be served a plate of *salumi* (also known as *affettati*). *Salumi*, not to be confused with salami, is a general name for cold cuts, salami, and cured meats. This will typically include some of the Tuscan highlights such as *prosciutto* (usually *prosciutto crudo*, not *cotto*), salami and *finocchiona*, which is a salami seasoned with fennel seeds. Other, more specific *salumi* may also be included such as *lardo di colonnata* (a seasoned, aged lard from northern Tuscany, see tip 133); *prosciutto* or *salame di cinghiale*, meaning either a *prosciutto* or a salami made with wild boar meat; *prosciutto di cinta senese*, which is a *prosciutto* from an indigenous breed of Tuscan pig, called *cinta senese*; *bresaola*, or cured beef; *mortadella*; *pancetta*, and more. Another popular option is *crostoni*, or *crostini* (smaller than *crostoni*), which are slices of toasted bread, each with something different served on top. The most traditional is the *crostone toscano*, which is served spread with liver paté, but you will usually also find a *crostone* with *lardo di colonnata*, with black cabbage, mushrooms, tomatoes, or fresh olive oil (the famous *fettunta*). A cheese plate, which will typically include different kinds of *pecorino* cheese, possibly some goat cheeses, or even some gorgonzola, can also be served as an *antipasto*, but it will more commonly be either a second (main dish) or a dessert.

Primo

On the menu for the *primo* (the first dish) you will usually find either a soup or stew, like *ribollita*, or perhaps a bread salad, such as *panzanella*. However, the real stars of the *primo* section of the menu are, without a doubt, the pasta dishes, and the occasional *risotto* plate (*risotto* isn't typical of Tuscany but rather, of northern Italy). In fact, we often skip the *secondo* (main course) and focus on the pasta dishes, which are far more interesting and varied. *Pasta caccio e pepe* (pasta with caccio cheese and black pepper), *tagliatelle con ragu di cinghiale* (tagliatelle with wild boar ragu), *ravioli con ricotta e spinaci* (ravioli filled with ricotta and spinach, usually served with a butter and sage sauce), *gnudi* (nude ravioli, made of the filling without the actual pasta, served with a light buttery sauce), *pappardelle alla lepre* (flat, wide pasta served with rabbit ragu), *tortelli di patate* (potato-filled tortelli, served with ragu or other sauce), and *pici all'aglione con bricciole* (pici served with garlic and fried bread crumbs) are just a few of the typical first dishes you will find.

Secondo

For the main dish, the *secondi*, you will normally be given a choice of fish- or meat-based dishes, depending on the restaurant; though, in truth, most offer a selection of both. Tuscans love meat and, as such, meat dishes are treated with great importance. The *tagliata* (sliced steak served with different toppings: anything from *porcini* mushrooms to arugula and shavings of *parmiggiano reggiano*—parmesan cheese) is very popular, as is the famous *bistecca alla Fiorentina* (Florentine-style steak). This *bistecca* is a huge ordeal, priced by weight and served seared on the outside, bloody on the inside. If you like your meat well-done or if you simply don't have much of an appetite, then steer well clear of this dish. Also popular are *il peposo* (a beef stew), *arista* (pork roast), *bollito misto* (boiled beef), *caciucco*, (the famous fish and seafood stew from Livorno) and the *baccala* fish, which is served in different sauces.

Contorno

For the side dish, the *contorno*, you will often find *patate al forno* (oven baked potatoes), *patatine fritte* (French fries), *fagioli* (white beans), *spinaci* (spinach), *ceci* (chickpeas), *verdure alle brace/alla griglia* (roasted vegetables), *insalta mista/insalata verde* (a simple salad, though you should know that the Italian definition of a salad is very limited, usually involving little more than lettuce, a few other green leaves, and a couple of cherry tomatoes).

Cheese Plate

Personally, we can't get enough of the Tuscan cheeses. There are many recommendations in this guide for little *caseifici* (cheesemakers) who produce the very best of the best, places any foodie will appreciate. Even if you don't plan on driving across the countryside and doing some cheese tasting, you can still taste much of the best produce in shops and restaurants. A cheese platter will usually include a selection of the local *pecorino* cheeses served with marmalade and/or honey. The sweetness of the marmalade really brings out the deep flavors of the cheese, allowing you to more clearly appreciate the top quality produce of this region.

Pizza

Pizza, of course, is a hugely popular choice for many Italians. A meal in a *pizzeria* is much cheaper than a dinner in a *trattoria*. You can find *pizzerie* where you sit down at the table; while there are also places that sell slices to go, perfect for a picnic lunch or if you are short on time. We recommend choosing a pizzeria that advertises itself with the magic words *forno a legna* (real wood-burning stove). *Gusta Pizza* in Florence (Via Maggio 46), *Funicula* in Pisa (Lungarno Mediceo 32), *Pizza da Felice* in Lucca (Via Buia 12), and the pizza in the *Consorzio Agrario* in Siena (Via Piangiani 5, just off Via dei Banchi di Sopra) are all very good.

Vegetarians

There are a few precautions you should take when visiting restaurants in Italy as a vegetarian. First, you should know that most (but not all) soups are usually made with a meat or chicken stock. If you are unsure about the contents of a dish, just ask: *"Sono vegetariano, c'e' carne o pesce?"* (Pronounced, "Sono vegetariano, che carne o peshe?"). The Italian idea of vegetarian can be difficult, however. They have no trouble telling you if there's meat in the dish, but they often don't think it's a problem if there's chicken broth inside, or lard, or gelatine, or any other animal by-product. More than once we asked whether a certain dish was vegetarian, and were told that it was. On further investigation we found small pieces of salami in the sauce, or a distinct meaty flavor of the broth. When we enquired whether there was indeed any salami in the sauce we were often answered, "Yes, but just a little bit—for the taste!" by a rather offended cook. You should also know that most hard cheeses are prepared with *caglio*: rennet produced from cows. Some cheesemakers offer a cheese made with *caglio vegetale*, suitable for vegetarians. Vegetarians should also avoid anything containing *strutto* and *lardo*, both of which mean lard. It might seem strange, but *strutto* is sometimes found in breads, *focaccias*, and pastries.

Dessert

Italians have a talent for salty baked goods. Their *focaccias* and *schiacciatas* are famous world over. Italian desserts, on the other hand, can sometimes be a little disappointing, tend to suffer from a lack of imagination and are often rather heavy. With the exception of a real *ristorante*, desserts will typically be weak and not homemade. If they do make their desserts in-house, they will usually make a point of explicitly stating *dolci fatti in casa*, homemade dessert, on the menu. Peek around and look at the desserts served to others in the restaurant. If they look disappointing, skip them and head for a *gelato* instead. Strolling through quiet streets enjoying a good ice cream is often so much more pleasant than a heavy dessert in a *trattoria*.

If you are interested in trying the local desserts, here are a few options you will almost always find: *panna cotta* (cooked cream), *torta della nonna*, a cooked custard pie with pine nuts on top, and *torta del biscchero*, also known as *torta co' bischero*, which is a pie filled with chocolate, grapes, raisins, canned fruit, and pine nuts. The simplest dessert you will encounter are Tuscan biscuits, the *cantuccini* (known abroad as *biscotti*), which are typically served with a sweet local wine, the *vin santo*.

Tipping and the Coperto

To request the bill at the end of your meal simply ask the waiter for *"il conto per favore,"* pronounced as it is written. Once this is done, the issue of tipping arises. Restaurants in Italy charge what is called a *coperto*, which means a fixed fee for "opening the table." Contrary to what many tourists believe, it has nothing to do with how much bread you eat or whether you ask for water or not. It is rare for a restaurant to charge more than a 2 euro *coperto* for each person at the table, though be warned that if a restaurant is located in a very tourist-focused area, the price of the *coperto* will go up. Water is charged separately.

You may wish to leave a 10% tip at the end of a dinner. Only do this if you were especially pleased with the service, as it is not obligatory. Some restaurants, again mainly in the more popular touristy areas, have begun to add an automatic 10% service charge to the bill. This is added alongside the *coperto*, but it is not yet the norm. Tipping in taxis, hotels, etc. is totally up to you. To do so will be appreciated, but it isn't considered a major *faux pas* if you don't do it. The one case in which tipping may be a good idea is when someone goes out of their way to help you, in which case a tip is the best way to show your appreciation.

Italian Wine

There are many books written just on the complex and fascinating subject of Italian wines, so any introduction we give here is only meant to be used as a very general primer. If you are interested in a detailed account, we recommend writings by Kerin O'Keefe, Jancis Robinson, and Robert Parker, all of whom are extremely knowledgeable, interesting writers who have covered the subject in great depth. However, seeing as there are several recommendations in this guide for various wine tastings and tours, it would be foolish not to provide a general summary of the Italian wine industry.

The most famous wines in Tuscany are Chianti, Brunello, Nobile di Montepulciano, Morellino di Scansano, Carmignano, Vernaccia di San Gimignano, and Bolgheri (one of the leading Super-Tuscans).

Chianti

Tuscany's pride and joy, is divided according to the areas which make it. Chianti made in the area around Siena, for example, is called *Chianti Colli Sensei*. The most famous Chianti, and the one most worth your attention, is the *Chianti Classico*, which comes from the traditional growing area in the heart of the Chianti region. Chianti is made with 75–100% Sangiovese grapes, and the rest of the wine is made up of other local Tuscan grape variety – Malvasia and Canaiolo grapes.

Brunello

This is one of Italy's best known wines, and is especially beloved by the American market. The Brunello has a more austere and complex taste, but a good bottle of Brunello also enjoys a power and complexity few other wines can compete with. Brunello is produced in the area around Montalcino, a small town in the Val d'Orcia, and is always made with 100% Sangiovese grapes.

Nobile di Montepulciano

Unsurprisingly, this wine is made in the area around Montepulciano and consists of a mix of Sangiovese and Prugnolo gentile grapes. It is a smoother, more delicate, very elegant and deliciously drinkable wine.

Bolgheri DOC

Bolgheri DOC is a relatively new category of wines, Super-Tuscans made in the area around Bolgheri on the Tuscan coast with varieties of grapes that aren't originally Tuscan, such as the Cabernet Sauvignon. The current official formula for the Bolgheri specifies that these wines must be made with no more than 70% Sangiovese grapes, no more than 70% Merlot grapes, and no more than 80% Cabarnet Sauvignon grapes.

Super-Tuscans

Super-Tuscan wines were born when prominent growers (mainly from the noble Antinori family) began experimenting and making wines with grapes which were not autoctonous to Tuscany, such as Cabernet Sauvignon and Merlot. Officially, these wines did not fit into any of the common classifications (Chianti, Brunello etc.), and were thus classified as *vino da tavola*, or table wine, the lowest quality of wine. However, as time went by, and several American wine connoisseurs began expressing an interest in these wines, the Super-Tuscans' reputation changed and they were even re-categorized (as IGT). Today they are some of Tuscany's most famous (and expensive...) wines. The Tignanello (by Antinori) and the Masseto (by Tenuta Ornellaia), for example, are two of the most famous Super-Tuscans.

Wine Classification

All Italian wines adhere to the classification system set by the government. This system protects local production, so that a wine from the North of Italy, for example, won't be able to advertise itself as a Chianti, while also ensuring that certain quality standards are adhered to. This system defines four major categories:

> **Vino De Tavola**, or table wine, is the simplest wine available. Don't bother to waste your time with it.

IGT, stands for *indicazione geografica tipica*, and defines wine that comes from a specific geographic location. Though not the highest classification, there are some very good wines in this category. Most IGT wines are quite simple, but it is important to remember that many of the best and most expensive Super Tuscans are also classified as IGT, since they don't belong to any other category.

DOC, *denominazione d'origine controllata*, means you are guaranteed a product of a certain quality, from a specific area.

DOCG, *denominazione d'origine controllata e garantita*, marks the highest quality wines.

The best way to learn more about Italian wines is, quite simply, to drink them. In Italy, wine isn't considered a snooty hobby reserved for the rich, but rather a way of life and a popular, traditional passion. Most Italians grew up with wine on their family dinner tables, and have developed a palate from a young age. Many, and not necessarily foodies, are well informed about good produce.

Wine is such an important part of the Tuscan way of life, that we have included several tips on wine tours, estates, tastings and similar activities. These can be the beginning of a more serious learning endeavor, or just a fun, light, tasty experience. The choice, of course, is up to you. Personally, we adhere to the approach that wine should be an enjoyable, open activity. And while relying on the advice of experts, we also feel it should not be followed blindly. Wine is, after all, a matter of taste, and sometimes the wines that receive attention and the highest marks from authority figures in the field aren't necessarily the ones you might enjoy most.

Prices, too, can be misleading, and while they can offer guidance, they are not an automatic guarantee to the quality and taste of the wine. While we do very much enjoy an $80 bottle of Brunello, or a150 euro bottle of Sassicaia, the time we've spent in Tuscany has taught us that there is an incredible variety of absolutely excellent wines for $30 or less. (Try the entry level Chianti from Castello di Ama, Montepulciano Nobile from Salcheto, Brunello from Tenute Silvio Nardi, Bolgheri Rosso from Le Macchiole or Ser Lapo from Mazzei, all conveniently priced at under 20–25 euro.) You can even find very good wines for less than $20, which are, at the end of the day, what most Italians drink. Wine can be bought at an *enoteca* (wine shop), or at the supermarket. The larger supermarkets (but not the smaller ones) hold a respectable selection of local Chianti and Brunello bottles, as this is where most Italians go to do their shopping and then pick up a bottle or two for their party or family dinner. And while some of the wines will be no good, others will surprise you as far as their ration of value for money.

Booking in Advance

If there is a specific restaurant you want to try out, we highly recommend booking in advance. During the summer months restaurants in towns like Florence, Siena and San Gimignano are always packed to the rafters. The same goes for booking an *aperitivo* in a sought-after location, a room in a popular B&B, villa, or *agriturismo*. Booking can, in some cases, be done by e-mail, but if you are making a booking for that same day, a phone call would probably be better.

Italian Manners

Italians take manners very seriously. They pride themselves on their *buona educazione*, proper education, and appreciate it when others play by the same rules. It's considered rude, for instance, to ask for something without first saying *scusi* (meaning excuse me, pronounced "skuzi"). Starting a conversation with *scusi* and ending it with *grazie tante*—thank you very much (Note that the word is pronounced graziE, not graziA, as many tourists mistakenly say.)—will leave a good impression and help you get better service in hotels, restaurants, and attractions. The polite way to say goodbye is *arrivederci*, while the polite way to say hello when arriving somewhere is *buongiorno* or *buonasera*, depending on the time of day. Of course, like anywhere, a smile can go a long way.

That said, we have to admit that as polite as a tourist may be, service in Italy can be lacking at times. Though the majority of Italians we have met have been welcoming, be prepared for the occasional annoyed waiter. If it makes any difference, know that it's usually not personal; salesmen and waiters are often short with locals as well as foreigners (to many of the local businesses, a foreigner is anyone that didn't grow up on the same street and go to the same playschool as them). Sometimes you may get the feeling that Italians get better service, and occasionally you'll be right. Often however, it's not because you are being discriminated against, it's simply due to the language barrier. Most Italians don't speak English very well and keep their sentences as short as possible to avoid embarrassment.

Lastly, it is worth mentioning that Italians are very conscientious about fashion and style, and will usually prefer to dress up rather than down. Take a look around any given centrally located piazza in Italy on a Saturday night at the Italian women in skimpy dresses, 6-inch heels and perfectly done hair, and the Italian men in chic jackets and pricey shoes, and you'll immediately understand what we are talking about. Though not as stuck-up as starred restaurants in Paris, the more high-end restaurants in Tuscany do welcome more elegant attire. You will probably feel more welcome (and get better service) if you dress the part.

Sleeping in Tuscany

One of the most difficult tasks for a tourist is choosing a place to sleep. There are thousands of hotels, beds-and-breakfasts, *agriturismi* (a B&B with an active farm, usually producing olive oil or wine) and resorts in Tuscany. Most of the recommendations in this book are written with the idea of hedonism and decadence in mind, so you will find quite a few suggestions for impeccable hotels, fairy-tale resorts, historic residences, and chic little country retreats. However, we have intentionally not limited our recommendations to the modern hotels, nor did we favor the 5-star Disneyland-type resorts that have been built in recent years in Tuscany. On the contrary, charm and individuality were key factors. To us, much like restaurants, some of the best lodgings are the smaller, more intimate places that offer a glimpse into the romance of daily Tuscan life.

The main advantage of the high-end places, other than the question of style, is that the service they offer is often better and amenities; there is air-conditioning, Wi-Fi (though a hotel without Wi-Fi, today, is very rare), decent-sized bathrooms and bedrooms, comfortable beds, elevators and sometimes, though not always, a stronger guarantee of attentive, professional staff. The main advantages of an *agriturismo* or a B&B are that they feel more personal, authentic, and intimate.

Renting a villa or an apartment for a week or two in the Tuscan countryside, or in Florence, is a very popular choice, too. We would recommend consulting websites such as homeaway.com, homeinitaly.com, discovertuscany.com, tuscany-villas.it, or luxuryretreats.com to find a wide array of homes, villas, and apartments for rent. We also highly recommend checking the reviews of other travelers on websites such as TripAdvisor and booking.com before you book.

If renting an apartment, be sure to ask what the price includes to avoid unpleasant surprises. Is there a minimum number of nights? Does the price of the room include all cleaning charges? Will you be charged separately for electricity, gas, or heating? How much? Does the price include a weekly change of linen and use of the laundry room and Wi-Fi? Does the price include parking? Is the apartment properly furnished and adequate for daily cooking and living? This last question is especially important if you plan on shopping in local markets and cooking for yourself most nights.

Whether you rent a villa, a room in a B&B, *agriturismo*, or book a hotel, location is always important. Some places are located deep in the beautiful countryside, which is wonderful if you plan to stick to your immediate surroundings, but can be a problem if you have some more serious sightseeing planned. If you plan on leaving your rented room or villa daily and touring a different part of Tuscany each time, then you should rent a place that, firstly, isn't too far from the places you plan on touring. The truth is Tuscany isn't that small; it will take you about two and a half hours to get from Pisa to the Val d'Orcia for example, two hours to reach Arezzo from Lucca and two hours to drive from Florence to the Maremma. Secondly, don't choose a completely remote B&B from which you have to drive for 40 minutes every morning just to reach the main road. Finally, if you are planning some intensive sightseeing in different parts of Tuscany, consider booking two or even three different accommodations, rather than renting a place for an entire week. For example, a B&B south of Siena for touring Siena itself, the Val d'Orcia, the *maremma* and even Chianti, and a villa near Lucca if you want to tour Lucca, Pisa, the Garfagnana, Bolgheri, and more. It will save you a lot of driving hours.

Florence

 Enjoy an Aperitivo with an Unmatchable
View of Florence

It is clear that in one vacation a person cannot follow all of the suggested tips in this guide. There simply is not enough time, plus, tips are a matter of taste. Some of our suggestions may be your style, others won't be. But if there is one thing you should definitely do, it's follow the advice in this tip.

Aperitivo is one of the best parts of an Italian vacation. A perfect way to get your appetite working, this light, informal drink sets the ambiance for the rest of the evening. Since it is typically served pre-dinner you can enjoy the view of Florence in the soft afternoon light. Depending on the location you pick, you'll see the incredible Duomo and the historical center or you can peek down at busy people rushing by in the ancient streets, but all of the bars listed below offer fantastic drinks in sophisticated settings with great views.

So, where can you go for an aperitivo to remember? here is a list of our favorite spots for a romantic, stylish and tasty aperitivo.

The Sesto Restaurant at the Top of the Westin Hotel

The Westin Hotel is famous for its restaurant with glass walls and a 360-degree views. Come here for lunch or for an early dinner or, of course, an aperitivo. The contrast between the restaurant's clean, straight glass architecture and the colorful, rounded medieval and Renaissance buildings and piazze below provides a perfect backdrop for a relaxed pre-dinner drink.

The Westin also offers a €25 lunch deal which means you can enjoy the scenic restaurant even if you don't want to spend a lot of money on a 4-course dinner. Booking in advance (which can be done online) is not obligatory but recommended in high season, as this place is very popular. Obviously, there is not much point in coming here when the weather is terrible and you can't see anything because of rain and fog.

The 6th Floor Terrace of the Stylish Continental Hotel

The Continental prides itself on its two restaurants—the Fusion Bar and *Borgo san Jacopo*—but we are here to recommend their terrace experience. *La Terrazza* bar is located at the top of the medieval Consorti tower and looks out onto Florence's most famous bridge, the *Ponte Vecchio*. Sipping a cocktail over the Arno River at sunset is an experience not to be missed! Book a table well in advance, and as close to the edge as possible.

The Panoramic Terrace at *Minerva Gio*

Initially, Thursday nights were *aperitivo* night during the summer months at the Minerva hotel (The "gio" in *Minerva Gio* stands for *giovedi*, Thursday). However, today the hotel offers daily *aperitivi* for all in the high-season. This is a younger place and drinks are served around their panoramic pool, on the rooftop. Mingle with young professionals, enjoy the view of the *Duomo*, chat with locals and relax to the sounds of good music played by the DJ. This is a place to see and be seen.

The Beautiful *Terrazza Brunelleschi* in the Baglioni Hotel.

This beautiful, top floor restaurant is connected to an American bar and the garden on the terrace, three large and welcoming spaces from which to enjoy Florence from above. In the summer months (late May–late September), it becomes perfect for *al fresco* dining with a view. The *Baglioni* is one of Florence's more exclusive hotels, so expect to find a crowd of businessmen and well dresses locals and tourists.

The Popular and Panoramic VIP Bar at *Piazzale Michelangelo*

The VIP is located right next to the famous and scenic *Piazzale Michelangelo*, and, as you can imagine, offers quite a view. This spot is hardly as sophisticated as the others, but what it loses in style it makes up for with unparalleled views. To reach VIP from *Piazzale Michelangelo*, walk down the stairs, turn right, and you'll see the panoramic terrace called *"Terraza delle cinque Paniere"* and the bar itself. Alternatively, head out to Flo, another bar with a view just off Piazzale Michelangelo, and a smarter crowd.

SE·STO Restaurant (Westin Excelsior Hotel) ★★★★

Piazza Ognissanti 3, Florence.
Tel: 055-2715-2783,
www.sestoonarno.com.
Aperitivo is served until 9:00 p.m.

The Continental ★★★★

Vicolo dell'Oro 6r, Florence.
Tel: 055-2726-5806,
www.lungarnocollection.com.
The terrace is open daily, 4:00-11:00 p.m.,
except during bad weather. Advance
booking is recommended for groups larger
than four.

Minerva Hotel ★★★

Piazza Santa Maria Novella 16, Florence.
Te:. 055-272-30.
www.grandhotelmonerva.com.
An *aperitivo* is served at the hotel bar
year round (6:00-9:00 p.m), but the
panoramic *aperitivo*, on the terrace, takes
place during the summer months only.

Grand Hotel Baglioni ★★★★

Piazza Unità Italiana 6, Florence.
Tel: 055-235-80,
www.hotelbaglioni.it.
The hotel often organizes events and
themed evenings, contact in advance to
find out if anything is happening during
your visit.

VIP Bar ★★★★

Viale Giuseppe Poggi 21,
Tel: 334-345-5559,
www.facebook.com/pages/Vips-Bar-Firenze
Hours of operation: March-May, 9:30
a.m.-8:00 p.m.; June-September, 9:30
a.m.-midnight; October-November, 9:30
a.m.-8:00 p.m. During bad weather the
VIP will close down, even in-season.

¶¶|02 | **Enjoy a Meal** in One of Florence's Best Resaurants: Il Santo Bevitore

A favorite with savvy local diners, *Il Santo Bevitore* offers a modern interpretation of Tuscan classics and is considered by many to be one of the best restaurants in town. The place has a fashionable vibe and artwork of young Florentine artists often lines the walls, but don't worry that you will be surrounded by overly hip Florentines scowling at you as for ordering the "wrong" bottle of wine. In reality the clientele here is very mixed, from business people to a younger, more alternative crowd. The service is attentive and friendly. As for the food, the menu offers some surprising twists on traditional dishes. This isn't the most typical Florentine restaurant you will find, but it is loyal to its origins. Try the pasta with *cacio e pepe* (cacio cheese and black pepper), *maccheroni* with *ossobuco ragu*, the stuffed calamari (the menu is seasonal, and may change), as well as the delicious desserts. Make sure you make a reservation, and consult the staff to pick the best dish for your taste.

IL SANTO BEVITORE ★★★★
Via di Santo Spirito 66r, Florence.
Tel: 055-211-264,
www.ilsantobevitore.com.
HOURS OF OPERATION:
Monday–Saturday, 12:30-2:30 p.m.,
7:30-11:30p.m. Sunday, 7:30-11:30 p.m.
Closed for the second half of August.

03 Book a Night at One of Florence's Top Hotels: Il Salviatino

A grand 15th-century villa set on a hilltop in a suburb of Florence overlooking meticulously kept gardens bathed in Tuscan sunshine and providing spectacular views of the city. Interested? We thought you would be. Stylish and smart, *Il Salviatino* offers one of the best experiences in Tuscany. The hotel itself is stunning; a Renaissance-era villa which has been meticulously restored and converted into a dazzling boutique hotel. Strewn with fine artwork and furniture, this unique spot got the recognition it undoubtedly deserves in 2011 when it was named the premiere boutique hotel in Italy by the World Travel Awards.

Its surroundings are equally enchanting. Sitting at an impressively scenic height above Florence, the town of Fiesole is where the rich and famous buy their exclusive gated Florentine villas. Home to Roman ruins and Renaissance monuments, staying here gives you a view into the city's storied past, as well as its luxurious present.

Prices here can be steep. But you won't be disappointed. Alongside the attentive and professional staff, is a spa and gym; and the rooms are equipped with espresso machines, rain showers, and handmade linen, giving you the luxurious experience you deserve for what is, admittedly, a hefty bill.

The food in the hotel's restaurant is good, but what sets the restaurant apart are the events they regularly organize. Brunches, themed dinners, *aperitivi* and more; you don't have to be a guest to log onto their website and check out what's on. A gourmet Sunday brunch, for example, may be a perfect opportunity to visit this astonishing hotel and elegant gardens, and enjoy its beautiful view of Florence, without having to pay a fortune.

Il Salviatino ★★★★★
Via del Salviatino 21, Fiesole, Florence.
Tel: 055.904.1111,
www.salviatino.com

04 | **Catch an Opera Show** at St. Mark's Anglican Church

St. Mark's is a beautiful Anglican church in Florence. It's not just lovely to visit but also quite famous, thanks to the series of performances it hosts that have drawn thousands of opera fans over the years.

The most famous operas, such as La Bohème, Tosca, La Traviata, Rigoletto, The Marriage of Figaro, The Barber of Seville, Carmen, Don Giovanni, The Magic Flute, and Madame Butterfly form the base of their repertoire, but they also perform traditional Neapolitan songs. Another great feature is that they provide English explanations and opera notes, which make the show much easier to follow even if you don't speak Italian. For opera lovers and opera novices alike this is great fun. All shows are by professional opera singers in full costume.

St Mark's Church ★★★★
Via Maggio 16, Florence.
Tel: 055-294-764,
www.stmarksitaly.com.
Find out more about the monthly program and book here:
www.concertoclassico.blogspot.co.uk

Book an Organized Wine Tasting Tour,
with a Guide and a Driver

Self-driving wine tours give you the freedom to choose your wine, but driver-led wine tours give you the freedom to choose how much of it you will drink. The advantages of booking a tour led by someone else are clear, and in Tuscany, the options are endless. Before booking, you should always be clear about what you hope to see, so ask questions to understand what the program includes. Many of the smaller tours are flexible, so check if it possible to build your tour around the specific wineries you may be interested in. Here are three of our favorites:

Italy and Wine is one of the best options available. This company offers several different excursions, but the common denominator is the enthusiasm and passion the organizers bring to it, embracing the wine, the vineyards, and local traditions with a knowledge that is hard to rival. The company is headed by Vittorio del Bono Venezze, a sommelier with over 10 years' experience and an intimate understanding of wine and Italian culture, and the tours themselves are led by experienced sommeliers. Tours are offered in a number of different areas, including Chianti, Montepulciano and Montalcino (where the famous Brunello is made). Check their website for more details on the different options available.

At around 260 euro per person Italy and Wine tours aren't cheap. The price does go down with larger groups, however. Alternatively, book one of their wine tasting lessons which last about an hour and a half, and cost a more affordable 35 euro. The tastings take place in Vittorio's wine tasting academy in Florence, and are a perfect activity for those who are interested in learning more about wine and wine culture. It's also a great option for visitors with limited time, who have no intention of driving outside of Florence to visit the different estates.

Wine Adventure is another popular option. Lead by Alessandra Chiti, a sommelier and a passionate wine lover, the tours are available in English, French and Spanish. A full day tour lasts eight hours and will cost about 190 euro per person (if you are a couple). The price decreases with a larger group and goes down to 100 euro per person for a group of eight. Interesting and well executed Tours of Chianti, Montalcino, Brunello and San Gimignano are available and all include a mini-wine school which provides a brief education for the uninitiated.

Finally, **Fun in Tuscany** offers a much lighter approach, mostly geared towards a younger crowd. These tours of the Chianti region start at 90 euro and, though somewhat touristy and not led by wine connoisseurs, are a thoroughly enjoyable (and efficient) way to pass the afternoon. The guides lead visitors through Chianti and swing by San Gimignano for a Tuscan lunch followed by some sumptuous ice cream at Dondoli Gelateria. Food, wine, and ice cream—what's not to love? And to top it all off, the tour ends at the Piazzale Michelangelo where, with a full stomach, you can enjoy a view of Florence by night.

Italy and Wine ★★★★
contact through their website:
www.florencewineacademy.net.
NOTES: Wine lessons are held Monday-Thursday, year round, at 6:30 p.m., near Pitti palace.

Wine Adventure ★★★
Tel: 0577-309-132,
Cell: 334.9363253.
Booking is done through their website: www.winetouradventure.com

Fun in Tuscany ★★★
Via Bernardo Cennini 6, Firenze.
Cell: 338-592-2682 or 392-633-9101,
www.funintuscany.com.
NOTES: tours leave at 9:30 a.m., advanced booking required.

06 | **Book an Apartment** with the Best View Imaginable in Florence

The **Florence with a View** apartments enjoy views that few can compete with. Staying in the Santa Maria apartment, it feels like all you need do is open the shutters and reach out to touch the Duomo. The large windows let in an abundance of light into the luminous apartment and of course grant you a delectable view of Florence's busy streets below. A quiet evening glass of Chianti, shared with someone special and soaking in the night's ambience from this exceptional viewpoint is one of the most tranquil experiences this beautiful city has to offer. The San Giovanni apartment is very impressive too.

You can get a sense of each residence from the pictures on their website, though pictures can never do these views total justice. On top of the view, the apartments themselves are stunning. Spacious, eminently comfortable, and classically designed; the furnishings are the definition of elegant luxury. This, in our opinion, is better than any hotel. The fact that so many of the apartments' original, 150 year old fixtures have been preserved, including a beautiful, hand carved Indian ceiling, marble work and wooden floors, adds to the charm. Surprisingly, prices here are absolutely reasonable, making Florence with a View one of the best accommodation option in town. Make sure you book well in advance, as it is rare to find an opening in high season.

Florence with a View Apartments ★★★★★
Via Roma 3, Florence.
Tel: 055-582-961,
www.florencewithaview.com

¶|07 | **Try Some** of Florence's Best Ice Cream

The debate over Florence's best ice cream shop is a heated one. Each of the big name *gelaterie* has hordes of fans that fight for the honor of their personal choice. Without wanting to get involved in the conflict, we're willing to raise our heads above the parapet long enough to present a short list of our favorites. Four names are included here, in no particular order—simply our recommendations after years of tasting. As it should be, each has its own unique style and taste. From new, delicious, modern concoctions to the regular beloved traditional flavors, these are the parlors that for us do it best. The rest is up to you to judge.

Grom is a chain of ice cream shops and normally, we would never recommend a chain. However, if the ice cream really is excellent, then why should we resist? Creamy, rich, and very satisfying, Grom's gelato is a treat. Ask for a sample of any one of their flavors, the staff will be happy to oblige. They are based in Torino and in recent years have opened shops in several major towns in Italy, as well as in the United States and Japan. One can be found right by the Duomo in Florence.

Vestri is a small shop that has been mentioned in this guide in another tip. We discovered their ice cream by accident one day, and we have returned to enjoy it several times after that. The small shop is easy to miss, unassumingly located in a fairly regular street not far from the Duomo, but their charming logo, with its angelic blue tones, will catch your eye. Don't be surprised that no ice cream is on display. Instead, like many of the best *gelaterie*, they keep their *gelato* in enclosed aluminum cans, which are only opened to serve customers, thus keeping the ice cream fresher and smoother.

Carraia is one of the more popular ice cream shops in Florence. The location is slightly away from the heart of the *centro storico*, just off the Carraia Bridge, and its grey exterior isn't particularly attention grabbing, but inside awaits a well-priced selection of rich, smooth-tasting flavors that manage to be deliciously creamy without being too heavy. Though you won't find wholly innovative or unique flavors here, they have perfected the traditional favorites. Try their *cioccolato fondente*, or dark chocolate. Trust us, it's worth the indulgence.

De Neri is another Fiornetine institution. Named after the street where it is located, this place is very popular with the locals. All their delicious treats and delectable ice creams are charmingly laid out behind the counter, and the general feel of the place is that of a neighborhood *gelateria* that hasn't changed much since the '60s. Their ice cream is a little on the heavy side, very traditional, but also very good, and their *semifreddi* (a half-frozen dessert, resembling an ice cream cake) are excellent. However, if you prefer a lighter, smoother taste, you might enjoy other places more. Make sure to grab a few extra napkins on your way out, you'll need them to get the tint of their sweet-tasting more chocolatey than chocolate ice cream off your lips!

Gelateria Grom ★★★★
Via del Campanile, Florence.
Tel: 055-216-158.
HOURS OF OPERATION:
Daily, 10:30 a.m.-midnight
(until 11:00 p.m. off-season)

Gelateria Vestri ★★★★
Piazza Gaetano Salvemini 11, Florence.
Tel: 055-234-0374,
www.vestri.it
HOURS OF OPERATION:
Monday–Saturday, 10:00 a.m.-7:00 p.m.
Sunday closed. August Closed.
Hours may vary off-season.

Galteria La Carraia ★★★
Piazza Nazario Sauro 25r
(just off the Carraia bridge),
Tel: 055.280695,
www.lacarraiagroup.eu
HOURS OF OPERATION:
Daily, 10:00 a.m.-midnight (hours may vary, or shop may close, off-season)

Gelateria Artigianale Dei Neri ★★★
Via dei Neri 22r,
Tel: 055 210034.
HOURS OF OPERATION:
Daily, 9:00 a.m.-midnight (hours may vary, and shop may close off-season).

08 | **Taste Some Excellent Wine** in the Famous Cantinetta Antinori

Cantinetta Antinori is one restaurant which tends to divide people. Owned by the famous Antinori wine producing family and part of a chain of restaurants in similarly luxurious locations such as Vienna and Moscow, some say this spot is overpriced for what it offers while others rave about their excellent quality wines. We find ourselves somewhere in the middle, although admittedly, we may be biased as Antinori wines happen to be among our favorite Italian producers.

On the positive side the restaurant's setting is beautiful. It is located in Palazzo Antinori, a historic 15th-century edifice. The layout inside is quaint, comfortable, well lit, and spacious; a tasteful setting in which to enjoy your meal. The real draw however, is the wine. The Antinori family is one of the great wine producers in Italy with a remarkable history stretching back hundreds of years and estates throughout Italy and the world. They make wines of exceptional quality, many of which can be sampled here for a range of prices. On the other hand the limited menu can be a little disappointing and overpriced.

We'd recommend coming here if you want to enjoy a superior wine list and don't plan on leaving Florence for any wine tasting excursions or tours. If you don't want to have a full meal here, you can organize your own *aperitivo*, order some starters, and ask the knowledgeable staff to make some good wine suggestions.

Cantinetta Antinori ★★★★
Piazza Antinori 3, Florence.
Tel: 055 292234,
www.cantinetta-antinori.com
HOURS OF OPERATION:
Monday-Friday, 12:30-2:30 p.m., 7:00-10:00 p.m.
Closed on weekends. Closed for the last 3 weeks of August. During the high season (mid-April to late September), may open for two Saturdays a month.

🏃 | 09 | **Discover Two Hidden Gems** off Florence's Standard Museum Route

Is it possible that Florence, with its five million tourists a year, has any remaining hidden treasures, any concealed gems waiting to be discovered? Surprisingly, the answer is yes. Florence tends to see tourists, especially those who haven't got much time, go to the same, well-known museums and attractions, while completely skipping other parts of town. But for the curious and adventurous, two more surprises hide along the roads less traveled.

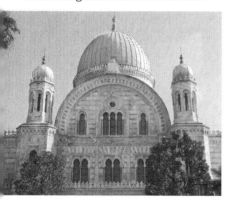

Both are located far enough from the center to deter the crowds, but make no mistake, they are both easy to reach and definitely worth visiting. One is a small museum, the **Museo Stefano Bardini**; and the other is the Jewish Synagogue and Museum, **Sinagoga e Museo Ebraico**.

Museo Stefano Bardini, named after its creator, the Italian antiquarian Stefano Bardini, is a secret many art lovers would gladly keep to themselves. The collection is housed in a convent that was renovated and transformed in neo-Renaissance style in 1881 by Bardini to accommodate his collection and business. In his glory days, Bardini had a number of laboratories for the restoration of his precious items, and buyers and art lovers would come from afar to buy antiques. After Bardini died, the museum was left to the city of Florence. Today, it houses a delightful and fascinating collection of over 2000 antiques and crafts—ancient, medieval, renaissance, and 18th-century art, paintings, medals, bronze sculptures, oriental rugs, and more. Much of the museum's charm comes from its intimate setting, and of course, Bardini's excellent eye in creating his collection. As you discover room after room of delightful and diverse pieces in the elegant and refined space, you will be drawn further into its warm, inviting environment; you may even be reminded of the Poldi Pezzoli museum in Milan. The wonderful view of the city from the Bardini villa gardens is an added bonus. Watch out for events and temporary exhibitions that regularly take place here. The near-by Villa Bardini is the perfect place to end your visit and stop for an afternoon snack or a relaxed *aperitivo* (often accompanied, in the summer months, by live music).

The Jewish Synagogue (known in Italian as either *Synagoga* or, sometimes, as *Tempio Israelitico*) may seem a little difficult to visit—due to threats, the security detail around the site is strict. However, the effort is absolutely worth it. Once you enter, the chaos of the tourist strewn city outside is forgotten, and you are engulfed in beauty. Built in Moorish style, with Arabic, Byzantine, and Romanesque elements, the synagogue was inaugurated in 1882, about 20 years after the emancipation of the Italian Jews. The community had set out to build a temple that would be worthy of the beautiful city of Florence and have

surely succeeded. The massive green dome, which can be seen a long way in the distance, was once gilded. Inside, the walls are decorated with Moorish arabesques and geometric patterns. Superior craftsmanship can be found in every corner.

Interesting and informative organized tours are available daily (every half hour in high season) of the synagogue and the museum. Tours need to be booked in advance.

Museo Bardini ★★★★
Via dei Renai 37,
Tel: 055-234-2427,
www.museicivicifiorentini.comune.fi.it/bardini.
HOURS OF OPERATION:
open year round, Friday-Monday, 11:00 a.m.–5:00 p.m.

Synagogue and Jewish museum ★★★
Via Farini 6,
Tel. 055 234-6654,
www.moked.it/jewishflorence/synagogue-and-museum.
HOURS OF OPERATION:
June-September, Sunday-Thursday, 10:00 a.m.–6:30 p.m. Friday and the eve of major Jewish holidays: 10:00 a.m.–5:00 p.m. Closed on Saturday; October-May, Sunday-Thursday, 10:00 a.m.–5:30 p.m. Friday and the eve of major Jewish holidays, 10:00 a.m.–3:00 p.m. Closed on Saturday and on major Jewish Holidays year round. Last entry 45 minutes before closing time.

ᵞᵞ 10 | Book a Fun and Informative Cooking Class, or Invite a Private Chef to Your Villa

So many B&Bs and *agriturismi* nowadays offer their guests some sort of cooking classes. In many cases, they are fun and worth trying. Most people don't suddenly plan on becoming a chef thanks to this class; it's just an enjoyable way to experience, hands-on, the Tuscan kitchen, and learn the Italian basics: from how to make pasta to how to correctly stir the bubbling ragu, just like a real Italian grandmother. A day of cooking can be not only a welcome break from all the sightseeing, but also quite a memorable experience from your Tuscan trip. There are a number of recommended cooking classes in Tuscany in this guide (see tips 36, 37, 44 and 62, for example). The following list is dedicated to some of our favorites in Florence:

Accidental Tourist offers a fun and accessible cooking class, focusing on making fresh pasta, in a nice setting—an 800-year-old villa located in the hills above Florence. These courses are very popular

and are perfect if you just want a short and simple experience, have fun for a couple of hours, and then move on to other activities. A class costs about 80 euro per person and should be booked well in advance, especially during high season.

A more sophisticated and certainly more in-depth possibility is **Faith Willinger's Cooking Lessons for Foodies and Culture Lovers**. Faith, a food critic and journalist, has been living in Florence for more than two decades and is knowledgeable about Italian culture and food. Her ice cream crawl (a tasty tour of Florence's ice cream shops) and her lunch lessons (guided visit to the market, shopping for fresh produce and then cooking together) are excellent. This is full-day experience; groups are small and you will enjoy an eight-course meal.

If you want a private chef to come over to the apartment you rented in Florence and cook you an authentic Italian dinner, that can be done

too! **Chefs Ginny and Fiamma** offer private lessons and personal live dinners, during which they can come to your rental apartment (provided it is properly equipped with a functional kitchen) and hold a private cooking lesson or cook a personalized meal. A live dinner is cooked for a group of 6 people at least, and costs around 80 euro per person. The menu is decided upon in advance, based on the participants' taste and requirements. Cooking lessons (2.5 hours long) can be organized for a minimum of two people (at a cost of 150 euro per person, and the price goes down to 100 euro per person for a group of 6).

Accidental Tourist ★★★
www.accidentaltourist.com

Faith Willinger ★★★★
www.faithwillinger.com

Kitchen Chez Nous ★★★
www.kitchencheznous.com

11 Try Some of the Best Chocolate
in Florence

We have to admit we are chocolate lovers. And similar to a dedicated follower of fashion, we believe chocolate should be enjoyed by season. So whether you are visiting in winter or sightseeing in summer, there are three options you have to try.

In summer, visit **Vestri**, a well-known local establishment. We come here for their rich chocolate and cream ice cream (And a couple of squares of their hand-made chocolate, of course…).

During the winter months, we migrate to **Arte del Cioccolato**, a small local spot with sumptuous hot chocolate, the perfect way to survive a cold Florentine morning.

Lastly, year round we are drawn to one of Florence's best loved and iconic cake shops: **Pistocchi**, which is located about 1.5 miles from the historical center, in Via Ponte di Mezzo. Pistocchi's concentrated, luscious chocolate cakes are famous across town, and are the perfect

shameless teatime indulgence. Their classic Torta al Cioccolato is the most famous on the menu, but the newer inventions, such as the Torta al Peperoncino (chocolate and chili flakes) and the Torta al Caffe are excellent, too. There are several other tastes from which to choose—white chocolate cake, chocolate with pears cake, Sicilian orange-cake, and more. They also sell products you can take home with you, such as a *gianduia* cream (a chocolate spread), that puts even the ever popular Nutella to shame.

Vestri ★★★
Piazza Gaetano Salvemini 11, Florence.
Tel: 055-234-0374,
www.vestri.it
HOURS OF OPERATION:
Monday–Saturday, 10:00 a.m.–7:00 p.m.
Closed in August.

Arte del Cioccolato ★★★
Piazza santa Elisabetta 2r, Florence.
Tel: 055-217-136,
www.artedelcioccolato.it.
HOURS OF OPERATION:
Monday–Friday, 7:00 a.m.–8:00 p.m.;
Saturday–Sunday, 8:00 a.m.–8:00 p.m. In August, open until 9:00 p.m.

Torta Pistocchi ★★★
Via del Ponte di Mezzo 20, Florence.
Tel: 055-051-6939,
www.tortapistocchi.it.
HOURS OF OPERATION:
Monday–Friday, 8:30 a.m.–6:30 p.m.
Closed in August.

12 **Book a Spa Treatment** in the Center of Florence

After a day spent tramping around Florence's hot, busy streets, of standing in lines for what feels like hours, and perhaps even ushering young children through the mania; it's probably a good guess that you'll be a bit worn out. As you stare at your swollen feet, too tired to move, or to consider all the beautiful things you still want to see tomorrow, a good massage seems like the only viable solution. Even though Tuscany's best spas, those which feature hot thermal water pools with a fabulous view and an endless range of treatments, are located outside the city, deep in the Tuscan countryside, there are a number of excellent urban spas too, less than 10-minutes from wherever you are staying in Florence, for a range of prices.

The very best hotels in Florence all have excellent spa services. Most aren't cheap, but if you want to treat yourself to some extra pampering, and soothe that aching body, they are the place to go. Alternatively, book a session at one of the city's smaller private spas (there are many outside of hotels), which also offer wonderful solutions for re-energizing the weary tourist in you.

The Four Seasons is probably the best choice in town, and has recently been elected as the best urban spa in Italy. Their top notch treatments are all executed using products made especially for them by the antique Santa Maria Novella pharmacy, a Florence institute. Guests enjoy

high quality treatments in elegantly designed rooms, as well as free use of the pool and the hot tub. Be warned, though, that the prices for all this are very high. Their full body treatments average around 550 euro while the starting price for a massage is 100 euro for just twenty minutes. Consult their website to find out more.

Soulspace, minutes from the duomo, has some reasonably priced massages and offers a large number of relaxation and beauty treatments. From aromatherapy to revitalizing treatments, water cocoon, four-hand massages, treatments designed specifically for pregnant women and new mothers, and much more. The space itself has a modern, comfortable design with an emphasis on neutral colors to help you relax. A number of special offers are available on their website as is a full list of their treatments and massages.

Silathai is a lovely place in Piazza Pitti, offering Thai massage, reflexology, and relaxing Swedish massages, a much softer method than the Thai style. Pleasantly decorated with warm golden hues and Eastern religious iconography, the staff here is friendly and it is more reasonably priced than the hotels. They speak English, too, which is another useful advantage if you need to tell an overly enthusiastic masseuse to calm down with your back massage!

Centro Manipura is located a little outside Florence's historical center, but it is still easily accessible. It's definitely worth considering if you are looking for an economic solution, as prices here are a fraction of the cost of many of the top end hotels. Shiatsu, essential oil, and Thai massages, as well as foot reflexology

and other treatments, can be enjoyed for just 45 euro an hour or 80 euro for two hours.

Finally, at the more luxurious end of the scale is **The Continental** which has a lovely spa, run according to the Daniela Steiner method. With a perfect location right by the Ponte Vecchio, this place will immediately put you in a pampered mood. Massages start from 140 euro and of course a series of beauty treatments, facials, and pampering is available, in a clean and modern space. If you fancy a drink to round off your relaxing experience, then head up to the hotel's Skybar after for an equally refreshing glass of wine and views overlooking Firenze.

The Four Seasons ★★★★★
Borgo Pinti 99, Firenze,
Tel. 055-262-61,
www.fourseasons.com
Booking in advance is required.

SOULSPACE® Wellness Center ★★★
Via S. Egidio 12, Florence.
Tel. 055-200-1794,
www.soulspace.it
Booking in advance is required.

Silathai Thai Massage Center ★★★
Via De Serragli 63r-65r, Florence.
Tel. 055- 217-559,
www.silathaimassage.com
Booking in advance is required.

Centro Manipura ★★★
Via G. Zanella 3r and Via Masaccio 222
(two locations).
Cell: 333-537-1957 (Filippo),
www.centromanipura.com
Booking in advance is required.

Continental spa ★★★★
Vicolo dell'Oro 6r, Florence.
Tel. 055-272-65966,
www.lungarnocollection.com
Booking in advance is required.

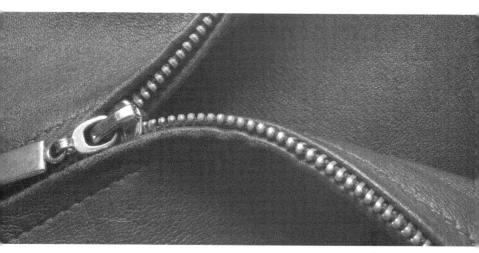

 13 | **Buy a Good Quality Italian Leather Jacket** in Florence

Good-quality leather jackets are a staple of the classic Italian wardrobe. We are not talking about those made-in-China, back alley, no-quite-sure-this-even-leather imitations, but something characteristic, timeless, and Italian.

While stores stocking authentic leather bags can be found dotted across Florence, finding a leather jacket specialist can be trickier.

The shops in and around the famous leather market in Piazza San Lorenzo are usually the first stop for buyers, and the shops around Santa Croce church are usually the second. Some of these shops have very good choices and are worth exploring, but if you are looking for something special—an investment piece—you are unlikely to find it there. For a special item, head out to one of these known boutiques:

Janniderma is one of the best-known boutiques in town and a popular venue for those looking for a quality jacket with a dramatic design. The shop also offers custom designs for the creative (or the brave!). Whether you are a fearless fashionista with a passion for flair or an intrigued buyer on the hunt for something a little different, Janniderma is worth stopping into. Check out their online collection to get a general sense of their style.

Another one of our go-to options is the **Pelletteria Bottega Fiorentina**. Their showroom is located in an elegant 16th-century building, right next to Piazza Santa Croce, and the quality is excellent. The designs are smart, and most items are handmade by designers from Florence. Custom made clothes are available, too.

Similarly, **Il Fiorentino** offers a more high-end collection, which can also be completely customized. Bags and leather jackets are all exclusively hand made by local artisans, using quality materials. Stop here if you are interested in a classic but still vibrant look.

Yet another option, with good quality jackets in a more causal but elegant style can be found in the **La Pelle** boutique. The service here is friendly and professional, which makes the whole experience that much more pleasant. In business for over 30 years, their chic aviator-style jackets are a particularly good buy.

Janniderma ★★★
Via dè Benci 10,
Tel: 055-234-6173,
www.janniderma.com.
HOURS OF OPERATION:
Daily 11:00 a.m.–7:30 p.m.

Pelletteria Bottega Fiorentina ★★★
Borgo dei Greci, 5r,
Tel: 055-295-411,
www.bottegafiorentina.it
HOURS OF OPERATION:
Monday–Saturday, 10:00 a.m.–6:00 p.m.
Closed on Sunday

Il Fiorentino ★★★
Lungarno Corsini 48, Florence.
Tel: 055-239-8325,
www.ilfiorentino.com

La Pelle ★★★
Via Guicciardini 11r,
Tel: 055-292-031,
www.lapellesrl.it
HOURS OF OPERATION:
Monday–Saturday, 9:30 a.m.–7:00 p.m.
Sunday usually closed, but may open in high season (call first).

🍴 | 14 | **Lunch like a True Italian** in Florence

For us, the perfect quick summer lunch has to be simple, authentic, and delicious. Choosing the right place can be tricky, though. After hours of walking around, it is more than tempting to crash, tired and swollen-footed, at the nearest pizza shop or bar and buy an even more tired-looking sandwich. But in a city like Florence, where one can choose from so many quality eateries, settling for such a mediocre solution would be a real shame. When picking a place for a light lunch on the go, we stick to one basic rule: we always go for places which we know pride themselves on good quality *materie prime*—i.e, quality produce. When a spot has high-quality, fresh local produce, everything else just seems to fall into position. In Florence, there are four particular places in which we regularly seem to end up, and the quality of their *materie prime* is only the first reason.

On the Oltrarno, we love **Il Santino**, in Via Santo Spirito. This tiny eatery has a warm, intimate feel that makes us feel immediately at home. You can find a small but quality choice of cold cuts and cheeses, tasty sandwiches, and a nice wine list—perfect for a light lunch or an *aperitivo*. Seating is very limited, so try to go early before it fills up. Adjacent is **Il Santo Bevitore**, an excellent restaurant with the same owners.

Though swarming with tourists, and recommended in just about every tourist guide, we cannot deny that the sandwiches in **l'Antico Vinaio** are really great and merit the hype. This takeout sandwich spot is the perfect stop if you want something cheap, quick and delicious. You won't be disappointed by their huge *panini* and salsas that explode with flavor. The fact you can wash it all down with a glass of red wine for two euro is a prospect that is sure to revive even the weariest tourist. This place is seriously popular, but the long line moves quickly, so don't despair. While you wait, you can always eavesdrop on locals fervently discussing politics and football.

Another place with tasty sandwiches on offer is 'Ino. Seating is limited and the décor is somewhat austere, but the location is perfect (just off the Lungarno, not far from the Uffizi gallery and the Galileo Galilei Science Museum) and the quality of the produce is very good, especially the cheeses and the cold cuts.

Last, but not least, is I Fratellini. A tiny, inconspicuous hole in the wall with an eternal line placed right in front of it, I Fratellini is a famous local establishment. Hungry locals and ravenous tourists line up for the tasty sandwiches which offer the perfect filler in the middle of the day. There is no place to sit, but feel free to stand around in the alleyway while you munch, and even wash it down with a glass of wine—both the sandwich and the wine are refreshingly cheap. Sink your teeth into one of their tasty *panini* with *porchetta* or with *prosciutto* and *pecorino* cheese. Vegetarians will enjoy the dried tomatoes and *pecorino* or the vegetarian mix.

For a more substantial meal, but still simple and unassuming, we head to one of these two centrally located, reasonably priced, and delicious restaurants. Near Palazzo Vecchio, we like Osteria i Buongustai, a small and simple but very well-liked eatery. It can be difficult to find an empty seat here and once you taste the food, you'll know why. Their platter of *antipasti* is particularly nice, and while any one of their homemade fresh pasta dishes is recommended, we particularly like the ravioli. Run and staffed entirely by women, the atmosphere is rarely less than lively.

Il Caminetto, on the other hand, offers a more serious dining experience, and the food is good enough to make us reconsider our rule of never trusting a restaurant that is closer than 500 yards from a major tourist attraction (in this

case, the Duomo). Try their pasta with truffle, the rosemary infused risotto with Chianti jelly (it tastes much better than it sounds) or the fried pecorino cheese served with fresh pears. Their lunch menu, for around 16 euro, is very reasonable.

Il Santino ★★★
Via Santo Spirito 60r, Florence.
Tel: 055-230-2820.
HOURS OF OPERATION:
Daily, 12:30 p.m.–11:00 p.m.

l'Antico Vinaio ★★★★
Via dei Neri 65,
Tel: 055-238-2723.
HOURS OF OPERATION:
Tuesday–Saturday 10:00 a.m.–4:00 p.m., 6:00-10:00 p.m.; Sunday 10:00 a.m.–4:00 p.m. Monday closed.

'Ino ★★★
Via dei Georgofili 3r, Florence.
Tel: 055-219-208,
www.inofirenze.com.
HOURS OF OPERATION:
Daily, 11:30 a.m.–4:30 p.m.

I Fratellini ★★★
Via de Cimatori 38r, Florence.
Tel: 055-239-6096,
www.iduefratellini.it
HOURS OF OPERATION:
Daily, 9:00 a.m.–6:00 p.m.

Osteria i buogustai ★★★
Via dei cerchi 15r (just off Via dei Corsi),
Tel: 055-291-304.
HOURS OF OPERATION:
Monday-Friday, noon–3:30 p.m.;
Saturday, noon–10:30 p.m.

Ristorante il Caminetto ★★★
Via dello Studio 34r, Florence.
Tel: 055-239-6274,
www.ilcaminettofirenze.it.
HOURS OF OPERATION:
Daily, noon–3:00 p.m., 7:00-10:30 p.m.
Off-season closed on Wednesday.

🏃 15 | **Visit a Little Gem in Florence** – The Antique Gardens of Torrigiani

The famous Boboli Gardens are beautiful and a must visit, but we have a special place in our heart for the Torrigiani Gardens, which appear like a mirage of green in Florence's chaotic historical center.

Spread across nearly 17 acres in the heart of Florence, this magical garden is still owned by two noble families who belong to the Florence elite of antiquity. It is also the largest private city-garden in Europe. The area was once a much smaller botanical garden, but was expanded in the 19th century and turned into an elegant English garden. The Torrigiani Malaspina and the Torrigiani Santa Cristina families do a marvellous job in preserving this special place and a family member personally leads each tour. A visit today includes a tour of the ancient botanical plots, with trees and plants from all over the world; of the woods surrounding the family crypts and a look at some very suggestive sculptures. Activities such as painting classes and gardening

lessons are occasionally organized, consult the garden's website to find out more.

Booking a private tour here may be slightly difficult, it will probably be easier to organize if you are a small group. And while there are cheaper and more accessible gardens to visit, this is a truly special experience and in our opinion worth the time and effort.

Giardino Torrigiano ★★★★
Via dei Serragli 144, Florence.
Tel: 055-224-527, Cell: 349-286-8449,
www.giardinotorrigiani.it
Call in advance to ask what tours are available.

🏃 16 | **Dance the Night Away** at Some of the Best Clubs in Florence

Tuscany's nightlife can be a little confusing. Though the local clubs aren't exactly as famous as the choice venues in Milan and Rome, Tuscany does pride itself on some trendy places of its own. Summer, obviously, is when the scene comes to life. As soon as the weather is warm enough, numerous hotspots open, from little beer gardens in the city to champagne bars in the top hotels to dance-'til-you-drop discotheques right by the beach. It is also quite common for the largest bars in towns like Florence and Pisa to open a temporary summer spaces by the river. And the beaches of Viareggio, Pietrasanta, Forte dei Marmni and Lido di Cammaiore (in northern Tuscany) and Albinia, Castiglione della Pescaia, Porto Ercole, Talamone, and many others (in Southern Tuscany) are awash with live music and events.

The scene changes greatly from town to town, but generally speaking, Florence, Forte dei Marmi (Tuscany's leading glitz and glamour resort town) and the coastline tend to offer much better, vibrant choices. To find out more about the best lounge bars, clubs and beach discotques in Forte dei Marmi and the area, see tip 127.

Florence, naturally, offers the best selection for a fun night out. The **Flo'**, for example, is one of the few *aperitivo* bars with a swanky, trendy vibe. It enjoys a great view (thanks to its coveted location, near Piazzale Michelangelo) and offers live and lively music that flows into the night. In the summer months, the Flo is open seven days a week. Check their website in advance to see if anything special is planned. Naturally, several

other spots compete for the visitor's attention. Many of the city's clubs and discotheques cater to a younger crowd—college students out for a night of clubbing, to be exact. This is unsurprising, given that Florence hosts thousands of foreign students every year. However, there are a few spots in town that are worth exploring, especially if you are interested in a night of partying, but without being surrounded exclusively by tipsy 19–26-year-olds. The **Yab**, **Otel,** and **Space**, for example, are all good options, even if you are old enough to remember the lyrics to some of *Nirvana's* biggest hits. Space is entirely dedicated to electronic music. The upstairs dance floor resembles a refurbished industrial warehouse, and the atmosphere here is free and fun. This is a place for dancing, not impressing. Yab, on the other hand, is all about fashion. Beautiful people come here to see and be seen. Stylish girls show off their micro-mini skirts while the men smart up and parade their Armani jackets and expensive taste in alcohol. Otel is more sophisticated than the other two, and caters to a slightly older crowd. This place is perfect for a dinner and a show, followed by some dancing and mingling, while surrounded by an enjoyably decadent atmosphere. Energetic, stylish and somewhat more luxurious, come here if you want to drink and then tear up the floor in style.

If you prefer a more alternative scene, Florence does offer a number of options (though, admittedly, selection is limited). Catch an impromptu live music show at

Piazza Santo Spirito while sipping some bubbly wine, enjoy a live jazz concert at the **Pinocchio club**, swing by Piazza **Sant'Ambrogio** during the annual mini-jazz **festival** (www. firenzejazz.it), and don't forget to check with the local tourist office to see what festivals and events are happening during your stay. If you are visiting Florence in June to September, it is very likely that at least one interesting event is scheduled.

Flo'
Piazzale Michelangelo 84, Florence.
Tel: 055-650-791,
www.flofirenze.com

Yab
Via dè Sassetti
Tel: 055-215-160,
www.yab.it

Otel
Viale Generale Dalla Chiesa 9, Florence.
Tel: 055-650-791,
www.otelvariete.com

Space
Via Palazzuolo 37, Florence.
Tel: 348- 776-8434,
www.spaceclubfirenze.com

Pinocchio Jazz
Viale Giannotti 13, Florence.
Tel: 055-683-388
www.pinocchiojazz.it

¶ | 17 | **Treat Yourself to a Delicious Brunch**, or Relax with a Cocktail, in the Four Seasons Hotel in Florence

With its wonderful location, beautiful gardens and two-star Michelin restaurant, the Four Seasons is considered to be one of the best hotels in Florence.

The royal suite, for example, is probably one of the most incredible suites in the world. The stunning original frescoes and vaulted ceilings make you feel like you are nothing short of a member of the Medici family at the height of your power. Even the regular rooms are beautifully decorated and offer lovely views over nearby medieval streets or into the internal garden.

While a night at the royal suite is probably over budget for most people, there are ways to enjoy this luxurious hotel without breaking the bank. One way is to book a seat at their famous **Sunday Brunch**. Off-season, from October to July, the hotel offers delicious weekly brunches that have become very popular with locals and tourists alike. At 78 euro, the buffet brunch is still very costly, honestly, but it's a fun experience. Call ahead on Monday to book for the upcoming Sunday, as places tend to run out quickly.

Alternatively, if you are visiting during the summer months, or if you prefer an evening drink, afternoon tea or a glass of wine while listening to the soft piano playing in the background, then a drink at the hotel's **Atrium Bar** is a must. The Atrium is one of the smartest bars in town, regularly drawing in a crowd of businessmen, artists, and well-heeled locals and tourists. Sumptuously decorated with oak cabinets and elegant lamps, which provide a soft lighting, this space will help you quickly slip into a perfect mood. Naturally, the cocktails here are professionally prepared.

One last thing: the Four Seasons isn't the only place for a tasty Sunday brunch. The famous Sestro Restaurant (see tip 1), located at the top of the luxurious Westin Hotel, also has a very popular Sunday brunch, as well as a jaw-dropping view (www.sestoonarno.com)

Four Seasons Hotel ★★★★★
Borgo Pinti 99, Florence.
Tel: 055-262-61,
www.fourseasons.com.
NOTES: Brunch is served from October to late June, on Sundays only, in the Palagio restaurant, between noon and 3:00 p.m. The Atrium bar is open daily, 9:00 a.m.–midnight/1:00 a.m.

¶¶ | 18 | **Discover Three Hidden,** Modern and Innovative Florentine Restaurants

Tuscany is known for its no-frills, hearty, and slightly rustic cooking, and Florence is filled with such restaurants. But if you have had your fill of *ossobuco* and tagliatelle and want to sample a more elegant Tuscan cuisine, then there are some wonderful options—even for those who don't want to blow their entire budget.

Acquapazza is one of our favorites, and is located just 10 minutes from Santa Maria Novella, near Fortezza da Basso. Chef Filippo Germasi prepares delicacies such as marinated red prawns, seared scallops with artichokes, crispy polenta and cinta sense, linguine with lobster, and one of our favorites: risotto with scampi. Main dishes are around 20 euro, there is a good wine list, and desserts are excellent. Book a table in advance. There are better seafood restaurants in Tuscany, but in Florence this is one of the best.

Il Santo Graal is another good option. The simple décor belies the innovative kitchen, which is run by a group of young chefs who pride themselves on the smart and delicious menus. This place is more affordable than Acquapazza, but it still has that extra little twist to distinguish it from the typical neighborhood restaurant.

Finally, **La Bottega del Buon Caffe** is a fantastic, intimate, family-run restaurant. The family believes that fresh produce is at the heart of a good kitchen and specializes in local, seasonal dishes. The result is always enjoyable and the wine list plays a perfect complement. A classic tasting menu will cost about 45 euro. Add four glasses of wine to match each course and the price rises to 65 euro. The gourmand menu is 60 euro. We especially enjoy their veal tartar, served with vegetables and olive oil ice cream, the roasted squid served on a cream of chickpeas, and the ravioli made with a chestnut flour and filled with *parmigiano* cream (though the menu is seasonal, and may change). This isn't the place for groups larger than six, as the seating is limited, but it can't be beaten for cozy, intimate dinners.

Acquapazza ★★★
Via Cosimo Ridolfi 4r, Florence.
Tel: 055-475-430,
www.acquapazzafirenze.it.
HOURS OF OPERATION:
Monday-Saturday, 12:30-2:30 p.m.;
7:30-10:30 p.m.

Ristorante il Santo Graal ★★★
Via Romana 70r, Florence.
Tel: 055-228-6533,
www.ristorantesantograal.it
HOURS OF OPERATION:
Thusday-Tuesday, noon-3:00 p.m.,
7:00-10:30 p.m. Closed on Wednesday.

La Bottega del Buon Caffe' ★★★★
Via Antonio Pacinotti 40r, Florence. Tel: 055-553-5677
www.labottegadelbuoncaffe.com
HOURS OF OPERATION:
Monday-Saturday, 12:30-3:00 p.m.,
7:30-10:30 p.m.

 19 | **Treat yourself to a Stay** at One of Florence's Most Unique Hotels–Palazzo Magnani Feroni

Palazzo Magnani Feroni has everything you would expect from a 5-star hotel; each room is meticulously decorated with luxurious antique furniture, the location is spectacular—just minutes away from the Ponte Vecchio and the Boboli Gardens, and the staff is impeccable.

While there are more modern hotels in town, with better amenities, in our opinion, the Magnai Feroni makes up for whatever disadvantages it may have with heaps of charm. Architecturally speaking, this hotel is beautiful—located in a

Renaissance palazzo, guests enter a lobby (though the word "lobby" is really insufficient in this case) which is in fact an open art gallery, filled with antique statues and Renaissance works of art, as well as priceless frescos. The rooftop terrace and bar offer guests some wonderful views of Florence and are the perfect place for a sunset *aperitivo*. The inner courtyard, filled with plants and bathing in sunlight, will make you feel as if you were a character in an E. M. Forester novel. In fact, all of the common spaces are majestic: chandeliers hang from the roof, gilded frames adorn the walls, and regal dark hardwood covers the floors.

The rooms are equally beautiful and the marble bathrooms are a little small but elegant. Off-season you will often find special offers.

Palazzo Magnani Feroni, ★★★★
Borgo San Frediano 5, Florence.
Tel: 055-2399-544,
www.florencepalace.it

 | 20 | **Visit Parenti,** the Perfect Stop for Luxury Items in Florence

An elegant, upscale family business which has served the Florentine elite since 1865, Parenti is a shop bursting with history and luxury. If you are on a quest to find a truly memorable piece for yourself, or a gift for someone special, then this shop is a must-visit.

As soon as you walk in, you are surrounded by a unique, beautifully displayed collection. The luminous store holds an assortment of high-end articles from the likes of Saint Louis, Raynaud, Ercuis, Royal Crown Derby, William Yeoward Crystal, Alberto Pinto, and many more.

Though take warning, the price tags are not for the faint of heart nor the light of wallet. However, there are not many places where you will find a baccarat chandelier designed by Philippe Starck side-by-side with Art Deco crystal glasses or vintage Van Clef jewelry next to Alberto Pinto plates.

Parenti ★★★★
via Tornabuoni 93 r, Florence.
Tel. 055-214-438,
www.parentifirenze.it
HOURS OF OPERATION:
Monday-Saturday 10:00 a.m.-7:30 p.m.
Sunday 11:30 a.m.-7:30 p.m.

 ## 21 | Buy Exquisite Handmade Silverware and Chandeliers in Florence

If you are like us, then you love finding one-of-a-kind items while traveling. Of course, this cannot be just any item, but something rather special, even unique, stylish, and preferably handmade. Something original rather than a clone of the designs you can find in just about any tourist shop in Tuscany. For the right piece, we feel it is absolutely OKAY to splurge a little (or a lot…), for what will undoubtedly become a one-of-a-kind souvenir. If you are overcome by such an urge during your time in Florence, we would recommend three shops that have been attracting the local high society for many years.

Since its founding in 1955, **Brandimarte Argenteria**, located in the Oltrarno district on the west side of the River Arno, has been the place to go for high-end silver items. One of the most well-known silver brands in Italy, their work displays exceptional craftsmanship and a classic sense of style. Their products are not solely elaborate works of the utmost skill; they also make simple, practical items for the household, from egg cups to water servers for the kitchen table. Their tableware though, is particularly beautiful. Guided visits to their studio, to see the artists' work, are available. Call in advance.

Another fascinating shop is **Argenteria Sacchi**, filled to the brim with one-of-a-kind pieces (quite literally – each piece is unique) which are fit for royalty. Though this boutique does stock silverware from other manufacturers, too, their most prized pieces are those personally designed and produced by Sacchi's own artisans.

For chandelier lovers, or for anyone who appreciates unique glass pieces, go to **Ugo Poggi.** The shop opened its gates in 1922 and has been selling delicate china dishes, high class cutlery, and attractive dinnerware since day one. This is the kind

of place that wealthy Florentine families register for wedding gifts. Their elegant showroom is located in one of Florence's most expensive streets, Via Strozzi, ensuring its exclusive reputation. At the showroom, you can find their famous chandeliers, made from Murano glass, as well as ancient silverware and modern pieces, all of which are of superior quality and boast gorgeous designs.

Brandimarte ★★★★
Via U.Foscolo 6, Florence.
Tel: 055-230-411,
www.brandimarte.com
HOURS OF OPERATION:
Monday-Friday, 9 a.m.-1:00 p.m., 2:00-7:00 p.m.; Saturday 10 a.m.-1:00 p.m.
Sunday closed.

Sacchi ★★★★
Lungarno Acciauoli 82, Florence.
Tel: 055-283738,
www.argenteriasacchi.it
HOURS OF OPERATION:
Monday-Saturday, 9 a.m.-1:00 p.m.,
2:00-7:00 p.m.

Ugo Poggi ★★★★
Via Strozzi 26r, Florence.
Tel: 055-216-741,
www.ugopoggifirenze.it.
HOURS OF OPERATION:
Monday-Saturday, 10:00 a.m.-7:00 p.m.
Sunday closed. Off-season may be closed for lunch, from 1:00-3:00 p.m.

 # 22 | **Get Some Serious Shopping Done** in Florence

Florence is filled with tempting shops to grab a fashion lover's attention, everything from touristy little hubs filled with Florentine leather souvenirs to exclusive boutiques that sell the best Italian fashion. The very high-end options—such as Yves Saint Laurent, Bottega Veneta, Hermes, Gucci, and others—are concentrated in the area around Piazza della Republica, Via Strozzi, and the famous Via Tornabuoni. Still expensive and high-end, but slightly less so, are the shops in Via

di Parione (just off via Tornabuoni, near the church of Santa Trinita), Via del Moro, and, of course, the famous Via della Vigna Nuova (where every well-dressed Florentine man and woman goes). Don't miss **Zadig & Voltaire** (Via della Vigna Nuova 17), **Gianfranco Lotti** (at number 45), **Brunello Cucinelli** (next door, at number 47), and **Sartoria Rossi,** a perfect stop for men on the look for smart suits and fasionable shirts (at number 51). In the nearby streets, don't miss **Ottod'Ame**, in Via della Spada 19r, famous for their sophisticated, casual and urban chic look, and **Pineider**, in Piazza Rucellai, who have been making classic, quality leather bags for more than 250 years. Additionally, there are a number of interesting shops along Lungarno Corsini and Lungarno Acciaiuoli, which are sadly often overlooked by tourists. **Flo**, for example (Lungarno Corsini 30, near Il Fiorentino leather shop, see tip 13), is a modern concept store founded by three entrepeneurs, Elisabetta,

Guia and Serena, that combines a modern and exclusive style with a strong belief in social responsibilty and community values. Here you will find several fun yet refined items of clothing and accessories, all designed and produced exclusively by local artisans. Flo also makes a point of providing employment opportunities for disabled workers. **Madani** (Lungarno Acciaiuoli 28), just a few shops down the street, offers an interesting collection of hand made colourful and modern leather bags. Some fine leather items can be found in Boutiqe **Davide Cersai**, next door, as well as in the **Buti** shop at number 54r. Another must stop street is Via Roma, near the Duomo, where you will find the well-known **Miu Miu** and **Luisa Via Roma** stores. Luisa Via Roma, specifically, is perfect for those looking for the latest trends, from Dolce & Gabbana and Armani to Marc Jacobs and Giuseppe Zannotti. If you are visiting Florence in July, during the famous *Saldi* (seasonal sale), it is very likely that you will find a few interesting items for a reasonable price even in Via della Vigna Nuova.

For mid-range options, hit the streets connecting Piazza Santa Maria Novella and the Duomo, which are lined with popular fashion brands such as Stefanel, Sisley, Fratelli Rossetti, and others. The shops along Via Por S. Maria (the street which connects Ponte vecchio and Piazza della Signoria) are worth a visit, as are the many smaller (but interesting!) boutiques in the surrounding alleys. You will also find a number of interesting items in different styles, from hand made jewelry to alternative hip jackets to classic leather bags, in the many small boutiques along Via dei Cerchi, Via Santa Elisabetta, Via dei Tavolini, and the many tiny alleys off the principal Via dei Calzauoli (the

main street that connects the Duomo to Piazza della Signoria).

If you are looking for a one-stop shop, then you must visit **Coin**, a three storey mega-boutique, located on Via dei Calzaiuoli, 56r, just 200 yards from Piazza della Signoria, and **La Rinascente**, in Piazza della Repubblica. Both stock some of the best known local and international brands.

Naturally, don't miss the Leather Market near Piazza San Lorenzo (just a few minutes from the Duomo) and the small but very interesting boutiques in the Oltrarno neighborhood, especially along **Borgo San Jacopo** (located just off the famous Ponte Vecchio).

If your time is limited and you are looking for a local to help you navigate the streets and direct you to the best shops for your taste, you can always schedule an appointment with a professional personal shopper. Maren Erickson (www.florenceshop4it.com), for example, is a well-known local figure. Aware of a tourist's need to balance the draw of the shops and the many attractions of a town like Florence, she offers custom-designed shopping expeditions through town.

Lastly, remember that Florence is not the only place to shop. Via Filungo in Lucca, Corso Italia in Pisa and Via dei Banchi di Sopra in Siena are all well-known shopping streets, filled with fashionable options.

 # 23 | **Buy Excellent Leather Bags** in Florence

Florence is famous for its leather industry. The leather market near San Lorenzo church is a popular stop for tourists and there are numerous shops all around town, competing for visitors' attention. Unfortunately not all shops offer the same quality, and some merchandise is even fake. True Tuscan leather-making is an honorable local industry that has been a point of pride for hundreds of years. Knowing where to go to get the real thing is important. The truly good boutiques may be pricier, but at

least they guarantee a beautiful and quality product, an investment piece that is not only fashionable but one which will last for years.

There are a number of excellent shops you should check out. **Il Bisonte** is a popular choice and is famous for its handmade bags. Their style is modern, mostly. For similar style and quality, visit **Bojola**. **Leoncini** has been a popular stop for fashion lovers in Florence since 1963. They stock more luxurious, classic, handmade items, (including gloves, belts, and wallets) which will appeal to those with a refined sense of style. Bags here can be customized to your personal taste. For more options, consult tip 22 (shopping in Florence).

For the serious shopper, the Scuola del Cuoio and Genten di Firenze are both unmissable stops, not just to see their collections, but mostly, to admire the artisans at work.

The **Scuola del Cuoio** is a Florentine institution. Attached to Santa Croce church, people from all over the world come here to see masters in their workshops and to learn how to work leather. The school was opened after the Second World War by monks from the Franciscan order and leading artisan families from Florence to teach orphans the tricks of the trade and turn them into skilled artisans. The quality is superb and prices are very high. Check their website to learn more. Guided tours (14 euro) are available, and need to be booked in advance, but you can also enter and briefly tour the workshops for free. The Artisans are usually present and working in the workshop Monday–Friday, 10:00 a.m.–5:30 p.m.

Genten Firenze is a Japanese brand, with an all-Tuscan feel. They stock high quality, hand-crafted, and environmentally-friendly unique pieces. The store is located in the most prestigious shopping area in Florence, near Via Tornabuoni, inside the 13th-century Palazzo dei Cerchi. If you are ready to invest in handmade, classic, one-of-a-kind articles, consider making a stop here, too. On Saturday, the artists come to the shop to work, usually between 10:00 a.m. and 4:00 p.m. (also, sometimes on Tuesday at 10:00 a.m.).

Il Bisonte ★★★
Via del parione 31r, Florence.
Tel: 055-215-722
www.ilbisonte.com
HOURS OF OPERATION:
Monday-Saturday, 9:30 a.m.-7:00 p.m.

Bojola ★★★
Via dei Rondinelli 25r, Florence.
Tel: 055-211-155.
HOURS OF OPERATION:
Monday-Saturday: 10:00 a.m.-7:30 p.m.

Leoncini ★★★
Via del Pollaiolo, 172 A,
www.leoncinifirenze.com
Tel: 055.705498
open Monday-Friday, 9:00 a.m.-1:00 p.m.,
3:00-6:00 p.m.

Scuola del Cuoio ★★★★
Via San Giuseppe 5R,
Florence. Tel: 055-244-533,
www.scuoladelcuoio.com
HOURS OF OPERATION:
Fall/Winter, Monday-Friday 10:00 a.m.-
6:00 p.m., Saturday 10:30 a.m.-6:00 p.m.;
Spring/Summer: Monday-Sunday 10:00
a.m.-6:00 p.m.

Genten Firenze Boutique ★★★★
Vicolo de' Cerchi, 1 (at the corner of Via della Condotta), Florence.
Tel: 055-277-6472.
HOURS OF OPERATION:
Daily, 10:00 a.m.-7:00 p.m.

 # 24 Buy Quality, Handmade Gloves and Shoes
in Florence

For almost a century, Madova Gloves has produced quality designer leather gloves, and nothing else. Owned and operated by the Donnini family since 1919, this combination of tradition and highly specialized expertise ensures that if you are looking for gloves, either as a gift or as a souvenir of your time in one of the great countries for fashion in the world, then you will not be disappointed. Situated within a block of the Ponte Vecchio in the Oltrarno, Florence's quarter for artisanal goods, the small but well-furnished shop has a nice selection in different styles. Traditional and modern designs are available and everything is made from the excellent quality Italian materials. For such fine handmade goods, you would usually anticipate paying a small fortune, but the store's most pleasant surprise is the extremely reasonable prices it charges for its wares. Check their online catalog through their website.

For a pair of beautiful, traditionally-crafted shoes, remain in Florence's Oltrarno Quarter, which is famous for its artisanal shops and boutiques. One of the mainstays of this quaint neighborhood is the artisanal workshop of the Mannina family. The family has been crafting men's shoes since 1953 and are renowned for their skill, design ethic and precision. Whether you are after moccasins, boots, or classic calf leather shoes, this is the place to visit. We can guarantee you will walk away happy.

Madova Gloves ★★★
Via Guicciardini 1r, Florence.
Tel: 055-239-6526,
www.madova.it.
HOURS OF OPERATION:
Monday–Saturday, 10:30 a.m.–7:00 p.m.

Mannina Shoes ★★★
Via De' Barbadori 19r,
Tel. 055- 211-060, and Via Guicciardini 16r,
Tel: 055-282-895,
www.manninafirenze.com
HOURS OF OPERATION:
Monday–Friday 9:30 a.m.–7:30 p.m.

 ## 25 Buy Some Quality Paper Products
in Florence

For many people today it may be a rarity to put pen to paper for anything more than the weekly shopping list, however, it is impossible to deny the charm of a handwritten letter using the finest stationery. It is for this reason (and possibly because we are shameless romantics) that we keep a stock of high quality, beautifully designed notebooks, cards, and envelopes to hand. Who knows when you might need them? Thankfully, in Florence it is easy to fulfil this desire for lovingly designed paper products. The city boasts a plethora of specialist shops and the typical Florence printed paper can be found just about everywhere.

The real challenge, however, is to find a store that offers a genuinely unique touch. For something a bit more special, our favorite has to be **Scriptorium.** A small, family-run shop, Scriptorium is where Sherlock Holmes would probably do his shopping if he were on visit in town. There is much to choose from, but we especially love their elegant, lovingly-bound leather Tuscan-style diaries (which can be personalized, too), their beautiful pens, creamy paper, and elegant magnifying glasses. You can find this shop literally a minute from the Duomo, at Via dei Servi 5r. Their website, unfortunately, is very outdated, perhaps befitting a shop which is home to a rather medieval feel and name. As such, it is hard to understand what exactly they have in store without actually popping in for a visit, so we recommend checking it out for yourself.

For more regular goods at reasonable prices we recommend the chain store **Il Papiro.** Their shops stock good quality products and can be found in several locations in Florence and the rest of Tuscany, the likelihood is that you will come across one of their shops sooner or later. Their notebooks decorated with a traditional Florentine pattern

and their photo albums are especially beautiful, and make for a graceful gift or souvenir.

Interestingly, Il Papiro also offers a 3-hour tour of their workshop, which ends with a hands-on lesson, during which visitors will learn more about the techniques of marbleizing paper and traditional book binding. The visit and the workshop cost around 70 euro per person (the price goes down for larger groups), and can be reserved in advance through the store's website.

Scriptorium ★★★★
Via dei Servi 5r,
Tel: 055- 211-804,
www.scriptoriumfirenze.com

Il Papiro ★★★
Piazza del Duomo 24,
Tel: 055 281628,
www.ilpapirofirenze.it/

 # 26 | **Buy a One-of-a-Kind Piece of Art** in Florence

Hard stone mosaics—the product of honed craftsmanship and artisanal technique dating from the Renaissance—are a mark of Florence. But don't think that the tiny Museo Opificio delle Pietre Dure (the Museum of Hard Stones) is the only place where you can appreciate this work at its very best. From their artisanal shop in the center of Florence, **Scarpelli Mosaici** offer objects made using the very same techniques which result in equally impressive quality items. All the artifacts here are made by the specialist hands of master craftsmen Renzo and Leonardo Scarpelli. Their expertise produces goods on a par with those that have been popular with royal families in Italy and abroad for hundreds of years. Using stones sourced from the mountains and hills of Tuscany, from Prato to Chianti to Carrara, as well as others from abroad, what you will find here is very different from regular mosaics. Vividly colorful artworks that grab your attention with the sophistication of their artistic detail, they are most fittingly described as paintings in stone. The most incredible pieces are undoubtedly the tables, though so much of what you see in the workshop, from ornaments to artworks, floor tiles to broaches, is simply beautiful. Buying anything here is far from cheap, but rather an investment in a piece for a lifetime.

Yet another studio to visit, also specializing in unique *pietre dure* designs is **G. Ugolini - Il Mosaico Fiorentino**, in Lungarno Acciauoli (near the Ponte Vecchio). Filled with one-of-a-kind pieces, this tiny old-world, award winning studio is unique. The family who owns this business has been manufacturing its mosaics since 1868. Prices aren't cheap (a small mosaic will cost around 1200 dollars), but you will be taking home with you a little piece of history.

Lastly, **Pitti Mosaici**, located in the Oltratrno and within walking distance from Pitti Palace, has been run by the de Filippis family since the 19th century. The shop specializes in creating elaborate interior designs for clients from around the world who want décor worthy of a noble family, and who value the antique traditions. Make an appointment to visit the unique workshop, or stop by the main show room (located in Piazza Pitti 22, right in front of the Pitti Palace), to discover their elegant creations. Visit their website to see what they have done in the past.

Scarpelli Mosaici (Gallery and Laboratory) ★★★★
Via Ricasol i 59r, Florence.
Tel: 055-212-587,
www.scarpellimosaici.it
HOURS OF OPERATION:
Monday–Saturday 9:30 a.m.–6 p.m

G. Ugolini - Mosaics ★★★★
Lungarno Acciaiuoli 66r, Florence.
Tel: 055-284-969,
www.ugolinimosaici
HOURS OF OPERATION:
Tuesday-Sunday, 10:oo a.m - 7:00 p.m.

Pitti Mosaici ★★★
Sdrucciolo de' Pitti 5r, Florence.
Tel: 055-267-8730,
www.pittimosaici.com

HOURS OF OPERATION:
Tuesday–Sunday, 10:00 a.m.–7:00 p.m.

 # 27 | **Load Up On Some Traditional Italian**
Kitchen Gear

We love that feeling of remembering which comes when you pull out a baking tray or a saucepan you bought in that little Florence boutique, or when you chop the vegetables for a real Italian ragu sauce with a hand-made knife you bought in a small artisanal shop in a hidden Tuscan village. Equipping yourself with Tuscan tools is one of the best ways to bring back home with you some of that Tucan charm. Luckily, the region offers several good shops to choose from.

In Florence, we return again and again to **Bartolini** in the town's historical center, close to the leather market, which features a huge collection of kitchenware. Naturally, we don't focus on the international brands available, but try to hunt for the occasional unique items, and the classic Italian brands. This is a must stop for any cooking enthusiast. **Coltelleria Galli**, just off Via Tornabuoni, and **Coltelleria Bianda**, in Via Vigna Nuova (which

has been selling knives since 1820), are two of the few historical mom and pop shops which have survived the economic crisis and still boast interesting, quality, handmade, Tuscan style professional knifes. A visit here can be fascinating, even if you don't end up buying anything.

If you are a bit of a kitchenware enthusiast and feeling adventurous, drive up to Scarperia, a medieval

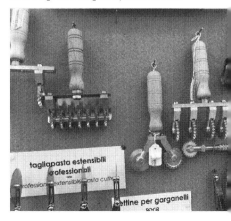

village in northern Tuscany (about 50 minutes from Florence), famous for its knife production. There is really nothing much to do here, but Scarperia has been sharpening its tools since the early 12th century, and there are several shops in the historical center still selling traditional knives. We especially like **Coltelli dell'Artigiano**, run by three master craftsmen. They have a large selection of on display, but will also make personalized knives to order. There is also a small private museum which is open on the weekends

Bartloini ★★★★
Via dei Servi 72R,
Tel: 055-291-497,
www.dinobartolini.it
HOURS OF OPERATION:
Monday–Saturday, 10:00 a.m.-7:30 p.m.

Coltelleria Galli ★★★
Via della Spada 26r,
Tel: 055-282-410.
HOURS OF OPERATION:
Monday, 3:30-7:30 p.m.; Tuesday-Saturday, 9:00 a.m.-1:00 p.m., 3:30-7:30 p.m.

Coltelleria Bianda ★★★
Via della Vigna Nuova 86r,
Tel: 055-294-691.
HOURS OF OPERATION:
Monday, 3:30-7:30 p.m., Tuesday-Saturday, 9:00 a.m.-1:00 p.m., 3:30-7:30 p.m.

Coltelli dell'Artigiano ★★★
Via Roma 77, Scarperia,
Tel: 055-843-0519,
www.coltellidellartigiano.it
HOURS OF OPERATION:
Monday, 3:00-7:00 p.m.; Tuesday-Sunday 9:30 a.m.-1:00 p.m., 3:00-7:00 p.m.

 ## 28 Purchase a Good Man's Shirt in Florence

Every suave man understands the importance of a crisp, good-quality shirt. Any such man would appreciate the style found at **Piero Puliti's** shop on the Via del Corso in Florence. The shop is small but possesses an old world charm. The shelves which carry Piero's wares are made of cherry wood, as is the exterior of the store. The walls inside are wallpapered and decorated with small portraits which one may would easily have found in a clothes shop in London at the turn of the century. The shirts are equally tasteful; simple yet utterly stylish. The ties meanwhile are all designed exclusively for the store by Piero. Like the shop itself the collection here is small. Still, the quality and exclusivity of the shirts and ties on offer and the reasonable prices easily makes this one of the best men's clothes stores in Florence. Have a look at their collection online, or if you're looking for fashion advice you can even send Piero an e-mail at info@pieropuliti.it. Other options worth exploring are **Sartoria Rossi** (in Via della vigna Nuova 51, see tip 22) and **Boggi** (Via della Vigna Nuova 17), both excellent boutiques. Sartoria Rossi, specifically, is a must stop shop. Over the last 40 years this family-owned business has built an excellent reputation. Today it is considered to be one of the leading brands for men in Italy, offering finely tailored, beautiful suits and shirts. Log on to their website to find out more.

Piero Puliti ★★★
Via Del Corso 51r, Florence.
Tel: 055-282-662,
www.pieropuliti.it
HOURS OF OPERATION:
Monday–Saturday, 10:00 a.m.–7:00 p.m.
Closed on Sunday.

Sartoria Rossi
Via della Vigna Nuova 51, Florence
www.sartoriarossi.it

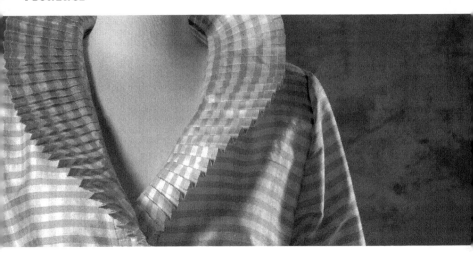

 29 | **Find Quality Linen** and Tablecloths in Florence

Ask any Florentine where to buy quality embroidered tablecloths or gorgeous night gowns and the answer will always be the same: **Loretta Caponi's Atelier.** Quality, as can be imagined, comes at a price, but do make a stop if you are looking for a special piece to take home. It is no accident that clients such as Princess Diana, Jackey Kennedy and Madonna were drawn to Caponi's sophisticated style.

TAF is another must stop for those looking for a special piece. Here you will find both traditional and modern hand made embroidered linen. Across the street you will find TAF's childrens' clothes shop, featuring some absolutely adorable items.

Another good choice is **Bussati 1842.** This Florentine shop is family owned and has been producing quality textiles for seven generations. Their elegant and simple craftsmanship has become popular across Italy and over the decades the shop has morphed into a chain. Browse their collection online.

Loretta Caponi ★★★★
Piazza Antinori 4r,
Tel: 055-213-668,
www.lorettacaponi.com
HOURS OF OPERATION:
Monday, 3:30-7:30 p.m.;
Tuesday-Saturday 9:00 a.m.-1:00 p.m.,
3:30-7:30 p.m.

TAF ★★★
Por. S. Maria 17 & 22,
Tel: 055-239-6039,
www.tafricami.com
HOURS OF OPERATION:
Monday-Saturday, 10:00 a.m-7:30 p.m.,
Sunday, 11:00 a.m-2:00 p.m., 3:00-7:00 p.m.

Busatti Firenze ★★★
Via Borgo San Jacopo,
Tel: 055-289-268,
www.busattipontevecchio.com
HOURS OF OPERATION:
Monday-Saturday, 10:00 a.m.-1:00 p.m.,
3:00-7:30 p.m.; Sunday 3:00-7:30 p.m.

Surrounding Florence

🏃 30 | **Visit Two of the Most Beautiful**
Medici Villas in Tuscany

Not all of the grand villas the Medici family built in Tuscany can be visited today, but of those which can, two in particular stand out as well-preserved, architectural treasures. One is La Petraia and the other is Villa in Poggio a Caiano.

La Petraia is perfectly positioned in the Florentine countryside and enjoys an impressive view of the city from its Belvedere Terrace. This is the perfect place to get away from the crowds—take a tour of the villa itself or simply walk around the beautiful late-Renaissance gardens. It is where the Medici family spent many of their vacations, escaping the city's heat (and intrigues…) and enjoying the quiet bliss, while still being close enough to the town to control their many businesses. The impressive tower is one of the oldest parts of the villa, a reminder of the mansion's past as a fortified residence when it was still owned by the Brunelleschi family. The gardens and the beautiful frescos

were added in the late 16th century and early 17th century. The front gardens, from which a panoramic view of Florence can be seen, are traditional Italian, and the garden in the back is English-style. Various rooms and hallways in the villa are still decorated with original frescoes and antique furniture and priceless art adorns the walls, but the most impressively decorated space is the fresco-covered courtyard.

Like many Medici villas, this was later used as an official residence of Italy's royal family—the Savoia, and King Vittorio Emanuele II, together with his wife, Rosa Vercellana, spent many summers here. Come to visit and you'll understand why this place was so loved. It isn't overly extravagant; just irresistibly charming. Admission is free and the villa is easily accessed from Florence.

Villa Poggio a Caiano is farther from Florence, located in a more hilly part of Tuscany. Built under the orders of Lorenzo (il Magnifico) Medici, the villa was designed by one of the leading architects of the time, and a close collaborator of the Medici family, Giuliano da Sangalo (who also designed the famous lion and griffin fountain in Montepulciano). The resulting villa was a huge success and the design was imitated by many architects working on other Tuscan mansions in the following years.

Decorating the wall inside are numerous works of beautiful art, by artists such as Filippino Lippi, Andrea Sansovino, Pontormo and Andrea del Sarto. Two of the most significant and lavish political marriages within the Medici family took place here—Cosimo the First wed Eleonora of Toledo, and Alessandro de Medici wed Margherita of Austria. Francesco the First and Bianca Capello were also married in this villa and died in it, both poisoned. This was even a favorite spot of Elisa Baciocchi Bonaparte, Napoleon's sister, who ruled as the Great Duchess of Tuscany from 1809.

Today the villa hosts a special museum with a wonderful collection of still life paintings, which can be viewed by appointment only. The villa and the royal bedrooms are beautiful, but can only be visited with a guided tour, which must be booked in advance. The residence has suffered somewhat from budget cuts. However, now that the villa has been recognized as a UNESCO World Heritage Site, we hope it will be restored to its past glory. The best time to visit is during one of the festivals that take place in the villa. Check the website to see if anything is going on during your visit. The gardens can be visited freely without a booking.

Villa La Petraia ★★★

Via della Petraia 40, Località Castello, Florence.
Tel: 055- 238-8717,
www.polomuseale.firenze.it/musei
HOURS OF OPERATION:
November-February, Daily, 8:15 a.m.-3:30 p.m.; March, Daily, 8:15 a.m.-4:30 p.m.; April, May, September, October, Daily, 8:15 a.m.-5:30 p.m.; June-August, Daily, 8:15 a.m.-6:30 p.m. Closed on major holiday, last entry one hour before closing.

Poggio a Caiano ★★★★

Piazza de Medici 14, Poggio a Caiano.
Tel: 055-877-012.
HOURS OF OPERATION:
The Villa complex (including the park, the gardens and the royal apartments) is open daily (closed on the second and third Tuesday of every month and on major holidays). Park and garden: October-March, Daily, 8:15 a.m.-4:30 p.m.; April-May and September, Daily, 8:15 a.m.-6:30 p.m.; June-August, Daily, 8:15 a.m.-7:30 p.m. Last entry, one hour before closing. Royal Apartments: Entry every hour, from 8:30 a.m. Last entry: November-February, 3:30 p.m.; March, October, 4:30 p.m.; April-May and September, 5:30 p.m.; June-August, 6:30 p.m. Entry to the Museo della Natura Morta (Museum of Still Life) is by guided tour only, and must be booked in advance. Tours leave once an hour (if a minimum number of people are present–usually around 10), starting at 9:00 a.m. (no tour at 1:00 p.m.). Last entry: November-February, 3:00 p.m.; March, October, 4:00 p.m.; April-May and September, 5:00 p.m.; June-August, 6:00 p.m.

 ## 31 | **Hit the Outlet Stores** in Tuscany and Shop for Real Italian Fashion

From fashionistas to shopaholics, if you're the kind of person who is serious about shopping then Tuscany's outlets are a must. Don't miss out on **The Mall**, which sits just outside the town of Leccio, roughly a 35-km drive from Florence. This is the perfect place to find stylish, high mark names such as Gucci, Salvatore Ferragamo, Valentino and Armani. If you have a craving for **Dolce Gabbana** you can find just what you're looking for, along with some real bargains, at their outlet right next to The Mall.

Prada lovers should head to the company's outlet store in Montevarchi, on the way to Arezzo. Though not very cheap, with reductions of usually around 30% on the wholesale price, you can sometimes find a good deal here, too.

High-end clothes from designers such as Max Mara, Galliano, Cavalli, Trussardi, Ferre, and other, less

exclusive brands, can be found in the relatively new **Fashion Valley Outlet**, which opened in 2011 in Scandicci, right outside Florence. Also on offer in this complex is a range of jewelry, sunglasses and watch brands, including Tag Heuer, Timex, Hugo Boss, and Nanis.

Fans of **Roberto Cavalli** will be interested in his outlet store in Sesto Fiorentino, about 20 minutes from Florence, though a good selection of Cavalli items can be found in The Mall and at The Fashion Valley Outlet, too. Fans of the Florentine designer **Ermanno Scervino** will want to check out his small but attractive outlet shop where the Ermanno Scervino Man, Woman, and Junior lines are all on sale. The store is located in Grassina, outside of Florence.

Your best choice if you are searching for a mix of high level and mid-level brands (like Levi's, Ralph Lauren,

Adidas, and Wranglers along with popular Italian brands such as Guess, Motivi, and Elena Miro), is to head out to the large outlet **Barberino del Mugello**, half an hour north of Florence, which is home to more than 90 shops. Another mid-level shopping outlet, similar to Barberino del Mugello is **the Valdichiana Outlet**, near Arezzo, though it has a smaller and less varied selection.

The Fashion Valley Outlet ★★★
Ruota al Mandò, Reggello (FI),
Tel: 055-865-7798,
www.fashionvalley.it
HOURS OF OPERATION:
Daily, 10:00 a.m.-7:00 p.m. Closed on Major holidays.

Barberino Di Mugello ★★★★
Via Meucci (exit the autostrada at Barberino and follow the brown signs to the "outlet", not to the town of Barberino itself).
Tel: 055-842-161,
www.mcarthurglen.it/barberino/.
HOURS OF OPERATION:
Monday-Friday, 10:00 a.m.-8:00 p.m.;
Saturday-Sunday 10:00 a.m.-9:00 p.m.

Dolce & Gabbana ★★★
Via S. Maria Maddalena 49, Incisa in Val d'Arno (FI). Tel: 055-833-1300.
HOURS OF OPERATION:
Monday-Saturday, 9:00 a.m.-7:00 p.m.,
Sunday 3-7p.m.

Ermanno Scervino Private Outlet ★★★
Via di Tizzano 169, Grassina (FI).
Tel: 055-649-24395.
HOURS OF OPERATION:
Monday-Tuesday, 3:00-7:00 p.m.;
Wednsday-Sunday 10:00 a.m.-7:00 p.m.

The Mall ★★★★
Via Europa 8, Reggello (FI).
GPS Coordinates: N 43° 42.130′, E 011° 27.804′.
Tel: 055-865-7775,
www.themall.it
HOURS OF OPERATION:
Daily, 10:00 a.m.-7:00 p.m. (June–August open until 8:00 p.m.).

Roberto Cavalli ★★★
Via Volturno 3, Sesto Fiorentino - Location Osmannoro (FI). Tel: 055-317-754,
www.robertocavallioutlet.it
HOURS OF OPERATION:
Monday-Saturday, 10:00 a.m.-7:00 p.m.

Valdichiana Outlet Village ★★★
Via Enzo Ferrari 5, Foiano della Chiana (AR). Exit off the autostrada at "Valdichiana". Tel: 0575-649-926,
www.valdichianaoutlet.it
HOURS OF OPERATION:
Daily, 10:00 a.m.-8:00 p.m.

Prada Outlet ★★★
Strada Regionale 69 (Levanella), Montevarchi. Tel: 055-978-9481.
HOURS OF OPERATION:
Sunday-Friday, 10:30 a.m.-7:30 p.m.;
Saturday, 9:30 a.m.-7:30 p.m.
(hours may vary).

 32 **Buy Some Great Olive Oil** from Gonnelli 1585

We love bringing the olive oil from Gonnelli 1585 home to our friends and family. The design of the Grand Cru selection oil is wonderfully dramatic—a square, cut-glass bottle, reminiscent of a 1930s whiskey decanter, perfectly placed into the black box with silver Gonnelli signature and red wax stamp—and is nothing short of regal. The olive oil inside this beautiful display is equally delicious. We recommend the Profuma d'Olive and the Piazza del Palio—both are aromatic and elegant tasting oils. Gonnelli also have a good selection of sauces and pastes, and guided tours of the 500 year old mill can be organized with advanced bookings.

The area where Gonnelli is located isn't usually a big tourist draw. However, a large outlet complex called The Mall is just 15 minutes away (see tip 31). The center, which stocks high-end, exclusive brands, draws shoppers from across Tuscany and is a favorite with tourists, too. If you are foodies on a shopping spree, or shopaholics with a passion for quality produce, combining these two sites may be a great way to spend an afternoon.

Gonnelli 1585
Via E. de Nicola 41, Loc. Santa Tea, Reggello (FI), Tel: 055-868-117, www.gonnelli1585.it
HOURS OF OPERATION: Monday-Friday, 9:00 a.m.-noon, 2:00-6:00 p.m. 3 stars

 33 | **Buy a Bottle of Laudemio**–The Highest Quality of Olive Oil

Exalted by gastronomic experts and celebrities alike, *laudemio* is, for many, the finest olive oil this part of the world has to offer. Traditionally, *laudemio* was the name given to best part of any olive harvest, especially reserved for the lord of the manor. For centuries, it has been said to represent the pinnacle of taste and fragrance that the Tuscan oil industry has to offer. In the 1980s, twenty one producers, many of whom can trace their lineage back to great Tuscan noble families of antiquity, came together to ensure the continuing quality and exclusivity of production. To find out more about the history of the *ludemio*, visit www.laudemio.it

Personally, we like the produce from **Castello di Poppiano**, one of the prominent members of the Laudemio Council. The Castello itself, owned by the Guicciardini family for nine centuries, is a 1000-year-old medieval fort which was heavily renovated in the 19th century. Located between Florence and Siena, in a wonderfully fertile and sun-soaked area, the olive oil produced on this estate is particularly fruity and aromatic, and has won a number of prizes over the years, including the Ercole Olivario National Contest, one of Italy's most esteemed olive oil contest, securing its reputation as one of the best oils in the country.

Another great option is the Frescobaldi *laudemio*. A centuries-old noble family with a fascinating history at the center of Florentine economic and political life, the Frescobaldis are mostly famous for their award-winning wines. Their oil, especially from the Ruffiana area north of Florence, is excellent, too. It can be bought on their estate, the beautiful **Castello di Nipozzano**. Drive out here to tour the impressive castle and enjoy the remarkable view of their grounds. While there, be sure to taste some of their lip-smacking *Chianti Nipozzano* (or better yet—the *Chianti Riserva*) and purchase the oil, naturally. Visits should be booked at least a week in advance. If you don't have time to head out to the estate, try to get to their shop in Florence on Via Santo Spirtito 11, near the Pitti Palace, where you can find all their products.

Castello di Poppiano ★★★

Via Fezzana 43, Montespertoli (FI).
Tel: 055-823-15,
www.conteguicciardini.it
Oil and other produce can be bought directly at the castle's shop. Hours of operation: Monday–Saturday, 8:30 a.m.–noon, 2:00–6:00 p.m.; Sunday, 2:30–6:30 p.m. (Though calling before leaving, especially off-season, is always recommended).

Castello di Nipozzano ★★★

Via di Nipozzano, Nipozzano, Pelago (FI).
Tel: 055-831-1050
GPS Coordinates: N 43 47.091 - Longitude E 11 28.297. Tours and visits need to be booked in advance.

Chianti

🏃 |34| **Visit the Chianti** Sculpture Park

The Chianti Sculpture Park was founded by Rosalba and Piero Giadrossi, a husband and wife team with a passion for contemporary art. This unique and beautiful open air museum, located just half an hour north of Siena, is filled with sculptures made by artists from around the world. The park was opened in 2004, and is set on seven hectares of woodland. We love coming here in the late afternoon to stroll around in the fresh, scented air. The park is the first initiative in a process that is meant to eventually transform Pievasicta, the hamlet in which it resides, into a B.A.C—*Borgo d'Arte Comtemporanea* (contemporary art hamlet). The philosophy of this park centers on combining art and nature, giving voice to different artists from 19 countries (and counting) around the world who use different materials and style to create their artwork. This is a real mosaic of art and nature. Among the artists who have their work on display here are Neal Barab and Benbow Bullock from the USA, Jeff Saward and William Furlong from the UK, and Nicolas Bertoux from France.

From June to August, you can extend the day by attending the weekly classical and jazz concerts. Arrive early to get a good seat. You can also combine a visit to the park with a tour of Vagliagli (a tiny medieval *borgo* 11-kilometers north of the park, with gorgeous views of the entire area from the top), or with a wine tasting session at one of the nearby estates in Castelnuovo Berardenga, Siena or Gaiole in Chianti.

Chianti Sculpture Park ★★★★
Loc. La Fornace 48, Pievasciata (near Castelnuovo Berardenga), GPS Coordinates: Long.E. 11° 22' 53" - Lat.N. 43° 23' 36".
Tel: 0577-357-151,
www.chiantisculpturepark.it
HOURS OF OPERATION:
March-November, open daily, 10:00 a.m.- sunset. Off-season (November-March), it is recommended to call first, as the park may be closed for visitors. Download detailed driving instructions from their website.

 35 | **Visit Castello di Ama** for a Unique Experience Combining Excellent Wine with Beautiful Modern Art

One of the region's finest wineries and also a contemporary art gallery, **Castello di Ama** is a personal favorite and a unique place that absolutely merits a visit. Since 2000, the winery has, in collaboration with Galleria Continua of San Gimignano, commissioned a number of installations which are strategically placed throughout the estate by the likes of Louise Bourgeois, Anish Kapoor, Michelangelo Pistoletto, Chen Zhen, and others. The modern art in the castle gives a visit here a different kind of feel than you normally encounter on the standard Tuscan wine tour.

The current winery was founded by a number of local families in the 1960s. In those days before wine tourism, this was still a poor area, but the families involved believed they could restore the medieval castle to its former glory and create an exceptional product, an award-winning kind of Chianti Classico. They were right, as since

that time their wines have won numerous accolades. Today the castle is run by Lorenza Sebasti and Marco Pallanti under whom the successes of Castello di Ama have continued. They have received several honorable mentions, and in 2005, were even chosen as the winery of the year by the prestigious *Gambero Rosso* guide. Undoubtedly, the greatest claim to fame was when, in a blind tasting, the Castello's l'Apparita wine beat the world famous Chateau Petrus.

There are different kinds of tours available, from the Ama Anthology tour, which offers exposure to the castle's different wines and olive oils, to the more specific Discovering the Crus tour, which focuses on different vintages of one of their four specific crus: Castello di Ama, Vigneto Bellavista, Vigneto La Casuccia, and L'Apparita. Tours and tastings must be booked in advance. Though the tours are highly recommended, as they enable you to explore the grounds and see all of the artwork, you can also freely visit the estate, buy a glass of wine from the *enoteca* and wander around the property, soaking in its beauty. You can also stop for a tasty lunch at the estate's small diner.

Don't leave without picking up a bottle of their wine to take home with you (we love the Haiku 2009, and the Al Poggio 2011, but even an "entry level" wine like the Ama 2010 is excellent), and of Castello di Ama olive oil, which is absolutely delicious.

Castello di Ama ★★★★★
Località Ama, Gaiole in Chianti,
Tel: 0577-746-031, Cell: 335.7746188,
www.castellodiama.com

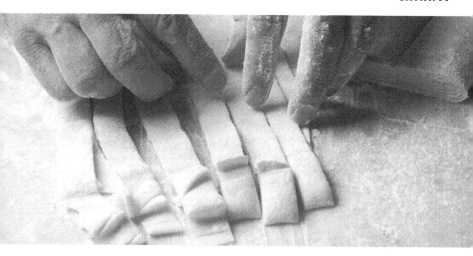

🍴 36 | **Book a Fun** and Delicious Cooking Class in Tenuta Casanova

Tenuta Casanova is a beautiful place, and their cooking lessons are some of the most fun in Tuscany. The 20 hectares of vineyards and burnt yellow farmland is located between Poggibonsi and Castellina in the Chianti region. The drive up to the estate, as you progress along a winding road surrounded by vineyards and cypress forest, will put you in the right mood for the culinary experience that awaits your arrival.

The cooking classes here are a full day activity. For six to seven hour visitors learn many secrets of Tuscan cuisine, beginning with the preparation of fresh pasta— from *ravioli* to *tagliatelle*. This is accompanied by good local cheeses and cold cuts. You will, of course, also make real Tuscan *secondi*—a main dish—usually meat-based; as well as a *contorno*—a side dish of traditional cooked vegetables. Rita, the friendly and charming chef leading the course, will even teach you the recipe for her famous *tiramisu*. All this is accompanied by tasting the wines produced in this estate.To round things off you even get a chance to try their 30-year-old balsamic vinegar served over ice cream. The classes cater to groups of eight maximum, so book in advance, as this attraction is popular. There is also an hour-long tour of the estate and the wine cellar, led by Silvio, which includes wine tasting as well as a chance to try their range of vinegars, olive oils, and honey. Remember, though, that the real highlight here is the cooking class. The wine here is by no means bad, but it wouldn't exactly rank among the top makers in Tuscany.

Tenuta Casanova ★★★★
Località Sant' Agnese 20, Castellina in Chianti. GPS Coordinates: latitude 43.476981, longitude 11.225875 (may appear in your GPS as "Caselle di Sant'Agnese").
Cell: 335-615-0760,
www.tenutacasanova.it

 37 | **Do Some Wine Tasting**, Dine, or Even Book a Cooking Class at Badia a Coltibuono

Badia a Coltibuono is one of the best-known wine producers in Tuscany, and even though their tours can be a bit touristy, we still think it's worth it to taste the goods. Even the simple wines from this mostly organic estate leave a memorable note on your palate. Their reasonably-priced and delicious Badia a Coltibuono Chianti Classico 2010, for example, is a regular guest on our dinner table and at parties, their Cancelli 2011 has caused excitement among wine connoisseurs, and the Slow Food Movement considers this estate to be one of the most important producers in the field. If the idea of a tour isn't your cup of tea, simply enjoy the wine tasting and pick up some bottles at the *enoteca*.

The Badia's restaurant is an obvious choice for lunch and is one of the best restaurants in the Chianti region. That's not just our opinion: it has been heralded by guides, travelers, and critics alike to be one of the region's

top 20 (for dinner, we prefer the restaurant at Castello Spaltenna, see next tip). We love how a modern touch is seamlessly melded with traditional Tuscan delicacies. Sitting outside in their garden, surrounded by wisteria plants and climbing roses, is particularly pleasant. Meat is an obvious choice in a place like this, in the heart of the Chianti area, but their homemade fresh pasta is excellent, too. Reservations are highly recommended, especially in high season.

Naturally, this scenic *agriturismo*, which today defines itself as a "wine resort", offers rooms and apartments to rent. The 1000-year-old abbey has been converted and restored, and guests can choose between former monk cells which have been transformed into comfortable lodgings, or one of the apartments on the premises. As far as amenities go, this isn't the most sophisticated lodging option in the area, but it definitely offers a unique charm.

Badia a Coltibuono ★★★★

Gaiole in Chianti, GPS Coordinates: 43.49490600, 11.44954830, Tel: 0577-74481,
www.coltibuono.com
NOTE: tours, tastings and cooking classes need to be booked in advance. Restaurant hours of operation: mid March–mid November (exact dates change yearly, check on their website), daily, noon-2:30 p.m., 7:00-9:30 p.m. (From 3:00 p.m. to 5:30 p.m., light snacks and drinks are served.) Reservations are recommended: 0577-749-031

ᚊᚋ 38 | **Visit Tuscany's Most Famous Butcher–**
And Stop for a Lively Dinner!

Dario Cecchini's **Antica Macelleria** draws quite a crowd and not only because of the excellent quality of the meat. His vibrant, larger-than-life personality has made Cecchini an institution in Italy. A true Tuscan host, he often welcomes his guests with a few lines from Dante's *Divina Commedia*. You may even be treated to a glass of Chianti and a piece of bread smeared with aromatized lard while you wait in line to get your teeth around one of his famous steaks. As the eight generation in a line of butchers, Cecchini comes from a strong tradition. It's just as well that the art of butchery is in his blood as he had no choice but to enter the family business when his parents died at a young age, leaving him to take care of the family. Giving up his dreams of becoming a vet (a little ironic, perhaps, given the restaurant's defiantly carnivorous philosophy), Cecchini combined this long tradition with his natural charm and PR skills, in the process, making himself famous at home and abroad.

In the evening, the small restaurant adjacent to the butcher's opens up and dinner is served. Here people will feast on beef tartar, fondly called "Sushi del Chianti", *affettati*, and, of course, the highlight of the meal—the traditional *bistecca Fiorentina*, the Florentine steak, a huge ordeal, seared from the outside, almost rare on the inside. The dining experience resembles a medieval feast: everyone sits together and gorges, wine is poured again and again into newly emptied glasses, and the smell from the roaring grill will, at some point, confuse your senses.

Dinners are held in season on Tuesday, Friday, and Saturday evenings, at 8:00 p.m., and, as Cecchini puts it, are recommended for those who have an appetite. The fixed price is very reasonable at 50 euro per person with wine included, though you can bring your own bottle if you prefer. There is also a vegetarian menu available, but it is very limited, and, to be honest, if you're looking for a vegetarian meal, this not the place to choose. Cecchini's is for proud meat-lovers, a self-proclaimed "Paradise for Carnivores". In any case, book well in advance, especially during high-season, as this place is popular.

Serious foodies may also be interested in Cecchini's three-hour workshop, which is held every Friday (very interesting but costly, at 200 euro).

If you have rented a villa or an apartment in the area, and are interested in buying a *bistecca Fiornentina* to take home and cook for your friends and family, make sure you book a few days in advance.

Antica Macelleria Cecchini ★★★★
Via XX Luglio 11, Panzano di Greve in Chianti.
Tel: 055-852-020,
www.dariocecchini.com.
HOURS OF OPERATION:
Daily, 9:00 a.m.–4:00 p.m., hours may vary off-season. Dinner is served at 8:00 p.m. and should be booked in advance

39 Visit the World Famous Antinori Cantine
A True Treat for Architecture Lovers as Well as Wine Enthusiasts

Since 1385, the wines produced by the Antinori family have been a symbol of quality and class. Today, the business is run by Marquis Piero Antinori and his three daughters Albiera, Allegra, and Alessia, who are the 26th generation to run the family business. The current owners stress both their connection to tradition and a desire to innovate and constantly improve the quality of their produce. This is no small brand. Just in Tuscany, the family owns a number of estates (and several others around the world), the most famous of which are Peppoli, Guado al Tassto (read more about this famous estate in tip number 96) and, of course, the world renowned Tignanello estate.

Visiting the newly renovated Antinori Cantina is, in our opinion, a must-do experience. At 20 euro per person, including a tasting of 4 wines, it is also a very good deal. The cantine is highly recommended not just for the wine, but also to admire the structure itself, which was beautifully designed by architect Marco Casamonti. In fact, the design has drawn considerable attention from architects and critics around the world, and was elected as one of the most interesting cantines in Europe by several critics. The tour itself is serious and informative, and despite the size of the groups (up to 20 people), manages to maintain a certain intimacy. The tasting at the end, of course, is delicious. As far as the wines go, buying a few bottles from one of the Antinori lines is a guaranteed success. For a (relatively) reasonable price you can get an excellent bottle, such as the Cervaro Della Sala, or Solaia 2010, which received excellent reviews by just about every major wine critic. Equally good value is a 2007 Tignanello, or a Marchese Antinori Chianti Classic Riserva 2009, which is a wonderfully balanced, reasonably priced, delicious wine,

and one of our personal favorites. Visits should be booked in advance, via Antinori's website: www.hospitalityantinorichianticlassico.it

Lastly, there is a restaurant on the premises, which is recommended for a quick lunch if you are visiting in September or October (when trucks come and unload the grapes into the winery in front of your eyes). But for a more serious experience, we would recommend dining at another Antinori establishment: **Osteria di Passignano**, a wonderful, delicious Michelin-starred restaurant, located just 20 minutes away from the estate (see next tip).

Antinori Cantine (Antinori nel Chianti) ★★★★★

Via Cassia per Siena 133, Loc. Bargino, San Casciano Val di Pesa. GPS Coordinates 43° 36′ 43:30″, 11° 11′ 29.76″.

CANTINE HOURS OF OPERATION: From April 1 to October 30, the cantine is open daily, 11:00 a.m.-6:00 p.m. (until 7:00 p.m. from June to late October). From July 1 to August 31, the cantine is closed on Sunday; November 1-March 30, the cantine is open Wednesday-Monday, 11:00 a.m.-4:00 p.m., closed on Tuesday. Note: A visit to the cantine during hours of operation will permit you to purchase wine and see the entry to the building, but you won't be able to tour the entire facility, or see its unique structure, without booking a tour in advance. Tours usually leave 8 times a day, from 10:00 a.m. to 5:00 p.m., every hour on the hour, and are available in English, too.

⅄ | 40 | **Book an Exclusive Tour** at the Antinori Badia di Passignano Wine Cellar (and End with a Memorable Meal at the Osteria di Passignano)

A visit to the vineyards and cellars of Badia a Passignano feels like a trip back in time. Located in the classic Chianti region, in a 700-year-old monastery and borgo which is still inhabited by Vallumbrosan monks, the area is suffused with history. The original Pasignano Abbey was built in 395 AD and maintained its reputation for centuries. In fact, Galileo Galilei was once a teacher there. As such, a tour here is no ordinary afternoon spent wine tasting; it is a truly special experience. Yet another estate owned by the Antinori family the tours here are more extensive than the classic cellar tour you will find in the previous Antinori estate.

The tours of the estate vary, and range from simple visits to more elaborate excursions which also include lunch. The "Badia a Passignano and the great Antinori wines", for example, at 180 euro, includes a four hour guided visit with an expert guide to the vineyards and the historic wine cellars in the abbey. You will learn about wine production, take part in some olive oil tasting and have dinner at the Osteria on-site. Your meal will be accompanied by some of Antinori's signature wines: Chianti Classico Riserva Badia a Passignano, Tignanello, Guado al Tasso, Brunello di Montalcino, and Solaia (all considered some of the best in

Tuscany). Considering the price of a dinner here and the price of the wines, this is actually a reasonable offer worth considering (do check the menu offered with this tour, first, to see if it is to your liking). Alternatively, a tour of the historic cellars in the abbey and a tasting of Chianti Classico Riserva, Solaia, and Guado al Tasso—all three of which are excellent award-winning wines— can be organized daily for a group of at least four people, at 4:30 in the afternoon, for around 80 euro. Prices, dates, and timetables change, so do check everything on their website, book in advance, and take the time to read their cancellation policy.

Whether you tour the estate or not, the *osteria* on-site is a highly recommended venue, perfect for a special lunch or dinner. Situated in a lovely renovated farmhouse, the dining experience here is one of the best in Tuscany, and justifies the Michelin star it holds. With modern dishes, beautiful presentation and a very local menu, you can enjoy dishes such as cannelloni filled with lamb, served on a lemony *zabaione*, roasted pigeon served with caramelized *tropea* onions, *baccala gnocchi*, and more (note that vegetarian options in this restaurant are extremely limited). A dish called "four versions of an artichoke", served in season, naturally, was one one of the best dishes we've had in Tuscany.

The small enoteca at the entry to the restaurant offers guests the possibility of organizing a little impromptu tasting. Of course you can also pick up a bottle to take home with you. The selection here is wide, including some quite rare bottles, but there is no need to spend a fortune; some medium range wines are available too. The shop is open Monday–Saturday, 10:00 a.m.–7:30 p.m.

Osteria Badia di Passignano
★★★★★

Via Passignano 33, Loc. Badia a Passignano, Tavarnelle Val di Pesa (the osteria is located right at the entry to the tiny village of Badia di Passignano. You will see it immediately on your right).
Tel: 055-807-1278,
www.osteriadipassignano.com
HOURS OF OPERATION:
Monday–Saturday, 12:15-2:15 p.m., 7:30-10:00 p.m. Closed on Sunday, and for winter break (usually late Janurary to early March, check website for details).

41 | **Spend a Week** at one of Tuscany's Most Beautiful Villas – "La Veduta di Vertine"

The fairy tale Tuscan experience: a lavish 16th-century Villa surrounded by olive groves, cypress trees, and rolling vineyards, where you can sit out by the pool under blue skies in the warmth of the golden sun, gently sipping a delicious glass of wine in the heart of the Chianti region. Before we tempt you any more, we should mention that the lowest price for just one night here is $3,200, and with extras included the cost can rise to $5,000. But if money is no object, then you absolutely must consider a stay in these incredible surroundings.

The villa is within walking distance of both Gaiole in Chianti and the medieval hamlet of Vertine and is a twenty-five minute drive from Siena, a fifty minute journey from Florence, and within an hour's distance of Arezzo, San Gimignano, and Montalcino. The Villa's stone exterior displays a typically rustic Tuscan charm and houses over 6,000 square feet of space. The four bedrooms and five bathrooms are spread between the main house and the guest house, both of which are decorated with a keen knowledge of how best to combine the traditional and the modern. Vaulted wooden beam ceilings, bricked archways, and large windows abound while the walkway up to the villa's entrance is charmingly covered in green vines. Inside you will find a full brick pizza oven, a wine cellar, exercise equipment and entertainment areas including a billiards table. The courtyard and gardens are even more tempting. Fruit trees and chicken coops provide fresh organic produce which you may peruse during your stay. The courtyard is fully equipped

for al fresco dining, including its very own barbeque and the gardens themselves are lovingly kept. The real stunner, though, is the outdoor heated infinity pool and its open views which stretch for miles over the graceful Tuscan landscape.

Children are perfectly welcome though pets are not allowed. A maximum of ten guests are allowed to stay while the minimum number of nights you must book fluctuates between three and seven, depending on the time of year.

As with many other luxury retreats, this villa is rented through agencies which specialize in such habitats. These websites offer many other marvellous villas and houses for rent, with equally beautiful views.

Consult the following websites to book, and search for "La Veduta di Vertine":

www.villasofdistinction.com

www.villasofdistinction.com

www.luxuryretreats.com

 42 Book a Moonlit or Morning Horseback Ride
across the Rolling Hills of the Chianti Region

The **Barardenga Riding School** in Podere Santa Margherita offers day tours as well as moonlit night tours across the rolling Chianti hills. Sadio and Donatella, the owners, have turned their passion for horses and country-living into their profession. They have opened an organic farm holiday and riding center in a particularly beautiful part of Tuscany. The views in this vineyard-covered part of Tuscany are spectacular.

A variety of riding itineraries in the countryside are on offer, but we suggest talking to the owners, and based on your experience (even if you have no experience whatsoever) they will find the perfect tour for you, starting with an introductory lesson. The summer moonlit tour is especially romantic and recommended. A whole day ride and picnic will cost around 110 euro. This place is no-frills but packed with charm.

Barardenga Riding School–Podere Santa Margherita ★★★
Strada del Ciglio 2, Castelnuovo Berardenga, Cell: 339-831-8519, www.chiantiriding.it

 43 **Soak Up the Rugged-Beauty** of the Chianti Countryside at the Fonterutoli Estate

The Marchesi Mazzei family is one of the oldest and most prestigious names connected to wine producing in all of Tuscany. Throughout the years they have won numerous awards for their wines, and having been in business now for 24 generations they have developed quite a pedigree. The heart of their production empire can be found at the Castello di Fontrutoli Winery. This breathtaking estate has been

in the family since 1435 and is surrounded by six hundred hectares of the mostly unspoiled nature, a rugged kind of beauty that makes it all the more charming.

Situated in the center of this spectacular landscape is the serene Mazzei castle. Built in the 1500s it has recently been impressively and respectfully refurbished, adding a chic, stylish edge without losing the village's rustic soul. A particularly notable job was done on the *borgo*, which before was falling apart. Best of all, there are twelve comfortable rooms available here in which you can stay.

There are many advantages to staying here, in this tranquil oasis located just five kilometers from Castellina in Chianti, but we are here to recommend first and foremost the wine yours held in this estate. This is one tour which should not be skipped if you are in the area, and the estate's wine cellar, which has been described by Decanter magazine and others as one of the most impressive in Chianti. Each tour lasts about an hour and twenty minutes, and even the constant arrival of tourist groups can't ruin the experience. Tours are available in English, French, or Italian and the maximum number of people per group is twenty. A tasting, held in their inviting little *enoteca*, follows the tour. The cost for four glasses is 25 euro. Also available on the estate are cooking classes while for those who want to explore the estate's sumptuous surroundings hiking, bike tours, and horseback riding can all easily be arranged.

The *osteria* on the premises offers good value, quite simple but satisfying takes on traditional Tuscan classics. Of course the opportunity to pair your meal with one of the family's renowned wines makes for a particularly memorable experience. Inside the restaurant is cleanly and neatly laid out, though the best spot is undoubtedly on the outside terrace with its views of the estate's olive groves, vineyards, and lush hills.

Fonterutoli estate and Enoteca (Marchesi Mazzei) ★★★★

Via Ottone III di Sassonia 5, Loc. Fonterutoli, Castellina in Chianti.
Tel: 0577-73571 or 0577-741-385,
www.fonterutoli.it
NOTE: all wine tasting tours of the estate need to be booked in advance through the Fonterutoli website. Tours usually leave four times a day (at 10:00 a.m., noon, 3:00 p.m., and 5:00 p.m., though hours may vary) Cooking classes are held daily (starting at 11:00 a.m.) and need to be booked in advance.

ENOTECA HOURS OF OPERATION: mid-March–November, Monday–Saturday, 9:00 a.m.–6:30 p.m., Sunday 9:00 a.m.–1:00 p.m., 2:00 p.m.–6:00 p.m.

OSTERIA HOURS OF OPERATION: Wednesday–Monday, 12:30–2:00 p.m., 7:30–10:00 p.m. Closed on Tuesday (sometimes closed on Monday instead, call first to make sure they are open). Reservations are recommended, and can be done by phone (0577-741-125) or by e-mail (osteria@fonterutoli.it). Both the Enoteca and the Osteria are closed during the major holidays, and closed for winter break, usually from early December to mid March, check website for precise dates.

44 Stay at **Villa Bordoni**–An Oasis of Beauty in Greve in Chianti

A dramatic country mansion, ideally located just outside of Greve in Chianti, halfway between Florence and Siena, **Villa Bordoni** offers ten beautiful rooms in a wonderfully renovated 16th-century villa. There is a certain rare refinement about this place, its interior is lavishly planned yet tastefully decked out with antique furniture that will never go out of style. The requisite modern conveniences such as LCD plasma TVs, mini bars, and WiFi connections are all present, but great care has been taken to integrate them unobtrusively into the tasteful, comfortable old-fashioned surroundings. An outdoor sports pavilion is available for guests' use so you may exercise in the serenity of the Tuscan countryside. You can also take advantage of the hotel's library and the outdoor swimming pool, as well as rent bikes, organize wine tastings and horse riding, or head to the nearby golf course of Ugolino. Make sure you book a room with a view!

The Villa has a long history as the residence of the Bordoni family, but as their fortunes dwindled, the family was forced to sell the dilapidated villa to David and Catherine Gardener, who have since done a fantastic job of reviving it. A particularly special time to stay is during the autumn, as the colors of the surrounding countryside change and glow with splendid vividness. There is also a cooking school on-site, which is open to residents and non-residents alike, and offers packages which include wine-tasting and dinner starting from 150 euro. The villa's main flaw is the unpaved road leading to it, making the daily drive somewhat stressful.

Villa Bordoni ★★★★
Via San Cresci 31/32, Località Mezzuola, Greve in Chianti,
Tel: 055- 854-7453,
villabordoni.com

 Taste Great Wine in a Real Castle

When it comes to wine tasting, we personally love the smaller places, the more intimate *tenute* (estates), where you can visit the lesser-known wine makers. In these spots, you can often find excellent, award-winning wines as well as a warm, local atmosphere. But it would be a shame to end your visit to Tuscany without visiting one of the region's largest and most famous castles, which have belonged to the oldest noble wine-producing families in the region for centuries and still maintain so much charm.

Both **Castello Brolio** and **Castello Meleto** are a notable and important part of Tuscan history and tradition. Both are citadels with histories that stretch back hundreds of years. In these two places, tradition, history, and great wines come together. Of course, these are not small discoveries hidden from scores of tourists but still, as visits that will certainly leave you impressed, we recommend them highly.

Castello Brolio is an enchanting place, even when large groups of tourists come to visit, which is often the case

during the summer months. Owned by the Ricasoli family since 1141, this stunning castle is the oldest winery in the world and today is a staple name in the Italian wine industry. You must taste their Chianti while in Tuscany for the simple reason that this is the family who first produced the Chianti wine. In 1872, Baron Bettino Ricassoli, who also served as Italy's second prime minister during his lifetime, came up with the modern formula for Chianti wine: 70% Sangiovese, 15% Canaiolo, and 15% Malvasia bianca grapes.

The castle itself is very interesting from an architectural point of view. What you see today is a reconstruction in a Gothic style which was ordered by Baron Bettino in the 1800s. Before this, the castle had been destroyed and rebuilt a number of times due to its strategic importance to the city of Florence. The most recent damage done was inflicted during World War II; shrapnel holes can still be spotted in the castle's façade. The setting is beautiful, with nature surrounding you in every direction. The castle is surrounded by 240 hectares of vineyards and beyond that are forests and rolling hills. To be up here can feel as though you have left the modern world behind. The view from the castle itself is lovely, on a clear day Siena can be seen in the distance. Inside the magnificent castle is a chapel and the family's crypt as well as numerous wonderfully decorated rooms. You can also take a walk through the castle's well-manicured gardens, though be careful at night, as legend has it that the ghost of Baron Bettino still stalks the grounds when there is a full moon—and he is cranky.

There are a number of tours you can book, all of which require a reservation in advance. The classic tour allows you to delve into the considerable history of the Ricasoli family. According to their own account, they are the fourth oldest family in the world. Alternatively you can take their wine production tour, which includes a visit to the cellars. There is also the private "gran cru" tour. Picking up a bottle from their *enoteca* is part of the fun, and you can choose from their many delectable wines, particularly the Rocca Guicciarda 2009, the Brolio 2010 or 2008 and the Casalferro 2010. You can stop here for lunch too, in the fittingly named Osteria del Castello, but to be honest, there are much better options in the area, from a culinary point of view.

Castello Meleto, on the other hand, is smaller but offers a more personable type of visit. Like Castello di Brolio this citadel is located in Gaiole in Chianti and has a history that dates back to the 11th century. Once the property of Benedictine monks, it later fell into the hands of a local noble family before eventually being given by Fredrick I Barbarossa to the Ricasoli-Fridolfi family. This family has owned it since the 1200s and in the intervening centuries, the castle has had an eventful history, largely due to its strategically important position between Siena and Florence.

Set among lush green trees and well-kept gardens, the castle is magnificent. A grand stone structure replete with turrets on two of its corners, it is surrounded by cypresses and a number of smaller buildings. The total grounds stretch for about 1,000 acres with 135 of that taken up by vineyards. Calm and serene, this is a truly stress-free location, perfect for a relaxing day out.

Tours of the castle can be booked in advance, or you can just stop at their *enoteca* for a tasting. We recommend a tour, to enjoy the beauty of the castle inside. A 30-minute tour will take you to the beautifully frescoed rooms on the main floor, as well as the impressive 18th-century wine cellar.

A number of apartments and B&B rooms are also available on the property, prices, which fluctuate greatly depending on the time of year, are available on their website.

Castello di Brolio - Barone Ricasoli ★★★★

Gaiole di Chianti. GPS: lat. 43° 24' 56" N long. 11° 27' 31" E (do not type Brolio into your GPS, use the coordinates instead). Tel: 0577-7301.
www.ricasoli.it
HOURS OF OPERATION:
The castle itself is private property and cannot be toured. The gardens, winery, and other public spaces can be visited with a guided tour. Tours usually take place March–late October, daily. Consult their website to find out more.

Castel Meleto, Gaiole in Chianti ★★★

GPS coordinates: LAT. 43.44992 | LONG. 11.42302, Tel: 0577-749-129. Enoteca hours of operation: April-October, 10:30 a.m.-6:00 p.m. Off-season, the enoteca is open occasionally, but on weekends only. Tours of the castle take place year round, daily (3-4 tours a day) and must be booked in advance. The 30-minute tour includes a visit to the castle itself, the historic cantine and the small theater on the premesis. Cooking classes, as well as specific tours, can also be organized. Naturally, advance booking is necessary.

¶¶ 47 | **Enjoy a Meal** at the Luxurious Il Pievano Restaurant, in Castello Spaltenna

An elegant, lovingly renovated 15th-century convent and castle, which looks like something taken out of a fairy tale, Spaltenna Castle is a perfect resort for a romantic weekend and for those who love the good life. Some of the rooms are a little small, but the ambiance is simply magical. The castle also boasts one of the most beautiful dining spaces in Tuscany (the Ancient lounge of Popes), filled with antique furniture and tapestry—fitting decorations for a nobleman's meal. In the summer, dinner is also served in the elegant cloister in front of the parish, right under the stars. Chef Fabrizio Borratinno has concocted some delightful dishes, such as suckling pig, served with an apple cream and potatoes; homemade pasta, served in a seafood broth; *chiannina carpaccio*; and more. There may be better restaurants in Tuscany, but very few can compete with **Il Pievano's** charm. Fixed and tasting menus are available (starting from 55 euro per person). The wine list is very extensive, and most of the herbs used here come from the castle's own organic herb garden. Il Pievano restaurant is open for dinner only. For lunch, you may stop at the second restaurant on the premesis: **Ristorante La Terrazza**, which is charming and delightful, though not as innovative as its big sister.

Castello Spaltenna
Via Spaltenna 13, Località Pieve di Spaltenna, Gaiole in Chianti.
Tel: 0577-749-483.

Il Pievano Restaurant ★★★★
HOURS OF OPERATION:
7:30-10p.m.

La Terrazza Restaurant
HOURS OF OPERATION:
12:30-2:30 p.m., reservations for both restaurants are recommended and can be done by e-mail (ristorante@spaltenna.it) or by phone (0577-749-483).

 ## 48 | **Sip an Afternoon Glass of Chianti** in La Bottega di Giovanni, a Charming Enoteca in Radda in Chianti

About 35-kilometers from Florence, the picturesque little commune of Radda is our favorite town in Chianti. Its surrounding area is dotted with castles and Romanesque churches while the views that can be enjoyed from this hilltop medieval village are beautiful. Still retaining part of its protective walls from the Middle Ages, the town itself is steeped in over a thousand years of history. Its narrow, winding streets are filled with eateries and charming little bars, one of which is **La Bottega di Giovannino**. Opened in 1965 by John Bernardoni, La Bottega has been a place where locals can enjoy a good glass of Chianti accompanied by some flavorsome cold cuts and cheeses ever since. Unfortunately the *salumi* here is no longer made in-house, though this slight loss of tradition is more than made up for by the owners' fine taste in local wines and by the high quality of produce that is used. The *enoteca* itself is still delightful. A tiny space,

which fills up quickly, it's perfect for a pre-dinner *aperitivo*. With mixed starters, daily homemade pasta specials, a wide range of wines to choose from and generous servings the restaurant is also perfect for a low-key, satisfying sunset meal.

Today the family business is run by John's children, Davide and Monica. The *enoteca* has also expanded into an adjacent B&B, which offers simple but perfectly comfortable rooms. The views from the B&B make it a good choice if you find yourself enchanted by Radda's delights. Wine tasting tours can also be organized through the wine bar.

La Bottega di Giovannino ★★★
Via Roma 6, Radda in Chianti,
Tel: 0577 738599,
www.labottegadigiovannino.it
Closed Tuesday, may close off-season.

 49 | **Enjoy** a Sumptuous Lunch with a Great View of the Chianti Hills

Excellent food, an incredible view and award-winning wine? Sounds like a good plan to us.

Unassumingly sat upon a panoramic hill, eight kilometers outside of Greve in Chianti, Ristoro di **Lamole** offers a perfect experience for lunch or an early dinner. The sumptuous vista is one of the restaurant's greatest assets. From the outside terrace you can see for miles over the green Tuscan countryside; the sunset here is stunning. Inside, the dining area is simple and comfortable, with plenty of space to enjoy your meal. We also love their kitchen philosophy: good, fresh produce, prepared and presented in a modern, elegant style, while still maintaining that old-fashioned Tuscan charm. Try dishes like the rabbit with fried vegetables, the *tagliatelle* with *porcini* mushrooms and the pig fillet, all of which are delicious. The desserts are very good, too, and combined with a bottle of their Chianti, you are sure to have a lovely time. Lamole isn't very cheap, but it isn't excessively expensive either, given the location and the standard of the cuisine. Make sure you book a table on the terrace to enjoy the view. Since this restuaurant is located deep in the countryside, it is highly recommended to make a reservation in advance, to let the owners know you are coming, especially if you are visiting off-season.

Lamole Restaurant ★★★
Via lamole 6, Greve in Chianti.
Tel: 055-854-7050,
www.ristorodilamole.it.
HOURS OF OPERATION:
Daily, 12:30-3:00 p.m., 7:00-9:30 p.m.
Hours of operation and days vary off-season.

🛏 50 | **Stay** at the Beautiful Borgo San Felice Resort

Situated in endless rolling hills covered in vines and olive groves which glisten in the summer sun, the area around the small town of Castelnuovo Berardenga is especially beautiful, even when compared with other parts of the Chianti region. At the heart of this area lies **Borgo San Felice**, just 15 km south of Siena. Originally a hamlet that dates back to the 8th century, this *borgo* was completely renovated and turned into an exclusive hotel, part of the Relais & Chateaux chain. The renovation was excellently executed; successfully maintaining the little village's authentic charm and respectfully restoring it to its original rustic beauty. This is a truly stunning high-end resort, offering its guests stylish rooms and a manicured yard with full amenities; including a tennis court, a spa, organized tours to local wineries and sightseeing trips. This isn't the place for those in search of an intimate, hidden B&B, but for guests looking for high-end options, this resort is a strong competitor.

Additionally, the *borgo* is surrounded by a wealth of excellent wineries which you can explore at your leisure, simply ask and the staff will point you in the right direction

Their restaurant, the sophisticated but expensive Poggio Rosso, which is run by Chef Francesco Bracacali, who already has two Michelin stars under his belt, is a good option for lunch or dinner. Their *nouvelle cuisine* interpretation of the Tuscan classics is best enjoyed on the comfortable outside terrace, though be warned: the menu here is different from other restaurants in the region. The emphasis is very strongly placed on innovation and, for some, it goes too far. Prices here tend to be higher, too. Check their website first and decide whether the cuisine on offer is for you.

Hotel Borgo San Felice ★★★★
San Felice, Castelnuovo Berardenga. GPS coordinates: 43°23'18.24 N , 11°27'30.94 E. Tel: 0577-3964,
www.borgosanfelice.it
The Borgo usually closes down during the winter months.

51 | **Book a Special Dinner** at La Bottega del 30

A tiny restaurant with a staff of only four, **La Bottega del 30** is an intimate countryside restaurant. It was opened in 1987 by husband and wife team Hélène Stoquelet and Franco Camelia, and ten years later, earned a Michelin star. Once you taste the food here, it becomes clear that it was well deserved. Hélène buys all the produce each morning from the local market and almost everything on the innovative menu is homemade, including the pastas and desserts. If they are in season, we particularly recommend any dish with white truffles. Though most dishes are purely Tuscan (sometimes even too Tuscan—the chef isn't shy about serving pig's liver, intestine and other such specialties), the occasional French influence can be noted in the menu. La Bottega del 30 is set in the small village of Villa a Sesta and can be hard to find. It requires driving on a gravel road so expect a bumpy ride on your way there. Once you arrive, however, the village and the restaurant

itself permeate an otherworldly ambience. The food is served in the dining room which is dotted with memorabilia and curiosities. And the wood burning stove used in the winter adds an extra intimacy.

Don't skip a quick visit to their tiny museum, which details rural life in the countryside around Villa a Sesta. The collection, housed in the ex-winery, represents the collective memory of this little Chianti village and is a testament to the love Hélène and Franco clearly have for their locality and business.

La Bottega del 30 ★★★★
Castelnuovo Berardenga, GPS coordinate: 43.384951 - 11.480284.
Tel: 0577-359226,
www.labottegadel30.it
HOURS OF OPERATION:
Wednesday-Monday, for dinner only. Booking in advance is highly recommended. Open for lunch, too, on request. Tuesday closed. Opening hours may vary off-season.

52 Book a Peaceful Night's Stay at the Fantastic Hotel Le Fontanelle

Perfectly positioned overlooking the rolling Chianti hills, **Hotel Le Fontanelle** offers a tranquil and memorable stay. Located in the countryside outside of Castelnuovo Berardenga, in a tiny village named Pianella, here you can enjoy perfect views of the golden morning sunlight pouring over the Tuscan countryside, take long walks or rent a bike to explore the numerous towns and hamlets in the area. In fact, the unique Chianti sculpture park (www. chiantisculpturepark.it) is less than 2 miles away. Chauffeured cars, which will take you to the local wineries in comfort, can also be booked.

The building itself is magnificent. Located in a masterfully renovated nobleman's house from the 13th century, the original stonework can still be seen, but now the rustic charm is blended with modern amenities. The rooms are equipped with WiFi and are simply decorated to provide a lovely environment in which to enjoy an evening glass of wine. The grounds of the hotel are well-tended and include a botanical garden. There are also indoor and outdoor swimming pools.

When it is time to eat, the restaurant La Colonna is a good choice. As is to be expected, the views from its windows are beautiful. This is the perfect place to sit back, relax and forget the world.

Hotel Le Fontanelle ★★★★
SP 408 (Km 14.7), Pianella, Castelnuovo Berardenga. GPS Coordinates: 43° 23′ 35″ N, 11° 24′ 42″ E. Tel: 0577-35-751, www.hotelfontanelle.com

Buy Some High Quality Meat, Cold Cuts and Sausages at Macelleria Falorni, One of the Best Butcheries in the Chianti Area

53

Combining the rolling hills and endless vineyards of the Chianti region with a tasting tour of Tuscany's finest meats and charcuterie is a meat-lover's dream. Luckily, this dream can easily be made a reality as the region offers its fair share of *macellerie* (butcher shops), which will satisfy even the most discerning carnivore.

Antica Macelleria Falorni, located in Greve in Chianti's bustling central piazza, is one such stop. The Bencistà Falorni family has been selling their meat since the 18th century and pride themselves on using local breeds, such as the *chianina* cow and the *cinta senese* pig, to prepare a variety of *salumi*. Here you can find *prosciutto dolce*, a sweeter version of the Tuscan *prosciutto*, *prosciutto di cinghiale* (boar *prosciutto*), which has a decidedly wilder flavor), along with a range of salamis. A wide array of pecorino cheeses, stored in a 17th-century ventilated cave to preserve the taste, are also available.

Antica Macelleria Falorni ★★★
Piazza Matteotti 71, Greve in Chianti.
Tel: 055-853-029. www.falorni.it.
HOURS OF OPERATION:
Monday–Friday, 9:00 a.m.–7:30 p.m;
Sunday and Holidays, 10:00 a.m.–7:30 p.m. (Fresh meat isn't sold on Sunday and Holidays between 1:00 and 3:30 p.m.).
Hours may vary off-season.

🍴|54| Buy Some Delicious Goat Cheese in the Charming Podere Fornaci

For us, goat's cheese is the best of cheeses. It's a taste that grabs all the senses—the creamy texture, the tart flavor, the distinctive smell and feel. Italy, being the land of sheep cheese or pecorino, and cow milk cheese, offers a far more limited choice of goat's cheese than France. But there are some wonderful little farms dotted across Tuscany serving up some excellent, artisanal goat cheeses.

Our favorite is **Podere Fornaci**, located right in the heart of the Chianti area—just two kilometers from Greve in Chianti. This farm is organic and puts an emphasis on animal welfare. From the outside it looks a little shabby but don't be put off, this is a fantastic little place with excellent cheese. Our favorites include the charcoal goat's cheese and the *Crosta Fiorita*, but let the owners know what type of cheese you prefer and they will match you to the perfect taste. To extend the day, you can take a tour of the farm and stay for a light lunch. Calling in advance is always a good idea.

Podere Le Fornaci ★★★★
Via Citille, 74 - 50022 - Greve in Chianti (FI), Tel: 055-854-6010,
www.poderelefornaci.it
e-mail: info@poderelefornaci.it
booking in advance required.

Siena

 55 | ### Stay at Siena's Best Hotel - Residenza d'Epoca Campo Reggio Relais

Though there are some wonderful *agriturismo* located outside of Siena, choosing a hotel within the city walls has its advantages. If you love touring the town on foot, a room close to the center is a big advantage. Plus, there is something to be said for choosing lodging that is part of the city; you get a much more intimate experience of Siena when you immerse yourself in its daily rhythm.

Our go to address is the **Residenza d'Epoca Campo Reggio Relais**. The views are the first thing that makes this place exceptional. Eating breakfast on the terrace you will be overwhelmed by the panorama of the city—a wonderful way to start your day of exploration. The décor inside is elegant and inviting, and maintains much of the old charm and slow rhythm Siena is famous for. This is a boutique hotel, located within a historical building, with just six rooms. They fill up quickly in high season, mainly thanks to the location, just minutes away from Siena's Piazza del Campo, so book well in advance, and ask for a room with a view of the town.

Campo Regio Relais ★★★★
Via della Sapienza 25, Siena.
Tel: 0577-222-073,
www.camporegio.com

⑂ | 56 | **Stop for a Fun and Chic** Aperitivo in Siena

If are looking for the perfect place to enjoy an afternoon cup of tea with a tasty piece of cake, or, better yet, a glass of bubbly prosecco and half a dozen oysters, **Cava De Noveschi** is the place to go to and enjoy a good vibe and relax while sightseeing in Siena. Given the restaurant's location a few minutes from Piazza del Campo, and right under the Duomo, you might reasonably expect this place to be another tourist trap with hiked-up prices and aloof staff. Thankfully, you'd be wrong.

A perfect spot to enjoy an *aperitivo*, and to rub elbows with the locals, make sure you take advantage of their long list of wines, cocktails, and champagnes. On a hot day the laid-back and friendly staff will help you feel relaxed in the small dining area's air-conditioned space, though if the sun isn't blazing outside we'd recommend one of the tables on the terrace in this prime location in Siena.

Cava de Noveschi ★★★
Via Monna Agnese 8, Siena.
Tel: 0577-274-878,
www.cavadenoveschi.it. Opening times: Tuesday–Saturday, 12:30-3:00 p.m., 6:30-10:00 p.m. (sometimes until 10:30 p.m.). Closed Sunday–Monday.

🍴 57 | Dine at the Delicious and Homely
La Taverna di San Giuseppe

La Taverna di San Giuseppe is one of the most popular restaurants in town. There are surely smarter places, but when it comes to good, hearty, traditional food, this place is excellent. From the moment you walk down the stairs into the long hall with its time-honored wood furnishings, candle-lit tables, and exposed brickwork, you get into the mood for some authentic Tuscan cuisine. The service here is extremely accommodating and knowledgeable without being snobby. The food is mouth-watering; they may be the usual staples but they are perfectly made. The meat dishes, anything with porcini and truffles, and the pasta are especially tasty. The location is also perfect, as the tavern can be found just 400 meters from the Piazza del Campo. Walk along via Dupré, until you reach the restaurant, which is right in front of the San Giuseppe Church. Reservations for this lovely restaurant are highly recommended; popular with visitors and locals alike, it's always full.

Alternatively, **Osteria le Sorelline** is another recommended Sienese eatry. Owned and run by a charming couple, this spot is casual and friendly but not over-simplified. The food is fresh and of good quality, well-prepared, and beautifully presented. The unassuming dining area boasts a friendly ambiance, while there are also tables available in the little laneway outside. All of this results in a thoroughly satisfying lunch. The fresh pasta here is delicious, especially the *pici*, the *tagliatelle*, and the *ravioli*, which are all homemade. For *secondi*, try the *tagliata* with porcini mushrooms. Their selection of aged pecorino cheeses with marmalade is very good, too.

La Taverna di San Giuseppe ★★★★
Via Giovanni Dupre' 132, Siena. Tel:
0577-422-86,
www.tavernasangiuseppe.it
HOURS OF OPERATION:
Monday–Saturday, noon-2:30 p.m.,
7-10p.m. Closed Sunday. Closed for the
last two weeks of July, and the last two
weeks of January.

Osteria Le Sorelline ★★★
Via dei rossi 76, Siena.
Tel: 0577-421-48
www.lesorelline.it
HOURS OF OPERATION:
March-October, open daily, 12:30-2:30
p.m., 7:30-10:30 p.m.; November-
February, closed Saturday for lunch and
Sunday for dinner.

 58 **Book a Walking Tour** of Siena with a Professional Guide

Though Siena can undoubtedly be enjoyed on a self-guided tour, it is also true that touring with the right guide can add a depth to the experience which cannot be rivalled. Navigating the medieval alleys of this fascinating town, from Piazza del Campo to the impressive Duomo to the San Domenico church, with a professional guide telling stories of the people who lived, worked, ruled and died here is a unique opportunity and treat, especially for history and art lovers.

Costanza Riccardi is both a licensed guide for the city of Siena, as well as a hiking guide, which means that, whether you are looking to embark on a city tour or explore the countryside, she will be able to help you. Her knowledge of local art and history and her passion for the traditions of her home town make her stand out among other guides.

We love the philosophy of **Tours Around Tuscany**, who offer personalized and professional tours of specific areas of Tuscany. Unlike other companies, that organize what are often superficial tours, with large groups, and try to cover too much ground in one day, this organization will happily take small groups, or even just a couple on memorable and intimate tours of Siena, the countryside of Southern Siena and the Chianti region.

Costanza Riccardi ★★★
Tel: 0577-281-605, Cell: 333-325-7717,
www.sienawalkingtours.com

Tours Around Tuscany ★★★
Tel: 0577-185-1602, Cell: 347-245-0225,
www.tourintuscany.com

 # 59 | Embark on a Fun and Professional Wine Tour from Siena

While the wine tours that leave from Florence are better-known (see tip 5), Siena stands its ground and offers its fair share of interesting excursions, too. This makes perfect sense—the Sienese Chianti is famous and delicious, and just a short drive from town you find some glorious estates and wine producing towns, such as Castelnuovo Berardenga, which lies 20 minutes west of Siena.

Though we love traveling around the wineries ourselves, touring with a guide has several advantages. The knowledge and experience of an expert guide are one obvious advantage, but we are also glad to know that we can taste whichever wine we want without having to worry about driving home after three (or six) glasses of wine.

Wine Tour in Tuscany is a very popular tour led by Donatella, a knowledgeable tour guide and sommelier, who is as passionate about wine as she is about her native town of Siena. Since she personally knows many of the area's producers, her tours are very individual and give you a perspective and closeness that others find very hard to match.

Donatella also offers cooking classes, organic food tours, city tours of Siena itself, and tours of castles, ancient hamlets (*borghi*), churches and other interesting monuments in the region. The wine tour, however, is the main draw. Tours can be personalized, and we love the fact that Donatella suggest visits to historical *cantines* too, which adds an interesting historical dimension to the day. Like most other tours, these excursions focus on the best known wines of Tuscany—a separate tour is offered to follow the path of the Chianti, Brunello, Vernaccia, and the Montepulciano wines (and even the super-Tuscans). The *Sunset Chianti Tour*, which includes a visit to two wineries, a sunset drive through the region and dinner in Greve in Chianti is very pleasant and quite romantic. Booking in advance is highly recommended.

Wine Tour in Tuscany ★★★★
Via Carlo Pisacane 166, Siena.
www.winetourintuscany.com

🏃 60 | Taste Some of Siena's Best Ricciarelli

For the locals, the debate over Siena's best *riccarelli* is as heated as the debate among Florence-natives over the city's best gelato. *Riccarelli*, the soft, moist, almond-based biscuit, dusted with powder sugar, has been a symbol of Tuscany since the 14th century, and is the second most famous biscuit in the region after the *cantuccino*.

Together with *panforte*—a heavy, dried, fruit-filled dessert, *cavallucci*—a harder, sweeter and more floury version of *ricciarelli*, and *pici* pasta—a thick spaghetti, traditionally served topped with fried breadcrumbs, *ricciarelli* biscuits have become a symbol of Siena. We have yet to meet a Sienese man, woman, or child who can't immediately tell you their favorite establishment to purchase a fresh batch.

As so often happens, the best places are outside the historical center and serve mostly locals. **Pasticceria Le Campane**, located about two miles from the center, is our top choice. If you have a free hour, a sweet tooth, and a car, drive here to try not only their *ricciarelli* but also the assortment of sweet treats on display.

Another good option, which doesn't require driving out to the suburbs, is **Pasticceria Sinatti** located on Via della Sapienza, near San Domenico church (about 10 minutes from Piazza del Campo, on foot). A third place is **La**

Pasticceria Nuova, which is even easier to reach, located just behind Piazza del Campo.

A good *riccarello* should always be soft and never contain flour. It should maintain a natural moistness from the almond paste. If packed properly, *ricciarelli* can travel well and will make a great gift for loved ones back home.

Pasticceria Le Campane ★★★
Via Caduti di Vicobello 37, Siena.
Tel: 0577-282-290.
HOURS OF OPERATION:
Monday, Tuesday, Thursday-Saturday, 7:00 a.m.-8:00 p.m. Sunday 7:00 a.m.-1:30 p.m. Wednesday closed.

Pasticcerie Sinatti ★★★
Via della Sapienza 36, Siena.
Tel: 0577-418-72,
www.pasticcerie-sinatti.it
HOURS OF OPERATION:
Tuesday-Saturday, 9:30 a.m.-1:00 p.m., 4:00-7:30 p.m. Sunday 9:30 a.m.-1:00 p.m. Monday closed.

La Nuova Pasticceria ★★★
Via Duprè 37, Siena.
Tel: 0577-405-77, www.lanuovapasticceria-siena.com.
HOURS OF OPERATION:
Monday-Saturday, 9:30 a.m.-7:30 p.m. Sunday 10:30 a.m.-7 p.m. (sometimes they open as late as 11:00 a.m. on Sunday).

Surrounding Siena

 61 | **Plan a Romantic Evening** in a Hidden Corner of Tuscany, starting with a Nocturnal Dip at the San Giovanni Thermal Spa

If there's a perfect way to end a day of sightseeing in southern Tuscany, this must be it: dinner at a small, intimate restaurant, simple but with delicious food, followed by a night dip at a spa that becomes magical after dark.

Terme San Giovanni (the San Giovanni thermal spa) is located in Rapolano, an area known for its thermal springs. The spa has five pools spread inside and outside the complex, filled with mineral rich water at 39°C . The outdoor pools are especially enjoyable to dip in, as they are surrounded by grassy banks which afford fantastic views over the Tuscan countryside. While the spa is open every day, it is really at the night that it becomes special. On Saturday nights in the summer, Terme San Giovanni morphs into a wonderfully romantic place. Come here before the sun sets and watch the light disappear across the horizon while soaking in the warmth of the pools.

The spa itself has a nice restaurant, but there are also some excellent options nearby. In a suburb of Rapolano called Localita Armaiolo, just 15 minutes from the spa, hides an excellent restaurant by the name of **Davide Canella**. Canella is the head chef and the owner and his food is modern and elegant. The fact that the restaurant is situated in a converted wine cellar which dates back to the early 19th century certainly adds to its charm and ambiance. We recommend the creamy risotto in Chianti sauce, the homemade pastas, the ricotta and pumpkin dumplings in pecorino and white truffle sauce, and the beef sirloin with herbs. Don't forget to top it all off with some excellent dessert.

Slightly further, in the direction of Arezzo, is **Il Goccino**. Located about 30 minutes away in the small, romantic village of Lucignana, the philosophy of this kitchen is tradition revisited which emphasizes seasonal and local produce. The result is a smart and delicious menu that uses local cuisine innovatively. Try their tasty lamb chops, fresh pasta, tartar (made with locally grown *chianina* beef), the *salumi*— mostly made with locally-bred *cinta senese* and *grigio del casentino* pigs, Tuscan soups, homemade ice creams and *semifreddi*. Though meat is a star in this restaurant, there are some very good vegetarian and vegan options available too and the chef will happily modify some of the dishes for vegetarian clients. Cooking classes can be organized with the restaurant's team of chefs, consult their website to find out more. On a hot summer night, book a place in advance on their lovely terrace!

San Giovanni Terme ★★★★
Via Terme San Giovanni 52, Rapolano Terme (SI).
Tel: 0577-724-030,
www.termesangiovanni.it
NOTE: the night spa is open till midnight. A dinner and an entry pass to the thermal pools will cost around 35 euro per person. Pool access without dinner (from 7:00 p.m.) will cost around 12 euro per person. Booking in advance is required (about 2-3 days ahead of your planned visit).

Davide Canella ★★★★
Ristorante Enoteca, Via del Finimondo 6, Loc. Armaiolo, Rapolano Terme.
Tel: 0577-725-251,
www.davidecanella.it
HOURS OF OPERATION:
mid-March to late October, Tuesday-Sunday, 12:30-2:30 p.m., 8:00-10:00 p.m. Monday closed; November 1-March 15, closed Sunday evening and Monday

Ristorante Il Goccino ★★★
Via Matteotti 90, Lucignano (AR).
Tel: 0575-836-707,
www.ilgoccino.it
HOURS OF OPERATION:
Tuesday-Sunday, 12:30-2:30 p.m, 7:30-10:00 p.m. Monday closed. May close off-season, call in advance.

62 | **Book a Unique Cooking Class** in the Countryside

Foodies and fans of the slow food movement may already know the name **Spannochia**. This organic farm is renowned for its slow-living attitude, its focus on local produce, sustainable consumption, and enthusiasm for the sharing of Tuscan traditions. Run by very professional staff, we highly recommend stopping by. There are a variety of ways to visit; you can enroll in a cooking class here, book a tour of the grounds, or rent an apartment or villa and use it as your Tuscan base for exploration. This isn't a luxurious resort, but rather, a place for those who wish to experience Tuscany from a different point of view—authentic but educated.

Spanocchia's reasonably-priced cooking class is a hands-on experience and a fine setting to learn how to make fresh pasta or other popular Tuscan *primi* (first course dishes). The class is led by Chef Loredana Betti who grew up on the farm, and begins with a morning tour of Spannochia's vegetable garden, with explanations of the growth cycles of the vegetables. Once you've built up your appetite in the fresh air, the cooking begins. Spanocchia focus on the staple dishes of the Tuscan cuisine, which usually include meat, but vegetarian options are available.

The tour of the grounds takes about two hours and you will explore the Castello itself, as well as the different agricultural activities, the gardens, and more. Other tastings and tours, focusing on produce such as honey, olive oil, and *cinta senese* (a local breed of pig) farming, among others, are available. All are reasonably priced, interesting and recommended for those who are passionate about Tuscan traditions. In fact, you can even book classes with Jessica, their education manager and a graduate of the slow food university in Pollenzo.

Lastly, Spannochia is located very close to the famous San Galgano abbey (see tip 64) in Chiusdino. Combining a cooking class with a visit to the abbey, and other attractions in the surrounding area, such as Rapolano thermal baths or the ancient town of Massa Marittima, could make for a wonderful day in a lesser-known, but beautiful, area of Tuscany

Tenuta di Spannocchia ★★★★
Chiusdino.
Tel: 0577-75 -261,
www.spannochia.org

63 | Visit the Splendid Monte Oliveto Maggiore Abbey and Sample Traditional Tonics Made by Monks

There are two Tuscan abbeys renowned for their Gregorian chants: Sant'antimo, near Pienza and Montalcino (see tip number 89) and **Monte Oliveto Maggiore**, near Asciano. Both are beautiful and offer a unique experience, but personally we prefer Monte Oliveto. While Sant'Antimo is impressive from an architectural point of view, Monte Oliveto Maggiore has a sense of peace that can't be rivalled.

Surrounded by woods and silence, traveling to Monte Oliveto Maggiore is like being transported into a different reality. Walking on the stone path from the parking lot to the main church, you are surrounded by oak, pine, and cypress trees, the occasional chirping bird, bushes and wildflowers, and the air is cool and crisp; it almost feels like time moves slower here. The abbey, which, was founded in the 14th century by Bernardo Tolomei (of the famous noble Tolomei family of Siena), is most famous for its fantastic

cloister decorated with frescos from Luca Signorelli and Antonio Bazzi (better known as Il Sodoma), but the chapels and the refectory are equally stunning. Once you have completed your visit to the chapel, it is time for the second part: the truly hedonistic experience.

Take the path down from the Abbey, following the signs directing you towards the canteen and the Azienda Agricola, their wine cellar and farm. The monks here offer tonics prepared using recipes which are hundreds of years old. Their Flora di Monteoliveto, for example, is a liqueur made from 23 herbs and flowers which grow on the land around the abbey. Touring the cellar is fascinating—big wooden barrels sit under vaulted, exposed ceilings, evoking a wonderful sense of history. Guided tours and tastings are available, but you have to book in advance. Check their website to find out more about the guided tours.

Monte Oliveto Maggiore ★★★★★
Loc. Monte Oliveto Maggiore, Asciano
(set your GPS to Loc. Chiusure, or to
Asciano. The abbey is located along the
SS451 road, 14 km from Asciano).
Tel: 0577.707611,
www.monteolivetomaggiore.it.
HOURS OF OPERATION:
Monte Oliveto Abbey is open year round.
Summer months, daily, 9:15 a.m.-noon,
3:00-6:00 p.m. Winter months, Monday-
Saturday, 9:15 a.m.-noon, 3:00-4:00 p.m.
Sunday, 9:15 a.m.-12:30 p.m.

A Mass accompanied by Gregorian
chants is celebrated on weekdays at 6:15
p.m., and on Sunday and Holidays at
11:00 a.m.

The Enoteca and Cellar are open mid-
March to late October, daily, 10:00 a.m.-
1:00 p.m. and 2:30-6:30 p.m.; November-
mid-March, Weekends and holidays only,
10:00 a.m.-1:00 p.m., 2:30-6:00 p.m.
However, it is recommended to come
before 5:15 p.m., as the guard tends to
close shop at 5:30 p.m. to attend mass.

Visits take place 4 times a day, at 10:00
a.m., 1:00 p.m., 2:30 p.m., and 6:30
p.m. (6:00 p.m. in winter). Advanced
booking is recommended, and for
groups it is mandatory.
Find out more here:
www.agricolamonteoliveto.com

 64 **Spend a Day Exploring** Charming Chiusdino, and a Night at the Romantic and Luxurious Terme di Petriolo Resort and Spa

Just 40 minutes away from Siena is a magical, fairy tale-like stone church. The **Abbey of San Galgano** in Chiusdino is a famous site, as much for the intriguing tales of its history as for the dramatic landscapes which surround it.

San Galgano was a functioning monastery up until the bubonic plague hit Italy in 1348. The deadly

epidemic devastated the monks and the resulting crime wave that spread across Europe forced the surviving monks to flee to Siena to escape local vigilantes. The last of the monks left towards the end of the 15th century and when lightning struck in 1786, destroying the roof, the church seemed to be beyond repair. However, this apparent misfortune transformed the church into an unexpected attraction as visitors came to the area to see the poetic, solemn yet elegant, roofless church.

After visiting the abbey you can walk up the hill to the nearby hermitage. The hermitage was home to Saint Galgano, an ex-Chiudsino knight, who retired here to spend his remaining days as a monk. He quickly realized that he no longer needed his sword and fiercely thrust it into a rock in act of his newfound pacifism. The sword-in-the-rock, which resembles a cross, lies protected to this day and serves as symbol of peace and faith.

After 6:30 p.m., you can't enter the site, but even from the outside it is impressive, especially when it glistens under the moonlight.

For a truly relaxing and decadent way to end to the day, pop into the nearby Petriolo thermal baths. The baths are just 20 minutes away and have been in operation since the Etruscan times. The Etruscans celebrated the numerous benefits of the thermal waters, as did later medieval and renaissance societies. The high sulphur level of the 43°C water explains the particularly strong odour of the baths. The sulphur combined with other minerals such as carbon, calcium and sulphate are very good for all types of aliments.

There is a free part of the baths, which we must admit is much more of a rustic experience, but still fun. For something slightly more sophisticated, book a night at the excellent **Petriolo Spa Resort**. The breathtaking views (take your breakfast out to the terrace) and the top-notch facilities of these stylish thermal baths make it easy to understand why the spa has been awarded five stars. There is a private pool exclusively for guests and a wonderful array of spa treatments is available. See specific information below for more details.

San Galgano Abbey ★★★★
Chiusdino (the Abbey is located mid-way between Chiusdino and Monticiano, follow the road signs to reach it), www.sangalgano.info.
HOURS OF OPERATION:
April-May, 9:00 a.m.-6:30 p.m. (7:00 p.m. Sunday and Holidays); November-March, 9:30 a.m.-5:30 p.m. (6:30 p.m. on Sunday and Holidays); June-September, 9:00 a.m.-8:00 p.m.

Eremo di Montesipei
HOURS OF OPERATION: April-October, daily, 9:00 a.m.-6:00 p.m. November-March, 9:00 a.m.-1:00 p.m. Opening hours tend to vary.

Petriolo Spa Resort ★★★★
Località Bagni di Petriolo, Civitella Paganico (GR), www.atahotels.it/en/petriolo/
NOTE: the spa is open daily from April 16 to November 2. Non-guests can buy a daily entrance pass (which allows entry from 9:30 a.m. to 6:30 p.m.) or an afternoon pass (2:00-6:30 p.m.). With this pass, you may enter the the two outside pools, the inside pool and the spa (treatments are excluded). A weekday daily pass costs 40 euro (afternoon pass: 30 euro), a weekend pass costs 60 euro (afternoon: 40 euro). Book 2-3 days in advance.

65 | **Book a Memorable Stay** at the Beauteous Castello delle Serre

The deluxe suite at the Castello delle Serre is one of the best kept secrets in Tuscany. Located in Serre di Rapolano, halfway between Siena and Montepulciano, the entire hotel is somewhat of a dream. Homely yet graceful, this ancient castle dates back to Bizantine times. The castello's suite is perfectly positioned at the top of a medieval tower, and spreads over three levels. The top level has a private rooftop terrace with a spectacular 360-degree view of the entire region, overlooking the magical hills of Asciano on one side, and the endless vines of Castelnuovo di Berardenga on the other. The elegant sitting area and bedroom have a charming sense of the pastoral luxury, like something enjoyed by noble families of years gone by. Other rooms in the hotel are very comfortable, too, and the staff is friendly and professional. The hotel's proximity to Siena (30 minutes) as well as the thermal baths of San Giovanni (www.termesamgiovanni. it), the Val d'Orcia, Montepulciano and even the Maremma is an added advantage, and make the hotel a great base for those planning on exploring Southern Tuscany. Booking this popular suite in advance is essential.

Hotel Castello delle Serre ★★★★★
Piazza XX Settembre 1, Serre di Rapolano.
Cell: (active from 9:00 a.m.-9:00 p.m.,
Italian time) - 338.7315802 (Antonio).
www.castellodelleserre.com

⊨ 66 | **Stay at the Incredible**
Fonteverde Spa Hotel

The **Fonteverde Natural Spa Resort** exudes luxury. The resort, which is set in a renovated 17th-century country estate formerly of the de Medici family, has 66 rooms and 7 suites. All of the rooms have been meticulously redesigned with sumptuous fabrics and deep colors, four poster beds, and draped curtains framing private balconies. However, the real forte of this resort isn't the hotel rooms, but the spa (which is also open to outside guests).

The Fonteverde spa is built around a thermal spring discovered by the ancient Etruscans and offers over 100 treatments. Five indoor pools and two outdoor pools are at the guests' disposal. The view from the thermal pools of vineyards and olive groves crisscrossing the Siena hills is magnificent, and reason enough for choosing this spa for a day of perfect pampering. Fonteverde really does go for the "wow factor", and for those planning on spending a day of true pampering, this is one of the top three choices in Tuscany. Soaking in the thermal pool under vaulted ceilings or lounging in the outdoor area while overlooking the postcard view is wonderfully relaxing. Their medical treatments are also worth exploring, including salt therapy to aid respiratory problems, Ayurvedic massage, or even hydro-massage.

Beauty treatments include anti-aging programs, naturopathy, and natural mud facials. Many of the treatments use locally sourced products, such as honey, mud, and olive oil—all of which are high in antioxidants.

Alternatively, a visit to Fonteverde's night spa is a highly recommended. Like many other spa facilities in the region, Fonteverde offers access at night for a bit of an after-dark treat. In our opinion, soaking at the thermal pool under the stars (and for a reasonable fee of 22 euro) and then enjoying the facility's beautiful *bioacqum* (thermal hydro-massage) is a perfect way to end a day of Tuscan adventures.

Prices here are obviously not cheap, but they are much more reasonable than in high-end spas in Florence and Siena, and in our opinion, Fonteverde offers better value for your money.

Fonteverde Tuscan Resort & Spa ★★★★★
Localita' terme 1, San Casciano dei Bagni (SI). Tel: 0578-572-41, www.fonteverdespa.com

Arezzo and Cortona

 67 | **Embark on a Truffle Hunting Adventure**
with Boscovivo

Boscovivo, a family-run, unassuming company located in the heart of the Arezzo Province, is in fact one of the best manufacturers of truffle-based products in Tuscasny. They not only offer a wide range of dips, spreads, seasoning salts, and truffle-infused goods, but also arrange tasting tours and activities for curious foodies. Their produce and activities have already won an honorable mention from the Italian Food Academy. Currently run by the charming and friendly Silvia Landucci, daughter of Alfredo Landucci, the founder of the company (whose photo is still featured on many of their products), Boscovivo are prepared to lead visitors on truffle excursions with professional truffle hunters and trained dogs, organize tastings, and recommend the best produce for you. Their attentive and welcoming manner is just one of this company's advantages.

Boscovivo Tartufi ★★★★
Via dei Boschi 34, Badia al Pino (AR).
Tel: 0575-410-388 or 0575-410-396.
www.boscovivo.it.
Open Monday–Friday, 8:30 a.m.–1 p.m., 2:30–5:30p.m. Organized visits and tastings can be organized according to a visitor's schedule, booking in advance required.

68 | Book a Night at the Exquisite and Historical Castelletto di Montebenicchi

High on a hill halfway between Siena and Arezzo, a 12th-century palace stares imposingly out on the Chianti valleys below. Castelletto di Montebenicchi, with its medieval architecture and fresco-adorned walls, is filled with history and tradition and luckily has opened its doors to the public as a truly impressive hotel.

Although the castle is large and commanding, the owners have maintained a sense of intimacy and great charm. The exposed brick walls show warm flicks of terracotta, especially against the light of the open fire, and the place is packed with paintings, tapestries, gilded mirrors, colorful rugs, and interesting antiques. The hot tub, sauna, and pool, as well as the kind and helpful staff, complete the experience. The hotel only has nine rooms so it's important to book in advance. If possible, go for a deluxe room or suite.

It should be noted that the *castelletto* is a little bit remote, frozen in time in the rural and tranquil Valdambra county in eastern Tuscany, making it, perhaps, more suitable for spending time and relaxing than for using as a base for exploration. But if you are looking for a complete getaway, this is the place.

Castelletto di Montebenichi ★★★★★
Piazza Gorizia 9, Montebenichi (Bucine).
Tel: 055- 991-0110,
www.castelletto.it

69 | Enjoy a Meal at the Best Restaurant in Cortona—La Bucaccia

To be honest, there are two restaurants we enjoy visiting in Cortona. One is **La Bucaccia**, and the other is **Osteria del Teatro**. While the food in Osteria del Teatro is excellent, the atmosphere is rather formal (and the decor a little weird). On the other hand, La Bucaccia is more vibrant and the food is top notch.

Although La Bucaccia has been discovered in recent years by travelers, and is now a popular stop in Cortona, somehow it hasn't lost an ounce of its charm. The restaurant is located in a converted 13th-century building, in a particularly picturesque street. Exposed stone walls and beams and soft lighting set the mood. The owners, Romano and Agostina Magi, are connoisseurs of local cuisine, and the menu reflects their passion.

Book well in advance and, if possible, a table outside on the small terrace overlooking the Valdichiana. Try their meat dishes, which are prepared from locally-bred cattle— the *chianina*—one of the oldest cattle breeds in the world. The ravioli and other fresh handmade pasta dishes are excellent too. Try their *gnudi* (a nude ravioli, which means a filling without the pasta itself, made of ricotta and spinach, and served with a pecorino sauce), or a heartier dish of meat filled ravioli (from *chianina* meat, naturally), served with a truffle sauce. The local specialities are the

punto forte (strong point) of this restaurant, so ask for the staff's recommendations, and any special dishes of the day. Don't forget to try their cheese platter, which contains mostly cheeses the owner produces himself. The wine list is good, too. Most of the wines on it are Tuscan, but if you want to be even more specific and choose a wine from this specific area, try a nice Syrah, Cortona's signature wine. La Bucaccia also offer cooking lessons, and, even better—cheese making lessons! Contact them to find out more.

Ristorante La Bucaccia ★★★★
Via Ghibellina 17, Cortona.
Tel: 0575-606039,
www.labucaccia.it.
HOURS OF OPERATION:
Tuesday-Sunday, 12:30-2:30 p.m., 7:00-11:00 p.m. Closed on Monday (except in July-August, when the restaurant is open daily). Reservations are advisable.

70 | **Book a Romantic Picnic** or an Etruscan-Themed Excursion with "Toscana & Gusto"

Cortona, for very good reason, is a popular destination. Charming (though very steep) streets lead you around the town made famous by Francis Meyer's *Under the Tuscan Sun*, and discovering the hidden little secrets of this well-preserved medieval town is always fun.

Once you have toured Cortona's various sites (such as the Etruscan Museum, the wonderful Diocesan museum and the Franciscan Hermitage, you will probably be looking for a great place to relax and dine. If it is a restaurant you are after, then Cortona, despite its petite size, will not fail you. There are a number of tasty options in town (see tip 69). However, a traditional *osteria* or *trattoria* is not the only option worth considering.

Toscana e gusto is a local touring company which organizes four course picnics for a minimum of two people. Prices start from €25 per person and include everything you might need. Guests who booked the service simply show up at a breathtaking spot and enjoy the food, the Prosecco, and the view. Regional wines are the perfect complement to the tranquil and decadent atmosphere. Picnics are available from late March to late October, and depend on weather conditions. Another very popular attraction organized by this company is their Etruscan tour, which will lead you on a discovery mission of Cortona's ancient past. These two activities can be matched and booked together.

Toscana e Gusto, Cortona ★★★
Tel: 0575-604-110, Cell: 349-851-2115,
www.toscanaegusto.com

71 | **Spend a special night** at Il Borro, Arezzo's Most Chic Resort

Arezzo and the Eastern Tuscan countryside have a certain silence and purity in the air which differentiates them from the Siena or Chianti Hills. Maybe the sense of calm comes from the fact that this part of Tuscany isn't on the usual tourist circuit. Or maybe it's because certain corners of this region feel untouched by time. As with many parts of Tuscany, this area has many spectacular views; secluded *agriturismi* dot the landscape, muddled with unpaved roads and unkempt fields. Monasteries, spiritual refuges, long forgotten churches, and secluded forests (such as the famous Camaldoli forest) further populate the region; quiet, tranquil, beautiful.

The Borro Resort Spa and Winery maintains this rustic tranquillity. Owned by Ferrucio Ferragamo, son of the famous designer Salvatore Ferragamo, who bought the property in 1985 from the Duke Amedeo D'Aosta, this resort offers luxury and sophistication. The surrounding grounds offer seven hundred hectares of soft hills, woodland, vineyards, olive trees, and an assortment of animals. When he purchased the property, Ferragamo set about renovating and rebuilding the 1000-year old medieval village on the estate and the manor house. Both were in a state of desperate

disrepair due to damage inflicted during the Second World War and the passing of time. Today, fully repaired and restored to its former beauty, the medieval village is particularly enchanting. Set right at the heart of the estate and dating back to 1039, you can feel the history in its pathways and buildings.

As you would expect from a luxury resort owned by one of Italy's top fashion industry families, **Il Borro** is suffused with luxury and sophistication. The amenities include horse riding, bike trails, tennis courts, cooking lessons, and wine tours. Alternatively, you can simply relax by the pool overlooking the sumptuous view and enjoy the wellness center and spa. The rooms are a chic blend of traditional Tuscan furniture and modern facilities.

Rooms here aren't cheap. If you do stay, you can choose between renting a villa on the grounds and staying in a suite or apartment in the medieval village. The most demanding guests will settle for nothing less than the exquisite Il Borro Villa. This historical gem is located right at the center of the estate and once belonged to some of the more renowned Tuscan families. The elegant restaurant on the premises—Osteria il Borro—is perfect for a romantic dinner, accompanied by one of the red wines produced by this estate, such as the Pian di Nuova Rosso or Il Borro Rosso, both of which are quite good.

Il Borro Resort ★★★★

Località Borro 1, San Giustino Valdarno.
GPS Coordinates 43.540709, 11.715324.
Tel: 055-977-2333,
www.ilborro.com.
RESTAURANT HOURS OF OPERATION:
Tuesday-Saturday, 7:00-10:00 p.m.;
Sunday noon-2:00 p.m., 7:00-10:00 p.m.;
Monday Closed. 4 stars

72 Book a Night at the Best Hotel in Cortona
Villa di Piazzano

Villa di Piazzano is probably one of the most famous hotels in Cortona. The villa is a 15th-century hunting manor, which has been converted into an elegant four-star hotel. It is just five minutes away from Cortona center, and enjoys wonderful views and a perfect tranquillity, matched with gracious service.

The villa is full of character and stories. The bell tower bears the coat of arms of the Medici family who controlled the area. When the former owner of the estate, Cardinal Passerine, died, it was turned into a convent. During WW2, this place served as the headquarters of the German army.

Today, guests can enjoy spacious, beautifully decorated rooms. There is a lush garden and walking paths lined with oak trees and jasmine floors. The pool is the perfect place to unwind. The hotel also offers cooking lessons.

Villa di Piazzano ★★★★
Località Piazzano, Cortona.
Tel: 0758-262-26
www.villadipiazzano.com

The Maremma

✗ | 73 | **Relax, Unwind, and Enjoy** the Perfect Thermal Water Dipping Experience in the Saturnia Spa

The restorative, tingling feeling of sliding into a hot thermal pool has no comparison. The medicinal properties of thermal spas have long been touted by locals, relieving everything from skin disorders to respiratory problems. There are several thermal spas and pools in Tuscany to visit (see tips number 61, 64, and 66) but not many of these stand out. **Saturnia Spa**, on the other hand, is very different. Situated in the municipality of Manciano, at a central point in the wild Maremma, this magical, idyllic hotel and thermal spa is one of Italy's best resorts.

The elegant hotel offers many services, including the popular (and recommended) Michelin-starred Acquacotta restaurant on-site, but the best attraction, of course, is the stylish dip in the healing 37.5°C thermal waters, which are rich in calcium, magnesium, sulphur, sulphate and bicarbonate ions, and are frequently replenished by a volcanic spring. Relaxing in the warm waters is the perfect relief for tired feet after days of sightseeing.

The resort itself is effortlessly elegant. One hundred forty rooms are spread across two floors of a converted stone villa. A golf course, a full spa, regular pools and the beautiful views complete the luxurious, pampering experience.

Terme di Saturnia Spa & Golf Resort

Saturnia ★★★★★
 The resort is about 30 minutes from Scansano, there are signs leading to it along the main road. GPS coordinates: Long: 11.51435 East, Lat: 42.64949 North. Tel: 0564-600-111,
www.termedisaturnia.it

74 Discover a Stunning and Secret Beach
in the Maremma

The Maremma is an area of Tuscany that is perfect for nature lovers. There are little beaches here that are just magical to walk on at sunset, and if you combine it with a boat ride (see tip 75) or a hiking tour of the region (see tip 136), you are in for a very special day.

We have many favorite beaches here. When we are in the mood for a more sophisticated evening we drive down to Castiglione della Pescaia. When we are looking to spend a relaxing day in a secluded spot, we head out to Laguna di Orbetello (near Albinia). But when we want some Caribbean magic in Tuscany, there is just one place to go—**Cala del Gelso.** A stunning but somewhat inaccessible beach that locals swear by, often calling it the most beautiful beach in southern Tuscany, this is a hidden corner of tranquillity and bliss. If you aren't afraid of a short but steep hike, this is the place for you. Don't forget to wear comfortable walking shoes though—paradise doesn't come easy!

Cala del Gelso ★★★★
To reach the Cala, drive along the SP65 from Porto Santo Stefano, and turn right at km 5+900. There will be a small asphalt road on your right, drive down it until you reach a gate, and from there hike about 20 minutes down a rocky road to the beach.

🏃 | 75 | **Rent a Yacht or a Boat** for a Day (Or Even a Week!)

Porto Ercole and Porto Santo Stefano are two beach towns with seaports located in a region known as Monte Argentario, a cape in the Maremma, in southern Tuscany. Porto Ercole, famous for being the town where Caravaggio found refuge and eventually died alone and poor, is today a destination for Tuscany's rich. It's a glitzy place where they park their yachts before sailing for the day to tour Giglio Island (recommended) or the Tuscan archipelago. Nowadays, unfortunately, Giglio Island is infamous for the horrible Concordia accident, but other than that tragedy, it is a beautiful place to explore.

In contrast to the glamour and glitz of Porto Ercole, Porto Santo Stefano is more of a beach resort town, with lots of places offering boat tours. The tours take three to four hours at sea, and the itinerary depends on the tour operator and on your interests

(though most make a stop at Giglio Island, the most popular attraction in the area). Alternatively, you can be the captain of your own boat, rent a *gommone* (rubber dinghy) and take on the waters by yourself. The smaller boats don't even require a skipper's license and are inexpensive (about €120–200). In fact, heading out to sea for half a day, with a picnic basket filled with cold water, fruit juices, and sandwiches and touring Tuscany by sea sounds to us like a perfect plan.

If you have a skipper's license or you want to rent a boat with a skipper, several companies are available. We particularly like **Zeurino,** who both rent boats and offers guided tours, and **Zen**, who run a very professional service (their websites contain every piece of information you may need) and rent both yachts (about €120 to €2000 a day) and *gommoni*. In any case, look into a number of options before you choose the best company or tour for you. Naturally, these are not the only available options (see the technical information below for a number of other listings, too). As you walk along the water in Porto Santo Stefano, particularly along Viale Barellai and the promenade along the sea, or on the docks in Porto Ercole, you will see a number of signs for rentals and tours worth exploring. Naturally, Porto Santo Stefano and Porto Ercole aren't the only beach towns to offer boats for rent and tours. Most nearby beach towns, from Talamo to Orbetello, offer an array of such services. If you are interested in renting your own boat, instead of booking a short, guided tour, we do recommend booking in advance. In high season it can be difficult to find an available spot, especially if you want a specific boat or date or if you are interested in renting not only the boat but the services of a captain, too.

Zen Yachts
Cala Galera BOX 4, Porto Ercole,
Cell: 328-665-8431 or 328-703-8072.
www.zenyachts.it,
e-mail: info@zenyachts.it

Zeurino
Piazzale Candi 9 Porto Santo Stefano.
Tel: 0564-818-728
www.zeurinobarche.com
e-mail: info@zeurinobarche.com

Biba Boats
Loc. Santa Liberata, Orbetello.
www.bibaboats.net

Argentarola
Via Orlando Carchidio 8, Monte Argentario. Cell: 338-7026-689.
www.argentarola.com

76 Rub Elbows with Tuscany's Who's Who
at Porto Ercole

Whatever your style on the open waters, we can guarantee one thing: after a day at the beach, or out sailing, when you hit dry land again you will have worked up a hunger. If you are looking for some glitz and glamour to add to your day, choose Porto Ercole. Here you will find one of the best and most luxurious resorts in Tuscany—the **Pellicano,** which features a 2-star Michelin restaurant by the same name, led by Chef Antonio Guida. At around 300 euro per person including wine, the food isn't exactly cheap (and, if we must be perfectly honest, there are better value Michelin-starred restaurants in Tuscany). But the cuisine here is innovative, the setting is smart, and if you want to rub elbows with the Tuscan elite, this is the place to do so. You can, of course, also spend the night in the Il Pellicano resort itself. A master deluxe suite, with sea view and private pool will cost you 2500 euro a night and a double room with a sea view around 1000 euro . Naturally you will be able to pamper yourself at the exclusive spa with treatments such as citrus fruit antioxidants body ritual or the sea breeze massage and enjoy an array of beauty treatments, executed with products that were tailor-designed by the famous Santa Maria Novella antique pharmacy in Florence.

Alternatively, for a glamorous but much more reasonably priced option in the Porto Ercole vicinity, try **Dama Dama**. This restaurant is part of the Argentario Gold Resort Spa and boasts a beautiful panoramic terrace, overlooking the sea and surrounded by mountains—perfect for light, delicious lunches, cocktails, and sunset dinners.

In Porto Santo Stefano, try **La Fontina**, which serves refined, modern Tuscan seafood. It also has a great selection of meat from the Maremma, an area famous for its beef. Book in advance!

Hotel **Villa Domizia**, right outside Porto Santo Stefano, also has a reasonably good restaurant with a great location, overlooking the beach.

Naturally, there are several accommodation options available, at various prices. The elegant and inviting **Hotel Torre di Cala Piccola,** for example, set right on the cliffs of Monte Argentario, is one of our favorite options in the area. The hotel's terrace has a beautiful view of the bay, and the rooms are modern and pleasant. Relaxing poolside, practically on the beach itself, enjoying the spectacular vista, is a delight. The restaurant is fine (though we prefer other dining options in the area).

Il Pellicano Resort ★★★★
Località Sbarcatello, Porto Ercole.
Tel: 0564-858-111,
www.pellicanohotels.com

Dama Dama, Argentario Resort Golf & Spa ★★★★
Via Acquedotto Leopoldino, Porto Ercole.
Tel: 0564-810-292,
www.argentarioresort.it.
HOURS OF OPERATION (RESTAURANT):
Daily, 12:30-3:00 p.m., 7:30-10:00 p.m.
May close off-season.

La Fontina Restaurant ★★★
Loc. S. Pietro, Porto Santo Stefano.
Tel: 0564-825-261
www.lafontina.com
HOURS OF OPERATION:
April-mid-September, Thursday-Tuesday, noon-3:00 p.m., 7:30-10:30 p.m. Wednesday closed. Late September-March, Thursday-Sunday, noon-3:00 p.m., 7:30-10:30 p.m. Monday-Wednesday closed.

Hotel Torre di Cala Piccola ★★★★
Localita' Cala Piccola, Porto Santo Stefano.
Tel: 0564-825-111,
www.torredicalapiccola.com.
The hotel closes down off-season (from October to March).

77 | Visit the Castello Colle Massari Estates
and Taste Their Excellent Wines

The brother and sister team, Maria Iris and Claudio Tipa, who run Castello Colle Massari, have a magic touch. One of the best wine producers in Europe, their work was once again officially recognized when they were recently chosen as the best winery in Italy by the 2014 edition of the influential *L'Espresso* guide. Maria and Claudio first united their knowledge, noses, and expertise in 1998 when they opened the **Castello Colle Massari** estate in southern Tuscany, an area that was once snubbed by wine lovers and only in recent years is finally receiving the respect it deserves as more and more makers recognize its potential. Castello Colle Massari, located in the heart of the beautiful Maremma, is where they make their Colle Massari wine. After opening this first estate, they opened two more, and all three are important in a different way. The most famous is their **Poggio di Sotto** estate, in Montalcino, where they make their excellent Brunello wine (see tip 90). Their **Grattamacco** estate in Bolgheri, on the Tuscan coast, is where they produce the famous Super-Tuscan Bolgheri DOC (see tip 97).

All three estates can be visited, and tasting tours can be booked in each. Although there are more laid-back estates to visit in Tuscany, if you are passionate about wine and looking for a more professional experience, a visit to one of these is highly recommended.

The Castello Colle Massari estate is situated in the foothills of Mount Amiata, an area slightly out of the way for many visitors, who tend to stick to the central part of Tuscany without going south towards the Maremma. But this is a beautiful region, perfect for nature lovers, with plenty of good food, pleasant areas for hikes, beautiful beaches and a sense of tranquillity that you can't always find in other, more crowded, parts of Tuscany, especially during high season.

This huge 1,200-hectare estate is located just below the Brunello growing areas and is perfectly placed for growing Sangiovese grapes. With the very best of the grapes from their 110-hectares of vineyards they produced the Lombrone 2009, which received high ratings from many critics and is a wine you have to try if you make the trip here. A visit will also include a chance to see their modern cellar, covering more than 6,000 square meters, which was specifically designed to ensure the ideal environment for wine storage. You will also get to see the beautiful *tenuta* which somehow manages to be both strikingly imposing and rustic at the same time.

Booking forms for tours, and detailed explanations on how to reach all three estates, including GPS coordinates, can be found on their website (one website for all three estates).

Colle Massari Società Agricola
★★★★
Tel: 0564-990-496,
www.collemassari.it

🍴 | 78 | **Discover What International Celebrity Chefs** Have to Offer the Tuscan Tourist

As a rule, we tend to look for (and recommend to others) the work and produce of locals in Tuscany. This means that, for the most part, we try to stick to small and medium family estates that represent the real charm and tradition of the Tuscan wine industry, excellent little restaurants that combine lovely food with gracious service, and local artisans who add their own individual and modern twist to century's old techniques.

However, we cannot completely ignore the delights that foreigners have brought to the region. For example, in recent years two famous celebrity chefs have opened top quality establishments in Tuscany. Gordon Ramsay's **Contrada** can be found in the beautiful Castel Monastero resort (near Castelnuovo Berardenga) while Alain Ducasse opened **Trattoria Toscana** in the wonderful Ananda resort, near Castiglione della Pescaia, a particularly panoramic point along

the Tuscan beach. Due to the famous names behind the restaurants, the quality of their food and the beautiful locations of each, both eateries quickly gained public attention; Ducasse's restaurant even received a Michelin star. Both restaurants are physically run by local chefs, Contrada is run by Nello Cassese, and Trattoria Toscana is in the capable hands of Omar Agostini. If you are curious to taste cuisine associated with the celebrity owners then we recommend a visit.

Contrada is Castel Monastero's gourmet restaurant. There is a second restaurant on the premises, **La Cantina**, which is charmingly set in a red brick vault, with simple wooden furnishings and lit mostly by candle-light. Contrada however is obviously the jewel in the crown given its famous connections. It offers modern interpretations of classic Tuscan dishes, using excellent local produce, from the *salumi* to the olive oil, and an

resort itself is beautiful. The grand orange Villa sits on a strategic point in the countryside where you can see for miles in any direction. A lovely walk along a path lined with olive trees and rosemary bushes leads to the restaurant, setting the mood for an elegant meal. However, the restaurant is only open during the high season (June to September). This is a shame as it shows up the fact this establishment is really only meant for visitors, not locals, undermining its authenticity. Aspiring chefs will be glad to know that cookery courses can also be organized with the restaurant's team of professionals.

extensive but over-priced wine list. It's undeniable that the food is very good, but you pay a price for the celebrity name, and we have yet to decide if that justifies the fee.

Trattoria Toscana is also located in a beautiful, high-end resort, L'Andana. It is here, in what used to be the barn of this charming old mansion, on a vast 500-hectare domain, that Alain Ducasse has made true his Italian dream. The restaurant opened in 2005, and after just two years, it received a Michelin star. Prices aren't cheap, as you might expect, but the food is very good, with dishes such as fried zucchini flowers stuffed with crab meat; ravioli stuffed with potatoes, thyme and lemon; red shrimps and colonata; wood-oven-baked lamb; and more. A strong emphasis is placed on using high quality local produce. The setting of the eatery is very pleasant while the

Contrada Restaurant ★★★

Castello Monastero, Monastero d'ombrone (near Castelnuovo Berardenga),
Tel: 0577 570570,
www.castelmonastero.com
HOURS OF OPERATION:
Early May-late October, Tuesday-Saturday, dinner only, 7:30-10:30 p.m. Closed on Sunday and Monday. La cantina, Hours of operation: Early April-late November, open daily, 12:30-2:30 p.m., 7:30-10:30 p.m. Advanced booking advised.

Trattoria Toscana ★★★★

Anada Resort, Località Badiola, Castiglione Della Pescaia.
Tel: 0564-944-800,
www.andana.it
HOURS OF OPERATION: late May-late September (precise dates change yearly, check their website in advance), Tuesday-Sunday, dinner only, 7:30-10:30 p.m. Closed on Monday.

79 | **Enjoy a Tempting Meal** in Italy's Smallest Trattoria

La Tana dei Brilli (formerly known as La Tana del Brillo Parlante) is one of the most charming trattorias we've come across during our travels in Tuscany, and not just for its size. This tiny eatery, which can accommodate no more than 12 people at once, is intimate and magical. The décor is simple and enjoyably kitschy. Located just a minute from the impressive Piazza del Duomo, La Tana dei Brilli stands its ground in a town known for its fierce culinary rivalry (Massa Marittima, in the northern Maremma, which boasts a number of noteworthy restaurants, including Bracali, a two-starred Michelin restaurant, making this town a popular stop for foodies).

The menu is traditional but perfectly executed, and most dishes are a modernized version of owner Raffaella Cecchelli's father's recipes, which are over 50 years old. Here you must enjoy the fresh pasta (often rolled and cut in front of you) in delicate pecorino sauce, wonderful potato ravioli, *antipasti* plates with tasty *salumi* direct from San Miniato, a cheese *antipasti* made entirely with cheeses from the nearby Saba cheesemakers (one of the best in Tuscany—see next tip), braised pork, quality veal *tagliata*, and much more. The restaurant uses seasonal, high quality produce, and most pasta dishes are served in the large metal saucepans in which they were cooked. Don't miss the wonderful desserts—they may look rustic and simple, but wait until you actually taste them. Much like the rest of the menu, the list of desserts changes often, depending on the chef's inspiration. We have yet to taste a bad dish here, but we do suggest you always ask Raffaella what she recommends, so you don't miss out on the best dish of the day. To walk off your lunch, tour Massa Marittima itself. The Duomo is beautiful, and the artifacts in the nearby archaeological museum are interesting, too. Of course the best moment to visit town is during its famous medieval feast, the Balestro del Girifalco (see tip 136).

La Tana dei Brilli ★★★★
Vicolo del Ciambellano 4, Massa Marittima,
Tel: 0566-901-274.
HOURS OF OPERATION:
Friday-Sunday, 11:00 a.m.-2:00 p.m., 8:00-10:00 p.m. During the summer months, the restuarnt is usually open daily (but do call in advance to make sure).

80 Visit Saba Farm, and Taste some of the Best (and Healthiest!) Cheeses in Tuscany

You would be hard-pressed to find cheesemakers as professional, dedicated, or passionate as the Saba siblings. Angela and Antonio Saba attract visitors from all over Tuscany to their *caseificio* —not just because of the excellent taste of their produce, but also because theirs is the first cheese in Italy to actually lower cholesterol. The sheep are fed a special diet which includes a significant quantity of linen seeds, a good source of Omega-3. The result is an Omega-3-rich, tasty milk. Clinical trials conducted by a medical team in the University of Cagliari (Sardinia), have proven that those who regularly consumed Saba cheeses experienced 10% lower levels of cholesterol.

But the Saba family's cheeses aren't good just because of their health benefits—it is the taste that keeps visitors coming back here year after year. Originally from Sardinia, the Saba family has been in the business for more than 40 years and has become renowned across Italy for their creamy, refined, smooth pecorino cheeses.

The Angelico cheese is fantastic, as is the fresh cheese with pistachios. Note that the selection of cheese available (as well as how aged and ripe they are) depends on the period of the year in which you visit. Saba only uses its own milk, which means the selection of available cheese is closely connected with the production of the sheep on the farm. From October to June, fresh milk is available, so you will find cheeses such as as the 20-day-old *pecorino* (delicious!) and *ricotta* during this period. From Late July to October, there is no fresh milk, so you will find the more mature and aged cheeses (which are good, but not as good as the freshest produce, in our opinion).

Caseificio Saba ★★★★
Loc. Cura Nuova 74, Massa Marittima. Tel: 0566-918-059,
Cell: 340-304-2378.
www.sabaformaggi.it
open year round, Monday-Saturday, 8 a.m-7 p.m

 81 | ### Taste the Delicious Nobile di Montepulciano Wine in Montepulciano's Finest Enoteche

Underneath the beautiful streets of Montepulciano hides a second city of underground *enoteche* where deep red wine flows from large wooden barrels and ancient cellars are stocked to the brim with wine from local producers. If you don't have the time (or the will) to leave town and drive out to visit the wineries themselves (see tip 83 to find out more about the wineries), then touring the *enoteche* is the next best thing.

A good *enoteca* (or in the plural form *enoteche*), or wine-merchant, is a place to cherish. The advice an experienced wine lover from the area can give you is invaluable. Montepulciano is famous for its ruby red, elegant, fragrant Nobile di Montepulciano, one of Tuscany's most famous DOCG wines. Some of our favorite *enoteche,* where great Nobile di Montepulciano can be tasted, are listed in the next paragraphs.

Enoteca il Nobile is a good choice. They have an extensive selection of local producers, which you can taste by the glass. You can of course also pick up a bottle to go—perfect if you plan on a picnic or a dinner in your *agriturismo* or apartment. Alternatively, the food here is quite good, too.

Enoteca La Dolce Vita is another good choice. They have a great selection Nobile di Montepulciano (we like the smooth tasting Salcheto and the vibrant Poliziano), as well as Chianti Classico (try something from Castello di Ama or Fonterutoli, both excellent producers), and, of course, Brunello. In fact, the *enoteca* stocks over 3000 bottles in caves underground (including several good wines from other parts of Italy) and the staff is knowledgeable. Shipping can also be arranged if you are interested in buying several bottles and taking them home with you.

A third place is the well-known **Enoteca Contucci**, located right on Piazza Grande. You will be taken down to the medieval cellar which is stocked with huge wooden barrels filled to the brim with the deep red Montepulciano wine. The Contucci family has been living in Montepulciano for more than 1000 years and has been producing wine since the Renaissance. Their Nobile di Montepulciano 2007 Reserva, at just €23, is a bargain and pretty delicious!

Enoteca il Nobile ★★★
Via Di Gracciano Nel Corso 95, Montepulciano.
Tel: 0578-757-016,
www.vinonobile.eu
HOURS OF OPERATION:
Daily, 10:30 a.m.–9:00 p.m.
(Thursday until 7:30 p.m.).

Enoteca La Dolce Vita ★★★
Via di Voltaia nel Corso 80/82, Montepulciano. Tel: 0578- 758-760,
www.enotecaladolcevita.it
HOURS OF OPERATION:
Daily, 10:00 a.m.–7:00 p.m. Hours may vary off-season.

Enoteca Contucci ★★★★
Via del Teatro 1, Montepulciano.
Tel: 0578-757-006,
www.contucci.it
HOURS OF OPERATION:
Daily, 9:00 a.m.–12:30 p.m., 2:30-6:00 p.m. Hours may vary off-season.

82 | **Sink Your Teeth into a Quality Steak** in Montepulciano's Famous Osteria Aquacheta

For more than twenty years, the cool dark cellar of the **Osteria Acquacheta** in Montepulciano has specialized in satisfying the appetite of even the most ravenous carnivores. With a reputation as one of the best meat restaurants in Tuscany, the Osteria Acquacheta is perhaps rivalled only by Dario Cecchini's restaurant in Panzano, Chinati (see tip 38). The cellar which houses the restaurant has been transformed into a hearty, informal setting—on cooler nights, a roaring fire is lit to complete the atmosphere. Inspect your slab of steak before it is cooked and then watch as it is prepared in the brick oven at the end of the restaurant. The meat here is served in the Tuscan style, which to the uninitiated means rare, or at the very most medium; well-done is a concept Tuscans frown upon. The house wine is cheap and perfectly agreeable, though a nice bottle of Avignoensi Nobile di Montepulciano would certainly be better. You can also bring your own wine if you wish, and if it's a good bottle the owner, Giulio Ciolfi, will gladly waive corkage in exchange for a glass.

Osteria Acquacheta ★★★★
Via del Teatro 2, Montepulciano.
Tel: 0578-717-086,
www.acquacheta.eu
HOURS OF OPERATION:
Wednesday–Monday, 12:30–3:00 p.m.,
7:30–10:30 p.m. Closed on Tuesday. Hours may vary off-season. Reservations are advised, especially in high season, and can be made by phone only.

 # 83 **Visit an Award-winning Winery** and Taste Their Excellent Nobile di Montepulciano Wine

Choosing a vineyard tour can be a tricky business. Personally, we base our visits on a number of criteria, including the quality of the wine (of course), the professional information provided on the tour, the friendliness of the staff, and the surroundings; ideally looking for a vineyard that offers tasting on a terrace with a gorgeous view.

Generally speaking, it's hard to go wrong; your visit may not be perfect, but it will rarely be terrible. Even when the tour is badly run, the wines themselves will usually make up for it. When in Montepulciano and the surrounding area, we are usually drawn to a number of wineries that, in our opinion, offer both excellent Nobile di Montepulciano as well as charming views and ambiance.

The **Boscarelli Tenuta (Podere)**, run by the De Ferrari Corradi family, is definitely one of the best wine producers in the area. This estate is consistently mentioned on Italian top wine lists, and their Nobile Noccio 2009 has won a number of awards. Pair that with beautiful surroundings, a hospitable staff, and a very pleasant tour of the vineyards and the production facility, and you will understand why this place is high up on our list. Since the 1960s, the family has been using the same traditional blend to make its flagship wine: the Nobile di Montepulciano DOCG. We recommend picking up a bottle, of course, but don't limit yourself to the classics. Try a bottle of their multiple award-winning Noccio wine, too—a cru production, with select grapes from their very best vineyards.

Canneto has an interesting story. Unlike most vineyards in the area, which have been run by the same family for generations, this estate was bought by Swiss wine-lovers in 1987 and has been run by this group of passionate winemakers ever since. The estate is nestled into the western

grapes' flavor. If you want to treat yourself to their best selection, go for the Nobile di Montepulciano Reserve Grandi Annate 2007, a delicious, smooth, aromatic wine, with a great finish. You can drink it now, or let it age for a few more years and pop it open on a special occasion. The Nobile di Montepulciano DOCG is excellent, too. For a simple wine tasting, bookings aren't necessary—simply stop by during opening hours (see below) and taste some wine (free if you purchase a bottle). Cooking lessons, wine tastings with lunch on the panoramic terrace and organized tours must be booked in advance.

slopes of Montepulciano and the vines benefit from this climate. The resulting wine is excellent but isn't sold on a large scale so maintains a certain exclusivity. Expect the experience to be an interesting, albeit pricey one.

Avignonesi is another excellent choice, and one of our personal favorites. We recommend you take advantage of the knowledgeable team and book a tour of the grounds in advance. The tasting at the end of the tour is particularly enjoyable, since the wine is served on the panoramic terrace overlooking the hills.

Known for both their Nobile di Montepulciano and their rich tasting *vin santo*—a century old Tuscan dessert wine, usually served at the end of a meal together with *cantuccini* - this estate offers tasting tours that are worth the drive. Avignonesi take their wine, and tradition, very seriously. Each lot is fermented separately, solely with indigenous yeast, to maintain as much as possible of the traditional taste and characteristics of the

Boscarelli - Marchesi de Ferrari Corradi ★★★
Via di Montenero 28, Cervognano di Montepulciano.
Tel: 0578-767-277 or 0578-767-608,
www.poderiboscarelli.com
NOTE: Weekend visits must be booked in advance. Weekday visits should preferably be booked in advance, too, especially off-season.

Canneto ★★★
Via dei Canneti 14, Montepulciano.
Tel: 0578- 757-737,
www.canneto.com
NOTE: Canneto will begin offering tastings and tours as of May 2014, on weekdays only. Advance booking is highly recommended.

Avignonesi ★★★★
Via Colonica 1, Valiano di Montepulciano,
Tel: 0578-724-304 or Cell: 346-580-5310,
www.avignonesi.it
GPS Coordinates: 43.17306 N / 11.93306 E or 43° 10' 23" / 11° 55' 59" E.
CANTINE HOURS OF OPERATION:
May-October, Monday-Friday, 9:00 a.m.-6:00 p.m., Saturday-Sunday 11:00 a.m.-6:00 p.m.; November-April, Monday-Friday 9:00 a.m.-5:00 p.m.

84 | Dine at the Charming **Ristorante degli Archi** in the Heart of Montepulciano

Montepulciano is one of the prettiest hill towns in southern Tuscany. Set on a high limestone ridge of almost two thousand feet, it is home to one of the best preserved historical centers in all of Tuscany. A place famed for its wine production, Montepulciano also boasts a number of excellent restaurants among its pleasant streets that will surely tempt you with their delicacies. For lunch or dinner, try one of our favorites: **Ristorante degli Archi**. The combination of comfortable décor, attentive service and delicious food, not to mention their use of quality local produce and seasonal specialties, creates a natural grace and charm. Their pasta is hand-made, and their cheeses come from the nearby farms in the Val d'Orcia. Try the mixed *antipasti* starter of salami and cheeses, served on a large wooden platter, the *gnocchi* stuffed with truffle fondue, or the *pici* (a typical Sienese pasta) with white ragu. If you enjoy stronger flavors, the *caccio* and *pepe* (cheese and black pepper) pasta, served with *lardo di colonnata* (aged and spiced lard, a popular Tuscan delicacy) is a good choice, too. For the main course, try the rather sweet piglet with plums and *vin santo*, the beef with porcini mushrooms or the *bistecca fiorentina*. A bottle of a good Nobile di Montepulciano wine, will, of course, perfectly round out your meal.

Ristorante degli Archi ★★★
Piazzetta S. Cristofano 2, Montepulciano.
Tel: 0578-757-739, Cell: 388-930-8947,
www.ristorantedegliarchi.it
open daily (usually closes down during the winter months).

85 Dine and Spend the Night at the Unique Patriarca Estate

In the heart of Tuscany, awaits a very pleasant surprise. Near the small town of Chiusi is the charming four-star resort of **Il Patriarca**. The brilliant red façade of the building with its green-shuttered windows and terracotta roof stands out from the countryside like a beacon. The villa is elegant; the rooms boast four-poster beds with hard oak floors. And the view from the swimming pool is wonderful.

The Hotel's main restaurant – the Michelin-starred **I Salotti**, is run by Katia Maccari, a Tuscan-born chef who recreates traditional cuisine with a unique innovative twist. The meat and freshly-made pasta are especially good here, and sitting outside in the little gazebo is especially lovely in spring and summer. Alternatively, the hotel also offers a simpler (but still delicious) tavern-restaurant, called **La Taverna del Patriarca**. This place is perfect for carnivores, and their grilled

meats are quite delicious. Combining your stay here with a visit to nearby Chiusi, a town which prides itself on a number of interesting Etruscan monuments, will complete your memorable visit.

Il Patriarca ★★★
Strada Statale 146,
Località Querce al Pino, Chiusi.
Tel: 0578-274-407,
www.ilpatriarca.it

Pienza, Montalcino and the Orcia Valley

86 Indulge Yourself with a Magical Afternoon
Aperitivo or Dinner in Monticchiello

In a tiny medieval village ten minutes from Pienza you could have one of the most spectacular *aperitivi* of your trip. Naturally there are quite a few spots in Pienza itself which offer a perfectly pleasant *aperitivi* of their own, but, to put it simply, the small hamlet of Monticchiello offers some of the most spell-binding views in Tuscany, the perfect backdrop to a memorable meal, or drinks. This village, whose history stretches well back into the first millennium A.D., and which is currently home to less than one hundred inhabitants, is an absolute joy. Its old walls surround houses which are incredibly well-maintained, and its stone-paved streets are unusually spacious for a settlement dating back so far. The only drawback is that finding parking here can be a real challenge, even more so than in Pienza.

If it's a simple pre-dinner *aperitivo* or an afternoon snack you are after, then head to **Le Guardiola**. This place has the best location in town, with seating outside on the terrace providing an unforgettable view. The terrace looks out over the Val d'Orcia in the direction of Montalcino and Pienza. The lengthening shadows and changing colors that come with the sunset are a mesmerizing sight to behold. The food is simple and there isn't much choice, but for a light snack it's fine. In terms of drinks the options are significantly better with many fine local wines on offer, as well as some interesting artisanal beers and good coffee.

For a more serious meal, head to **Osteria la Porta**, which also has a terrace with a view (though not as good). Housed in a quaint and rustic building, the food here is tasty, for the most part; though, overall this eatery is a little touristy and not particularly cheap (a *primo* is about €12, while a *secondi* will cost you around €18). The service is friendly and the general atmosphere is

laid back and fun. Try their fresh pasta, particularly the *pici*. The *peposo* and the *maialino* in *crosta* are also recommended. The wine is better value than the food and the restaurant has a decent selection in their cellar. It goes without saying that a table as close to the view as possible is the best place to enjoy your meal here, so book in advance to secure your spot on the terrace! If you would like a longer stay to fully appreciate the views of this charming hill town, then inquire about one of two perfectly comfortable rooms available from the owners of the *osteria* or go onto their website where you will find details about all they have to offer.

La Guardiola ★★★★

Viale Marino Cappelli 1, Monticchiello (Pienza),
Tel: 0578-755-167,
www.barlaguardiola.it
HOURS OF OPERATION:
March-January, Monday-Friday, 9:00 a.m.-4:00 p.m. Saturday, 10:00 a.m.-9:00 p.m. Sunday, 9:00 a.m.-7:00 p.m. Tuesday closed. February closed. Reserve a place on the terrace, overlooking the view.

Osteria La Porta ★★★

Via del Piano 1, Monticchiello (Pienza),
Tel: 0578-755-163
www.osterialaporta.it
HOURS OF OPERATION:
Friday-Wednesday, noon-3:00 p.m., 7:30-9:30 p.m. Thursday closed. January 10-February 5 closed for winter break (precise dates may change). Reservations recommended, especially in high season.

🏃 87 | **Discover the Charms** of Pienza

Located in the UNESCO world heritage site of the Val d'Orcia, Pienza, which itself was declared a world heritage site in 1996, is known as the jewel of this magnificent valley. A delight for the eyes, the commune is surrounded by vistas that will make you sigh with happiness. A perennial favorite of travelers to Tuscany, these views define the romantic ideal of Renaissance pastoralism with age old farms, villages, towns and settlements sprouting out among the smoothly conical hills.

Sitting on a hill with views into the Orcia and Asso Valleys, Pienza itself holds undeniable charm. Once known as Corsignano, it was the birthplace of Enea Silvio Piccolomini, who later became Pope Pius II. Having spent many years away from his native town, the Pope returned after his papal coronation to find a village in which many of its inhabitants lived out a wretched existence. He dreamed

of turning the settlement into the ultimate idyllic Renaissance town, so under his orders, the town was completely rebuilt during the 15th century according to the principals of Renaissance architecture, as had been defined by renowned architect Leon Battista Alberti. The work was executed by Alberti's student, Bernardo Rossellino, and the results of his work are magical. The only thing that ruins this marvel is the hordes of tourists who come every summer to admire the town. If you can come off-season, consider yourself lucky, as this is the best time to appreciate this charming town.

The town's wondrous buildings center on the Piazza Pio II. Head straight for this Piazza and begin your tour with a visit to the Palazzo Piccolomini, the mansion which belonged to Pope Pius II's hugely influential noble family. Located on the west side of the piazza, this impressive construction was completed in 1463. The internal court

of the Palazzo is a wonder while the Italian gardens at the back of the mansion offer a beautiful view; one can even spot Mount Amiata, a favorite sight of the Pope, far off in the distance. On the south side of the piazza adjacent to the Palazzo Piccolomini, sits the Duomo. Its façade, one of the earliest completed in the Renaissance style, dominates the square. Inside you will find lovely altar paintings by famous students of the Sienese school including Giovanni Di Paolo and Vecchietta. There are other pleasant buildings which you can explore such as the Palazzo Vescovile and the Palazzo Comunale to complete the historical part of the tour.

A tour of Pienza's charming alleyways must begin with a good cup of coffee, or even a glass of wine accompanied by excellent chocolate cake, to set the mood. For both, stop at **Piccolomini caffe'**. Service here can be hasty and, at times, even unfriendly, but if you manage to get a table in their tiny courtyard in the stone alley outback, it's the perfect place for a relaxing nibble. The sandwiches here are good, but if you have a bit of a sweet tooth, go straight for their chocolate cake.

Made by one of Florence's leading bakeries, **Pistocchi** (see tip 11), it's divine. A number of artisanal beers and good local wines are also on the menu, to help wash it all down.

For a tasty light lunch, try our favorite place in town, **La Taverna di Re Artu**. Its traditional, honey-stoned exterior houses a very simple dining area of small circular tables under the exposed wooden cross-beams of the ceiling. The cold cuts, cheeses (including a tasty pecorino fondue) and bruschetta here are all delicious. The wine list is small compared to many other places in the area but the quality of wines they stock is undeniable. The same can be said for the range of micro-brewed beers on offer, making this a perfect stop for an enjoyable *aperitivo*, too.

For a more substantial meal, that includes pasta and meat, we would recommend **La Buca di Enea**. Tiny (book ahead to make sure you find an available spot) and delicious, this homely eatery is run by a husband and wife team who know their way around a good plate of pasta. Try their *papardelle*, *pici* and cold cuts, and then walk off your meal as tour the panoramic walls of Pienza, enjoying a truly spectacular vista.

There are several alluring little shops in Pienza, selling the typical selection of Tuscan ceramics, produce, table cloths and bags, but to be honest we are reluctant to recommend any of them. Prices here are high—higher even than San Gimignano—and the selection is rather limited. If Pienza is your only stop, however, we would recommend the town's main street, Corso Rossellino, for some light shopping. Selection here is better than other towns in the valley (Montalcino, San Quirico, Bagno Vignoni and more). We especially like the ceramic dishes in **Ceramiche d'Arte** in Piazza Martiri della Liberta' (located at the very beginning of Corso Rossellino). They stock some delightful handmade items which you won't find in other shops.

A great place to stay in Pienza is **La Bandita.** This boutique country house has received rave reviews from a number of international publications such as *Vanity Fair*, *The New York Times* and *Marie Claire*, and it's easy to see why. Chic and stylish, La Bandita is owned by a New York couple who have made their home in the val d'Orcia, and have brought with them a sense of style and sophistication. The location is stunning with the obligatory views of the remarkable landscape, which can be enjoyed while sitting outside or swimming in the beautiful infinity pool. The rooms are graceful and have air-conditioning, and if you are looking for a place inside Pienza itself, the same owners also have La Bandita Townhouse, at the very center of Pienza, which offers

12 beautiful rooms and a delightful restaurant (perfect for a smart lunch. Try the hamburgers!).

Piccolomini Caffe ★★★
Corso Rossellino 87, Pienza.
Tel: 0578-748-051.
HOURS OF OPERATION:
Friday-Wednesday, 8:00 a.m.-9:00 p.m.
Thursday closed; July-August, open daily.

La Taverna di Re Artu ★★★
Via della Rosa 4, Pienza. Hours of operation: Friday-Wednesday, 11:30 a.m.-8:00 p.m. Thursday closed.

La Buca di Enea ★★★
Via della Buca 10, Pienza.
Tel: 0578-748-653.
HOURS OF OPERATION:
Daily, 11:30 a.m.-10:00 p.m., hours may vary off season.

La Bandita ★★★★
Podere La Bandita, Pienza.
Cell: 333-404-6704,
www.la-bandita.com

¶¶ 88 Buy Some Delicious Pecorino Cheese at One of the High-Quality Farms around Pienza

If you are an Italian cheese connoisseur, then you have heard of Pienza. Pienza's most famous industry is its cheese, and the town's pecorino is a nationally known brand that has been produced in this area for centuries. And while production techniques are up to date, the core philosophy remains unchanged. In fact, when you are digging into some pecorino di Pienza, you can be almost certain that Pope Pius II, a Pienza native, enjoyed the same delicacy some 500 years ago.

Il Cacio di Ernello is one of our favorite cheese shops in town. Located just a few minutes from Pienza's main street, and a few meters from Pienza's main parking lot, this small, inviting shop sells cheese produced in Podere San Polo, a farm located just 4 km away, by Erenello Armellini and his family. They have a delicious array of pecorino cheese aged with different methods, as well as a surprisingly

creamyyogurt, made with a mix of sheep's milk and goat's milk. If you are interested in learning more about the cheese making process, tours of the farm and tastings can be organized.

Right next door to Ernello's shop is Pienza's small agricultural supermarket (*consorzio agricolo*), where you will find a selection of pasta, sauces, cheeses, and much more. When we come here, we always pick up a nice chunk of **Fattoria Buca Nuova's** *Pecorino di Fossa,* our favorite cheese from this award-winning producer. Aged in caves dug into tough rock (which provides natural ventilation) this cheese develops and rich but not overbearing taste with time. The *pecorino al Mosto,* is another delicious option. Matured for 120 days, 40 of which are spent wrapped in marc—the residue of pressed wine grapes—this traditional, strong-flavored cheese is one of the Tuscan

171

but is very good when lightly seasoned with truffles or chili flakes (*pepperoncino*), too. One of the best *marzolino* cheeses is the red variety (*marzolino rosso*). The typical red coloring comes from the tomato concentrate and oil wash used in production, which leaves a very delicate tomato aftertaste in the cheese itself, too. Don't forget to try their freshest available pecorino. SOLP's version is particularly delicate and rich tasting.

Il Cacio di Ernello ★★★★
Viale Mangiavacchi 41, Pienza. Tel: 0577.665321, www.degustazionidipecorino.it
HOURS OF OPERATION:
Tuesday, Thursday – Sunday, 9:30 a.m-12:30 p.m, 3:00 -7:00 p.m. Monday and Wednesday closed.

SOLP Caseificio Cheese Shop ★★★★
Via Dogali 6, Pienza. Tel: 0578-748695, www.pienzasolp.it
HOURS OF OPERATION:
Daily, 10:00 a.m.–7:00 p.m., opening hours may change off-season

classics, and goes very well with a glass of Brunello. In any case, don't forget to pick up some locally produced honey (the sunflower honey, *Miele di Girasole*, is especially good), handmade dried pasta, and a bottle of wine, too.

For some excellent *Ricotta*, that is fresh, full-bodied and will leave that delicate taste of creamy sheep's milk lingering in your mouth, head to **SOLP**. You can either visit their shop outside of pienza (drive 6 km on the SP146 towards Chianciano, you'll see the shop on your right) or simply enter their Pienza shop, on Via Dogali 6. You will also find a selection of pasta, marmalade, sauces, and *pecorino* cheese, naturally. In our opinions their *marzolino* cheese is especially good. This light, fresh cheese has been a favorite with Tuscans since Renaissance times and was especially appreciated by members of the Medici family. Today *marzolino* is immediately recognizable due to its slightly squashed, rounded shape. It is delicious in its original version,

🏃 89 | Be Conquered by the Magic of the Val D'Orcia and the Sant'Antimo Abbey

A world heritage USECO site since 2004, the Val d'Orcia is a part of Tuscany that oozes magic and charm and shouldn't be missed. The valley changes its colors with the season. A strong, vital green washes over the place in spring, a lunar-like yellow appears in May; but the most beautiful moment is shortly after the harvest, in the period between mid-May and mid-June, when golden wheat covers the hills, interrupted only by patches wildflowers.

Numerous writers, poets, and artists have been inspired by the Val d'Orcia, as have many filmmakers. Among the movies filmed in the area are Franco Zeffirelli's *Romeo and Juliet*, Ridley Scott's *Gladiator*, and Anthony Minghella's *The English Patient*. Driving through the area, it is easy to understand why the Val d'Orcia has been such a source of inspiration.

The valley has many great spots to spot; Pienza (see tip 87) is always popular; the *enotecas* of Montalcino selling the world famous locally produced Brunello wine are a must stop (see tip 90); and San Quirico Val d'Orcia, with its tiny streets is bursting with charm, and Bagni Vignoni, with its thermal pools and resorts, are two additional popular destinations. But one site that really shouldn't be missed is the Sant'Antimo Abbey (Abbazia di Sant'Antimo). The enchanting Romanesque abbey is cared for by Norbertine monks, who chant Gregorian hymns a number of times during the day. Listening to the chants, it feels like you are being transported back to the Middle Ages, the time when the church was built.

The complex once included 90 churches and 85 other buildings, including monasteries, and hospitals. According to local legend, the army of the Great Charlemagne stopped by the abbey, and many soldiers became very ill. During the night, an

angel appeared before Charlemagne and told him he should prepare a potion for his soldiers, mixing the grass from the abbey with wine. Miraculously, the soldiers were healed after drinking the concoction, so Charlemagne decided to finance the rebuilding and extension of the abbey to its current size. To hear the Gregorian chants, you'll have to come at 9:00 or 9:15 a.m., 12:45, 2:45, 7:00, or 8:30 p.m. during the weekdays, or at 9:00 or 11:00 a.m., 12:45, 2:45, 6:30, or 8:30 p.m. on Sundays and holidays.

Abbazia di Sant'Antimo ★★★★
Castelnuovo Dell'abate,
Tel: 0577.835659,
www.antimo.it

 ## 90 | **Discover the Enchanting World** of the Brunello Wine in Montalcino

It feels almost redundant to say that Tuscany is one part of the world that has a glut of vineyards and wine tours. In every area of the countryside, it is easy to find producers willing to open their gates and invite wine-loving tourists in, to admire their estate, their vineyards, their cellar, and their production facilities; and, of course, to buy their wines. This enviable overabundance means that not only choosing the right vineyard to visit but also the right wines to try can be challenging. Should you go for classic Chianti? What about the Super-Tuscans? How about the Nobile di Montepulciano? We love all of the wines mentioned above, but we cannot ignore the fact that the Brunello is not only one of Italy's most famous wines, it is also a symbol of Tuscany. No wine lover should leave the region without having toured at least one estate, and having witnessed. first-hand, the making of this beloved product.

When we seek a place to enjoy a good Brunello tasting, we want an estate which combines excellent wines (preferably award-winning. Yes, we are spoiled that way...) with a magical location. Luckily, **Tenuta Col d'Orcia** offers just that. Placed near the petite and gorgeous hilltop village of Sant'Angelo in Colle, right outside Montalcino, the winery grounds are picturesque and surrounded by ancient cypress and olive trees. The tour itself is even better. Informative and interesting, you will leave with a much deeper knowledge of wine than when you arrived. As for the wines themselves, their Brunellos rank among the very best in the area, especially the Brunello di Montalcino DOCG Riserva. The Nearco San'Antimo Cabernet DOC, a handpicked single cru made with the best grapes, is another must try, and one of our personal favourites.

Book the tour, which of course includes tastings, in advance. Alternatively, visit the *cantina*, taste a few wines and pick up a bottle to take home with you. The price of the

The Castello isn't just one fortress; it is in fact a large complex—an entire medieval village to be exact—with roots that stretch as far back to the Etruscans. The ostentatious Romanesque structure is now home to one of Tuscany's most exclusive hotels. With just fourteen uniquely-designed rooms, it can be very pricey. However, an outdoor swimming pool with sumptuous views of the Tuscan sunset, a perfectly manicured garden covered in delicate white roses, a peaceful reading room, top of the line sports and spa facilities, cooking classes, and even hot air balloon rides ensure that if you can afford it, your stay at Castello Banfi will be one you will never forget, for all the right reasons. Similarly, tours of the castle and its grounds or tastings in the beautiful *enoteca* aren't cheap, but they are interesting, impressive, and professional. Booking in advance is highly recommended, as this estate is popular.

tasting at the *cantina* varies according to the wines you want to try.

Naturally, Tenuta Col d'Orcia isn't the only place that offers visitors the chance to tase top notch Brunello wine. **Banfi Castle** is one such choice. With a beautiful, narrow, cypress-lined road, and vine-covered hills stretching out in every direction, the drive up to Banfi castle alone is memorable. The 7,100 acre estate is magnificent, perhaps even more impressive because, up until about 25 years ago, the majority of it was covered in forest. However, once the Mariani family acquired it, they set about transforming the land into not just one of the major producers of Brunello in Tuscany, but also a superbly luxurious resort. A walk through the grandeur of their vineyards is pleasurable, while the view of Monte Amiata, southern Tuscany's highest peak, is wonderful.

The jewel in the crown is the Castello itself, originally known as Poggio Alle Mura (which, to this day, remains the name given to the Brunello produced by this estate).

Biondi Santi is another important contender for the wine enthusiast's attention. One of the most famous Brunello producers in the world, this is, in fact, the first family to produce this esteemed wine according to its modern formula. A visit to this estate is a special experience. The tour is quite short, but interesting and informative nonetheless, and the setting is nothing short of magical—a tiny, romantic estate which is still inhabited by the noble Ricassoli family, ivy clad walls and hidden little trails come together to create a unique atmosphere.

Admittedly, the Biondi Santi Brunello is very expensive. It has been named as one of the leading wines in the world by several magazines. (The 1955 Brunello was chosen as one of the 12 best wines of the 20th century, and you can still purchase one of the 228 remaining bottles from that year for the small fee of €5700.)

A Biondi Santi Riserva (produced only during exceptionally good years with grapes which come from vines that are at least 25 years old), will cost a few hundred euro, and a 20-year-old *Riserva* bottle will easily cost a couple of thousand euro. If you are unwilling to spend a fortune, you can still enjoy a nice classic bottle of a Biondi Santi Annata, produced yearly, which will cost around €80 a bottle. The Biondi Santi wines are produced according to very traditional techniques, and are aged in huge barrels, so that as little of the wine as possible comes in contact with the wood. Production is kept on a very small scale, and these wines are famous for their extraordinary aging potential (a good *Riserva* bottle will easily last for 40–50 years in your cellar).

Poggio di Sotto is another obvious choice. This estate is a name connoisseurs swear by. Set in between Mount Amiata and the Orcia River, the view from Poggi di Sotto is alluring and calm, and much of the estate is planted with olive groves. Production here has a rather low yield, mostly due to the very refined process of grape selection. Particularly notable are their 2006 and 2007 Brunello and Brunello

Riserva, each of which won several awards and mentions. We also love their Rosso di Montalcino, which is, in many respects, very similar to the Brunello, but much more reasonably priced.

Lastly, we would recommend three additional excellent producers, which absolutely merit a visit, even if you only have time for a quick stop at their enoteca to pick up a bottle. These are also names to keep in mind when ordering a bottle of Brunello in one of the restaurants in the area. **Tenute Silvio Nardi, Lisini** and **Le Chiuse** all produce a memorable, deep, complex, award-winning Brunello wine. Lisini is probably the best known among the bunch, but all three are highly recommended, and Silvio Nardi also offers organized tours and tastings, which can be booked through their website.

Col d'Orcia ★★★

Via Giuncheti, Montalcino.
Tel: 0577-80-891,
www.coldorcia.it
OPERATING HOURS:
the cantina is open Monday-Saturday,
9:00 a.m.-12:30 p.m., and 2:00 p.m.-5:00
p.m. Tour and tasting must be booked a
few days in advance.

Banfi Castle (Poggio alle Mura) ★★★

Montalcino.
Tel: 0577-840-111,
www.castellobanfi.com
Guided tours and tastings must be
booked in advance: March 1 to October 31
(holidays excluded), Monday-Friday, tour
leaves at 4:00 p.m.; January 7 to February
28 and November 4 to December 20,
Monday-Friday, tour leaves at 3:30 p.m.;
You will need your own car to participate
in the tour, since the cantina is located
about 5 km from the castle itself and they
don't offer transport. Booking: 0577-877-
505, reservations@banfi.it. Alternatively,
taste some of the castle's best known
wines in the handsome enoteca, which
is open daily, 10:00 a.m.-7:30 p.m. (until
6:00 p.m. in the winter months.

Biondi Santi ★★★

Tenuta Greppo, Montalcino. Tel: 0577-
848-087,
www.biondisanti.it
(check their website for driving
instructions). Tours should be booked in
advance. Tastings in the cantina are not
available.

Poggio di Sotto ★★★★

Montalcino, GPS Coordinates: N 42° 59'
32.71" - E 11° 31' 30.45".
Tel: 0564-990-496,
www.collemassari.it
Tours are available May-October, Monday-
Friday, 9:30 a.m-6:30 p.m and Saturday
9:30 a.m-1:30 p.m.; November to April,
Monday-Friday, 9:30 a.m.-5:30p.m. Tours
last for about an hour, and include a
visit to the cantines, as well as a tasting
(of the Brunello wine and the Rosso
di Montalcino). Advanced booking is
necessary.

Le Chiuse ★★★

Località Pullera 228, Montalcino.
Tel: 055-597-052,
www.lechiuse.com

Tenute Silvio Nardi ★★★★

Casale del Bosco, Montalcino.
Tel: 0577-808-269,
www.tenutenardi.com

Lisini ★★★

Podere Casanova, Sant'Angelo in colle,
Montalcino.
Tel: 0577-844-040, Cell: 366-633-86 77,
www.lisini.com

🍴 91 | Enjoy an Authentic and Homely Meal
in Montalcino

In the last two to three decades, as wine tourism has grown in popularity, Montalcino has transformed from a simple, often overlooked town to a prestigious tourist destination. Today Montalcino attracts wine-lovers who want to sample the world-renowned Brunello wine and the lesser-known Montalcino Rosso.

This lively, hilly little town is filled with busy *enotecas* and hectic restaurants, and the multitude of choice can be confusing for visitors. However, a few places do stand above the others, and for the most part offer a rounded and authentic dining experience, paired, naturally, with excellent local Brunello wine. All three places, however, are more suitable, in our opinion, for a simple lunch, not an exclusive dinner. For a special occasion, we would recommend leaving touristy Montalcino and heading towards Pienza, where there is a selection of better restaurants to choose from.

Il Pozzo isn't actually in Montalcino, but in a tiny, stunning village named Sant'Angello in Colle. Positioned ten-kilometers north of town, far from the touristic chaos of the center, Sant'Angelo is like a breath of fresh air. Right at the heart of the village awaits Il Pozzo. The food here is simple and authentic, though their menu doesn't maintain a consistent quality, and some dishes aren't as good as others. We enjoyed the fresh homemade *pici* pasta and their *bistecca Fiorentina*, but their baccala is too salty, and the *boconcini* in brunello sauce are no more than okay.

A slightly better restaurant, right outside of Montalcino, is **Osteria Crocina**, a popular spot with locals (in high season it's advisable to book in advance). The restaurant is warm and the food is wonderfully inviting – delicious antipasti, artichoke, and prawn gratin, freshly made *pici* with white boar sauce, and ravioli stuffed with sea bass in a creamy pepper sauce. Naturally, don't forget a nice bottle of Brunello to accompany your meal!

In Montalcino itself, our eatery of choice is **Il Grappolo Blu**. The menu of this modest, casual tavern is traditional and simple, but for the most part well-executed. Try their *bruschette*, the hearty pasta with mushrooms and the beef in balsamic sauce.

Trattoria Il Pozzo ★★★
Piazza Castello, Sant'Angelo in Colle.
Tel: 0577.844015,
www.trattoriailpozzo.com,
OPERATING HOURS:
Wednesday–Monday, noon–2:30 p.m.,
7:00 p.m.–11:00 p.m. Tuesday closed.

Taverna del Grappolo Blu ★★★
Scale di Via Moglio 1, Montalcino.
Tel: 0577-847-150,
www.ilgrappoloblu.it
OPERATING HOURS:
Daily, noon–2:30 p.m., 7:30 p.m.–9:30 p.m.

Osteria La crocina ★★★
Loc. La Crocina 1, Montalcino.
Tel: 0577-847-240, Cell: 347- 378-3955,
www.osteriacrocina.it.
OPERATING HOURS:
Tuesday–Sunday, 12:00 p.m.– 2:30 p.m.,
7:00 p.m.– 10:00 p.m.

🏃 92 | Visit La Foce Villa and Garden–A Magical Destination and Iris Origo's Home in Val d'Orcia

La Foce Villa and Garden is one of the best kept secrets in the Val d'Orcia. The villa was once the home of writer and biographer Iris Origo and the estate was a passionate obsession for her. Her book, *War in the Val d'Orcia*, accounts her time in the valley during WW2 and has enjoyed great success among critics and readers alike.

The estate is huge and includes multiple houses and annexes, cultivated fields, manicured gardens, woods teeming with wildlife, and a main villa which once served as a hostel for 15th-century pilgrims on their journey to Rome. You can rent rooms, apartments, and even the main villa. All accommodation options are pleasant, with beautiful views, adequate privacy, and spacious rooms. Each villa has a private swimming pool and there are tennis courts on the ground.

La Foce estate is just a few kilometers from Pienza in one direction, and the historical thermal bath town of Chianciano Terme the other way. In July, there is a chamber music festival held nearby. Even if you don't stay here, consider touring the charming gardens, a beautiful sightseeing spot in and of themselves. The Italian garden

was designed by Cecil Pinset, who also designed parts of Bernard Berenson's garden in Villa I Tatti in Fiesole (Florence). Note that the garden is open to the public once a week: on Wednesday afternoon, year round, as well as every first weekend of the month from April to November. It can be toured with a guided visit only.

La Foce ★★★★
Strada della Vittoria 61
Chianciano Terme,
Tel: 0578.69101,
www.lafoce.com.
Guided tours of the garden take place every Wednesday afternoon. From November to March: tours leave at 3:00 p.m. and at 4:00 p.m.; April to October, tours leave at 3:00 p.m., 4:00 p.m., 5:00 p.m. and 6:00 p.m.; Tours are also available the first weekend of the month from April to November. Tour leave at 10:00 and 11:00 a.m., noon, 3:00, 4:00, 5:00 and 6:00 p.m.

93 Book a Night at a One-of-a-kind Historical Agriturismo in the Val d'Orcia

The Sant'Anna in Camperna is quite unique. The *agriturismo* is located within a former Benedictan monastery which dates back to the 15th century. As soon as you walk in, a sense of protective solace comes over you—it feels like a space in which you can breathe and mediate. The interior maintains the delicate, simple style of an ex-monastery; the rooms are quiet and elegant, reflecting the fact that many of them used to be monk's cells. A treat few other *agriturismo* can compete with is the fact that the ex-monastery's original cloister is not only still intact, but also covered with wonderful frescos painted by Antonio Bazzi, who is better known as "Il Soddoma", the same artist who decorated Monte Oliveto Maggiore's cloister (see tip 63).

The *agirturismo* is just six-kilometers from Pienza, which means you are close enough to visit the town but far enough into the valley to enjoy the countryside. This is the location that director Anthony Minghella chose to shoot some scenes from his Oscar-nominated movie, *The English Patient.*

Sant'Anna in Camperna also organizes art classes and hosts concerts during the summer—contact them to find out what they have planned during your visit or to enroll in one of their classes.

Agriturismo Sant'Anna in Camprena ★★★★★
Località Sant' Anna in Camprena (Pienza), Tel: 0578-748-037, Cell: 338-4079-284.
www.camprena.it

The Etruscan Beach

 Explore the Wonders of the Etruscan Coast– Charm, Good Food, and Great Wines

The *Costa degli Etruschi*, the poetic name given to the section of coast that stretches from Livorno to Piombino, may not be as famous as Chianti or the hills of Siena, but it is one of our absolute favorite parts of Tuscany, a little slice of heaven just waiting to be discovered. So named because of the Etruscan settlements that once spread along its coastline, this surprisingly beautiful area offers a combination of fresh salty sea breezes, kilometers of tranquil, unspoiled beaches, and a number of charming little towns.

If you are a wine connoisseur, you are probably already familiar with this part of Tuscany, which has become a real hot spot in recent years; one of Italy's most expensive wines, the world famous *Sassicaia* is made here, and wine tours in this area are not only highly recommended but also very easy to organize.

Any visit of the Etruscan coast, whether low-key or indulgent, must start in **Bolgheri**. A small and sweet 900-year-old medieval village with no tourist attractions to speak of, it's a perfect place for a pleasant lunch followed by a stroll around the quaint alleyways. The drive leading to the Bolgheri will instantly put you in the right mood. A long, straight road lined with over 2000 cypress trees, it is perhaps the most serene approach to a town in this part of Italy (at the beginning of the road, on your left, you will find Bolgheri's tiny but very useful tourist office, where you can get information about local tours, tourist attractions, tastings, and more). When you reach the town, turn right and leave your car in the car park, as Bolgheri can only be entered on foot (ZTL). The castle, Bolgheri's most famous symbol, is today a wine- and olive oil-producing agricultural company.

If you are looking for a place for lunch, we would recommend **Osteria Magona**. Meat dishes are the specialty here, the *cinghiale* (wild boat) is particularly good. Of course there are also a number of the great local wines on offer to help wash everything down. Despite almost always being busy, the staff is friendly and will make you feel at home. The seating outside, in the little garden, is especially pleasant. Given that this is the most popular restaurant in town, it is recommended that you book a table in advance, particularly in the high season.

If you are looking for a unique culinary experience, you can lunch at the best restaurant in the area, and best known in all of Tuscany, the Michelin-starred **La Pineta**, (see next tip). Then, visit one of the leading estates, such as Guado al Tasso, Ornellaia, or Tenuta San Guido, to taste their world famous super-Tuscans.

Other sites worth exploring in the area before you dedicate your time to wine tastings include **Castagneto Carducci**. This small township is home to one of Italy's oldest family, the della Gherardescas, who lived in the castle which dominates the town, and which itself has a history stretching back over 1,000 years. While you're there, take a walk to the Piazzale Belvedere, which offers panoramic views over the pretty landscape and right down to the sea. Castagnetto Carducci hosts a number of *sagre* (food festivals) and fun little town events all year, find out at the local tourist office if anything special is happening during your visit. Another place of interest is the archeological site of **Populonia (Parco archeologico Baratti e Populonia)** located right next to the miniscule, but charming, town by the same name. Here you can see the remains of an impressive early Etruscan settlement, dating back to around 500 B.C. Particularly

interesting is the site's necropolis, or large cemetery, while the site's principal museum (located in Piombino, not Populonia itself), holds many of the original artifacts found at the site. Then, of course, there are the beaches. The nearby bay of **Baratti** offers a great spot for swimming and the pine trees dotted along the edge of the beach provide the perfect spots for you to laze in the shade, protected from the hot afternoon sun. **Vada**, **Punta Ala,** as well as the **California** beaches are all wonderful too, and are filled with sea-loving Italians who prefer these more authentic beaches to the high-end ones up in Pietrasanta, Viareggio, and Forte dei Marmi. Entire families and couples, naturally, come here to relax and work on one the most important Italian points of pride: a perfect suntan.

Osteria Magona ★★★★
Piazza Ugo 3, Bolgheri,
Tel: 0565-762-173.

Populonia Archeological Park ★★★★
Populonia. Tel: 0565-226-445,
www.parchivaldicornia.it
HOURS OF OPERATION:
March-May and October: Tuesday-Sunday, 10:00 a.m.-6:00 p.m. (until 5:00 p.m. on the last two weeks of October and the first two weeks of March), Monday closed; Janurary 19-February 28, Weekends only, 10:00 a.m.-5:00 p.m.; June-September, Tuesday-Sunday, 10:00 a.m.-7:00 p.m. (until 6:00 p.m. during the last two weeks of September), Monday closed. July-August, open daily, 9:30 a.m.-7:30 p.m. November 1-December 31, closed.

¶¶|95 Sit Back and Enjoy a Romantic Dinner by the Beach

Dining on the beach can be a cliché. But when done right, at a great restaurant, with good food, great wine, and good company, it can be magical. We have had our fair share of beachside flops, but these two cozy coastal restaurants have never let us down.

Located in Rosignano Castiglioncello, north of Vada beach, **La Lucciola** is a charming little restaurant, a perfect venue for a romantic evening by the sea. The menu is small and select with a strong traditional focus on fresh seasonal produce. We love that the food is based on whatever the fishermen caught that day, so you can expect to find weekly variations to the menu. Examples of some dishes we have indulged in include the *sformatino di polpo, patate and porri* (a squid, potato, and leek pie), the *millfoglie di polenta con gamberi e confit di pomodori* (a crunchy polenta, served with shrimp and tomato confit), *gnocchetti* with herbs and *bottarga*, the *paccheri con cozze* (homemade pasta with mussels), the filet of tuna, and more. A table at the end of the terrace will give you the best views, and guarantee a perfectly intimate evening.

La Pineta, on the other hand, is set on Bibbona beach, among a deceptively simple and somewhat rustic surroundings. But this Michelin-starred restaurant is one of of the best seafood venues in the region (together with Lux Lucis in Forte dei Marmi, see tip 125, and Lorenzo in Forte dei Marmi, see tip 128).

Effortlessly elegant and welcoming, we love coming here at night, when the soft sound of the waves breaking against the sand serves as a relaxing soundtrack to our meal. (Come here for lunch and you will see beach-goers parading their recently bought bikinis right in front of you; in our opinion, ruining some of the magic.)

The food here is perfectly executed and delicious, and their tasting menu is probably the best option. Enjoy dishes such as the *baccala* filled *ravioli*, a delicate salt-baked *rombo* fish with vegetables, spaghetti with squid and capers, and much more.

La Lucciola ★★★

Lungomare Vespucci 1, Castiglioncello, Rosignano Marittimo (LI).
Tel: 0586-753-192, Cell: 331-991-3528, www.lalucciolacastiglioncello.it
HOURS OF OPERATION:
In the summer, the restaurant is open for lunch and dinner, reservations are highly recommended. Off-season (September 15-late May) the restaurant is open for lunch only. Note: to reach the restaurant, park near Hotel Miramare, walk towards the beach, after 100 meters you'll see on your right a sign indicating the port and the restaurant.

Ristorante La Pineta ★★★★

Via Dei Cavalleggeri Nord 27, Marina Di Bibbona.
Tel: 0586-600-016,
www.lapinetadizazzeri.it
HOURS OF OPERATION:
early March-late October, Wednesday-Sunday, 12:30-2:00 p.m. 8:00-10:00 p.m. Tuesday open for dinner only (8:00-10:00 p.m.), Monday closed; November-February, Wednesday-Sunday, 12:30-2:00 p.m., 8:00-10:00 p.m. Monday-Tuesday closed. Booking in advance is highly recommended, bookings can be done by phone only, not via Facebook.

96 | Discover the World-Renowned
Super-Tuscan Wines

Bolgheri and the surrounding countryside is world renowned for producing many of the Super-Tuscans (read more about the Super-Tuscans in our introduction).

A visit to the high-end, famous producers of Super-Tuscans in the Bolgheri area will surely focus on three names - Tenuta San Guido, Ornellaia, and Guado al Tasso.

The Antinori family, who owns the magnificent **Tenuta l'Ornellaia** estate, was one of the first families to recognize the potential of Bolgheri. A standard Bolgheri DOC from this estate will cost around $200. Each year, the estate creates a limited edition vintage, in collaboration with a prominent modern artist who designs that year's label. A bottle from this vintage can cost up to $1000 at auction. The 2010 vintage, which was enveloped by a beautiful spiral sculpture designed by leading contemporary artist, Michelangelo Pistoletto, sold for more than $120,000 at auction. Other artists who have designed previous bottles include Rebecca Horn, Zhang Huan, Ghada Maer, and Luigi Ontani.

Tenuta Ornellaia can be visited, though be warned that their tours are rather pricey. You can stop by the elegant cantine to pick up a bottle, or book a guided tour of the grounds, which includes a tasting. The classic tour is available Monday to Friday, lasts three hours and costs around 80 euro, which is far from cheap, but it does include a visit to the production facility and the vineyard and, of course, a guided tasting. A number of personalized tours are also available, focusing on specific wines. The most

famous of these personalized tours is the Vendemmia d'Artists tour, which focuses on a tasting of five years of the Ornellia, from 2006 to 2010. Only ten of these exclusive tours are available a year, so book ahead!

Tenuta Guado al Tasso is a 750-acre estate famous for its flagship wine, the Guado al Tasso, a superior Bolgheri DOC. Try the 2010 bottle, it isn't cheap at 75 euro, but it enjoys a great reputation among critics. Other notable wines are the Bruciato, fondly described as the Guado al Tasso's younger brother, or the light and more mineral Vermentino, a fresh and crisp white, which is the perfect companion for an *aperitivo*. To be honest, it is very hard to find a bad wine on this excellent estate so try a few different varieties and see what you like best. Tours are usually not possible as the Tenuta only opens its gates to the public on special occasions. Still, make sure you stop by the estate's *bottega* and pick up a bottle, or buy some of their produce; a range of cured hams and sausages, organic tomato sauce, and more are available alongside the world class wines.

Even more famous than the Guado al Tasso is the prestigious Sassicaia wine, the best known Super-Tuscan of them all, produced by **Tenuta San Guido**. Made with 80% Cabernet Sauvignon grapes, the Sassicaia boasts such qualities that it is constantly featured in the top 10 list of Italian wines, winning numerous awards. The winery itself sits on a beautiful estate named after Saint Guido della Gherardesca who lived in the area during the 11th century.

Though a bottle of Sassicaia may be out of budget for most people, visitors can try other wines produced by this estate, such as the 2009 Guidalberto or a bottle of Le Difese from the same year. Today the estate is also famous for its impressive WWF bird sanctuary, known as the Bolgheri Oasis, on its grounds, which is a great sight-seeing destination for a nature lover. To combine your visit with a hike in the WWF reserve, check the info on their website, and call ahead to plan your visit as reservations are required. The Oasis is open from November to April, Saturday and Sunday, with two entrance times: 9:30 a.m. and 2:00 p.m. Reservations must be made by 5:00 p.m. two days before the chosen date. Reservations made by e-mail are valid at receipt of confirmation. E-mail: bolgheri@wwf.it, Cell: 334-7584832.

Tenuta Ornellaia e Masseto ★★★★
Località Ornellaia 191(located along the Via Bolgherese), Bolgheri, Castagneto Carducci.
Tel: 0565-718-242,
www.ornellaia.com

Tenuta Guado al Tasso ★★★★
Strada Aurelia Km. 267, Loc. Scalabrone, Donoratico (LI),
Tel: 0565-749-735,
e-mail: guadoaltasso@antinori.it

Tenuta San Guido ★★★
Loc. Le Capanne 27, Bolgheri, GPS coordinates: +43° 13′ 46.90″, +10° 35′ 7.86″.
Tel: 0565-762-003,
www.tenutasanguido.com

 97 | **Savor the Wonderful Super-Tuscans** of the Etruscan Coast Without Breaking the Bank!

Luckily, Tenuta San Guido and Ornellaia are not the only options competing for the wine enthusiast's attention. In fact, some of the lesser-known brands in this area are not only more reasonably priced, but are, in some cases, better, more complex wines, which are slowly gaining a wonderful reputation. For more mid-range touring, consider visiting the award-winning Grattamacco estate, Le Macchiole estate, Tua Rita estate and Michele Satta's estate. All of these produce highly recommended, excellent wines.

We love the **Grattamacco** wines, which have received several notable mentions and prizes. Their 2009 Bolgheri superior, for example, received a three cup rating from the prestigious *Gambero Rosso* guide. Currently owned by the Collemassari group (see tip 77), this estate was originally opened in 1977, at the beginning of the super-Tuscan frenzy. It sits on a hill between Castagneto Carducci and Bolgheri with a view of

the sea off in the distance. It's small, just 35 hectares, with 14 of those given over to vineyards and three for olive groves. Despite, or perhaps because, they have such a small plot of land to work with, the wines produced here are top notch and can stand proudly among many of the finest Super-Tuscans. Visits and tastings are available which you can book via their website.

Le Macchiole is not only an excellent choice, but also a personal favorite, and one of the best producers in the area, in our opinion. Another small estate, of only 22-hectares, the producers here are proud of their low-yield which is made from painstakingly chosen grapes. Try their flagship bottles, the Bolgheri Rosso DOC and the Paleo Rosso IGT, particularly the 2008 vintage. Their Messorio IGT 2008 received a perfect 100 score from the magazine *Wine Spectator*, which needless to say, is no mean feat. Run by Cinzia Merli, who used to run the winery with her husband before he passed away, the passion and enthusiasm for the production of high quality vintages is obvious here. Le Macchiole take pride in experimenting with different techniques and their hard work continues to pay off as they churn out delectable wines year after year.

In the middle to high range, we find **Tua Rita,** a company which isn't yet as famous as it ought to be. Though it is already esteemed among wine lovers, the general public is still not fully aware of the winery's produce. However, they are steadily gaining more and more attention and rightfully so. They have received top marks in recent years from a number of important tasters and magazines, and this year they were listed as one of the 50 best wines of 2013 by the magazine *Decanter.*

A family enterprise that has gradually grown over the last few years, their wines have a strong presence and complexity thanks to the conditions in the area. They grow on hills from which the Etruscans once extracted iron, and the growers say this gives the wine an iron-like nuance. You probably won't be able to try the Redigraffi 2000, the first Italian wine to be given a perfect 100 grade by Robert Parker. This wine is often sold in auctions for more than 500 euro a bottle. Still, though, for much less than that you can get your lips around the Syrah 2010, a single variety wine grown in their vineyards around the medieval town of Suvereto and is definitely recommended, or you can taste the equally lovely Giostro di Notri, their flagship wine.

Tours and tastings are possible, but must be booked in advance either through their website, or, better yet, by phone. Tours cost around 20 euro

per person and include a visit to the *cantine*, the vineyards, and a tasting of 4 wines. If you are interested in tasting one of the more prestigious labels (such as the Redigaffi), prices change considerably (about 70 euro per person).

Last but not least is **Michele Satta**. His wines are smooth and delicious, very drinkable, and for this, they rank among our favorites. Of course, the fact that his produce provides good quality for quite reasonable prices also helps sweeten the deal. Satta offers a tour of the small estate, but to be honest, it is short and not very well executed. Instead we recommend stopping by their *enoteca* and picking up a bottle (or two). Try the excellent Piastria 2012, a smooth and delicious red, or their Costa di Giulia, a fragrant and fun white, made with a mix of the typical local Vermentino grapes and Sauvignon. Satta also produce a lovely Vermentino, the perfect reasonably-priced Etruscan coast wine. The Vermentino is what the locals have been drinking for years. This is a single variety wine very typical to these parts of Tuscany. Fresh-tasting, flavorsome, and slightly acidic; perfect for an *aperitivo* or a dinner picnic by the beach. Naturally, other producers in

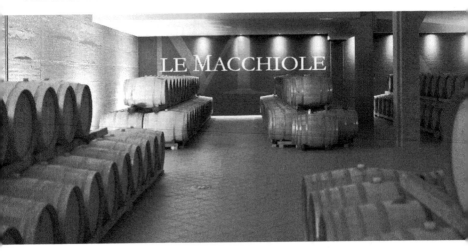

the area offer Vermentino bottles of their own.

Lastly, if you are not looking for a tasting, but rather a pleasant *enoteca* where you can enjoy a glass or two of some of the best wines in the area, we recommend **Enoteca Tognoni**. Right at the entrance to the charming village of Bolgheri (turn left immediately after you've walked through the village gate), here you will find a wide selection of excellent wines, from Guado al Tasso and Paleo to Solaia and others, and at any given moment there are 10 open wines which you can buy by the glass and taste without committing to just one brand.

Podere Grattamacco ★★★★
Castagnetto Carduci, GPS coordinates: N 43° 11' 10.51" - E 10° 37' 40.91".
Tel: 0564-990-496,
www.collemassari.it

Le Macchiole ★★★★★
Via Bolgherese 189, Bolgheri.
Tel: 0565-766-092,
www.lemacchiole.it

Tua Rita ★★★★
Località Notri, 81, 57028 Suvereto (LI),
Tel: 0565-829-237,
www.tuarita.it

Michele Satta ★★★★
Loc. Vigna al Cavaliere 61, Castagneto Carducci (LI).
Tel: 0565- 773-041,
www.michelesatta.com .
The cantine is open from mid April to late October, 4:00-6:30 p.m. Tours need to be booked in advance, at this number: 347 1734573

Enoteca Tognoni ★★★
Via Lauretta 5, Bolgeri,
Tel: 0565.762001,
www.enotecatognoni.it.
HOURS OF OPERATION:
November-March, Thursday-Tuesday, 10:00 a.m.-11:00 p.m. Wednesday closed.
April-late October, open daily, 9:00 a.m.-11:00 p.m. hours vary off-season

 98 **Book Your Stay** at the Incredible Castello di Magona

At around 25,000 euro a week, during high season, **Castello di Magona** is "slightly" out of budget for most people's private use. But it's always possible to dream, and there is no denying that the castle is one of the most luxurious destinations in Tuscany.

Castello di Magona is a Renaissance fantasy. Perfectly situated and marooned in rolling vineyards, the castle was built in the 16th century to house Leopold II, Grand Duke of Tuscany. Today, visitors can indulge in fantasies of nobility in the sprawling, meticulously restored estate, which boasts a pool, Jacuzzi, beautiful gardens, and 10 air-conditioned rooms which can host up to 20 people. If you are feeling extra royal, Castello di Magona also offers a full staff, including chambermaids, a chef, and a private concierge. The castle is renting out in the summer months on a weekly basis.

Castello di Magona ★★★★★
Via Venturina 27, Campiglia Marittima (LI).
Tel: 0565-851-235,
www.castellodimagona.it

Pisa and the Arno Valley

🏃 99 | **Discover Hidden Corners in Pisa** (From the Best Focaccia to Exclusive Boutique Shops)

Pisa is our home town, and one of our favorite things to do is to go on the hunt for hidden little places, not only in the city itself, but in the entire province. Much has been written about the Leaning Tower of Pisa, which is – together with the Duomo and The Battistero – one of the most beautiful architectural achievements not just in Tuscany but in all of Italy. We especially love visiting the tower at night. In the darkness, without any tourists around, the white stones softly glow and the pervading silence allows you the space to take it all in.

But there is much more to Pisa than just the tower, and even a relatively short tour of the city center can provide a thoroughly pleasing experience.

Start your day with a *cappuccino* at **Bar Capatosta** which is located in front of Teatro Verdi (and less than a minute from the town's main square, Piazza Garibaldi).

Michelle Paolicchi, who runs this place, makes the best cappuccino in town; so it's no surprise that, every morning, you can see all the lawyers from the nearby courthouse flowing in for that early caffeine fix. There is also a small but very tasty selection of *focaccia* sandwiches and *cornetti*, which, to the uninitiated, are essentially the chubby Italian version of a croissant. From here, continue walking along Via Palestro. At number 14 you will find **MYO' Vintage**, a small but wonderful vintage shop, filled with interesting dresses, tops and bags. Keep walking along the same street, until it becomes Via Giusti. At number 22 you will find **Panificio Primavera**, a small, deceptively simple looking bread shop, which happens to sell some of the best *focaccias* we've tried in Tuscany. They don't hold back on the olive oil here, in fact we suspect their oil to flour ratio is 2:1, in favor of the oil, so keep that bottle of anti-acid at hand. Try their *focaccia*

rustica, or the *lingue con origano*. Their *pizzette*, or small pizzas, serve as a delicious snack while the round *focaccias* with potatoes, onions, or tomato slices on top are gorgeous. You might be tempted to buy a few to bring back home with you, but these tasty little treats taste best when they are fresh.

Another essential stop is **Gelateria de Coltelli**, arguably the best ice cream shop in town. In this narrow, simply designed, inviting space, the ice cream is prepared with the finest ingredients. This *gelateria* focuses on quality, not quantity, which means you may not find 25 flavors like in the uber-popular ice cream parlor in Piazza Garibaldi, where most tourists go, but you will find genuine seasonal tastes made without any additives or artificial colorings. Only fresh seasonal fruit is used, and while that does mean that you won't find the same flavors year-round, it ensures that the ice cream celebrates the fruit's true, delicious taste. De Coltelli also prepares some excellent *granitas*; the strawberry *granita* with whipped cream is especially wonderful.

To walk all this tastiness off, take a stroll along the Arno River. Of the many Tuscan towns we have visited, Pisa has one of the best views of the river, thanks to the numerous colourful and medieval historic buildings that line its banks. Contrary to typical tourist wisdom, the best point in town to enjoy the view isn't Pisa's main bridge - Ponte di Mezzo, but the next bridge along - Ponte della Fortezza. Set against the clear blue Italian sky on a hot summer's day, it's a sight that you won't want to forget.

Next on the list, it is time to hit Pisa's two main shopping streets, which provide great opportunities for splashing out. Shopaholics will be in heaven hopping from store to store along Corso Italia, the main road leading from the train station to Piazza Garibaldi, and Borgo Stretto, the boutique-filled road that leads from Piazza Garibaldi to the Leaning Tower.

Corso Italia hosts some of the most popular mid-range fashion brands in Italy, including Zara, Motivi, Camaieu, and Twin Set, as well as a number of cute shoe and jewelry shops. In among the lovely tall buildings that stretch along on either side you will find a great amount of options, for every taste, from fashion-loving teenagers (try Pinkie, Bijoux Bijoux, Kiko) to older, more sophisticated buyers (check Furla, Max Mara, Marina Rinaldi, and Fiorella Rubino). Aside from the shops there's also a bunch of little cafes and eateries where you can leave any uninterested parties for a few hours while you shop in peace!

The medieval **Borgo Stretto**, is the more high-end option of the two streets. Among the colonnaded pavements you'll find expensive and more exclusive boutiques, such as Valenti, Pinko, Borbonese, and Versace. One of our favorite shops is, without a doubt, **Bottega Etrusca**, located right at the beginning of the street, two steps from Piazza Garibaldi. This jewelry shop stocks beautiful, handmade, one-of-a-kind pieces that you really won't find anywhere else. The shop is divided into two spaces, sitting across the street from each other. One mostly houses its jewelry collection while the other displays a very high-end assortment of home décor items, including serving sets by Hermes.

As you continue down Borgo Stretto you will find more shops as well as Pisa's most famous *caffe*—Pasticeria Salza, which we highly recommend. **Salza** first opened its door in 1898, and today, more than a century later, still retains that old world charm, serving excellent coffee and tempting sweets. The lengthy counter stretches around much of the inside of the café, displaying a tremendous array of gelato, chocolates, and cakes. There is also a pleasant outdoor sitting area where you can watch the world go by over an authentic Italian *espresso*. If you are lucky enough to visit on a day when they sell *tartufo*, a sinfully

creamy, chocolaty ordeal, make sure to try it!

For some quality antique shopping, visit **Galleria Antiquaria Il Gallo** and **Antiques di Alessandro Leoparti,** two elite shops hiding in Via San Francesco, just off Borgo Stretto. This is where Pisa's finest come looking for unique pieces of furniture and art. These shops are not cheap, but if this is your passion, there are some interesting discoveries here. For more modern, fashionable décor items, check the intriguing collection at **I Pazzi**, located across the street from the antique shops, in Piazza San Paolo all'Orto. Here you'll find a varied selection, from plates designed by Maurizio Catalan to sustainable wood-made wristwatches.

If you are leaving Pisa by train, make a stop at the tiny **Bottega del Parco**, located right in the middle of Piazza Vittorio Emmanuelle, just across from the train station. They sell fresh, organic produce from the San Rossore Natural Reserve and Park, located outside of Pisa. The reserve, which also houses the Italian president's summer vacation home, has made quite a name for itself in recent years, thanks to its quality produce, and their cold cuts and sausages are considered some of the best in town. If you have a preference for strong tastes then try their *finnocchiona*, a salami flavored with wild fennel seeds, which is excellent. Their prosciutto is similarly recommended, and they also sell honey and fresh pine nuts (a Pisa specialty).

Caffe Capatosta ★★★
Via Palestro 35 (just a few meters from Piazza Cairoli and the river).
HOURS OF OPERATION:
Monday-Friday, 7:00 a.m.-4:00 p.m., (off season opening hours may vary). 3 stars

Panificio Primavera ★★★★
Via Giusti 22. Hours of operation: Monday-Friday, 8:00 a.m.-1:00 p.m.

De Coltelli ★★★★
Lungarno Pacinotti 23,
Cell: 345.4811903,
www.decoltelli.it
HOURS OF OPERATION:
Daily, noon-9:00 p.m. Closed from November to mid-March.

Salza ★★★★
Borgo Stretto 46,
Tel: 050-580-144,
www.salza.it
HOURS OF OPERATION:
Tuesday-Sunday, 7:45 a.m.-8:00 p.m. (off-season may close earlier. May also be closed on Sunday).

Bottega del Parco ★★★
Piazza Vittorio Emanuelle,
Tel: 050-806-8019.
HOURS OF OPERATION:
Monday-Friday, 9:30 a.m.-9 p.m.;
Saturday-Sunday 10 a.m.-9p.m.

Bottega Etrusca ★★★★
Via Borgo Stretto 5 & 2,
Tel: 050-578-294 or 050-544-500.
HOURS OF OPERATION:
Tuesday-Saturday, 9:30 a.m.-1 p.m., 3-8 p.m.

Antiques di Alessandro Leporatti ★★★
Via San Francesco 64,
Tel: 050-580-101.
HOURS OF OPERATION:
9:00 a.m - 1 p.m, 4-7 p.m

Galleria Antiquaria Il Gallo ★★★
Via San Francesco 44,
Tel: 050-541-686,
HOURS OF OPERATION:
9:00 a.m - 12:30 p.m, 4:00 p.m-7:00 p.m

I Pazzi ★★★
Piazza San Paolo all'orto 2,
Tel: 050.544077,
www.ipazziblog.blogspot.it
HOURS OF OPERATION:
Monday 4:00-8:00 p.m. Tuesday-Saturday, 10:00 a.m.-1:00 p.m., 4:00-8:00 p.m. Sunday closed.

100 | **Lunch at Pisa's Best Trattoria**–Il Campano

If, after your visit to Pisa's leaning tower, you are looking for a place for lunch or dinner, then don't miss the best restaurant in town, **Il Campano**. Set in a delightful medieval building with a narrow outside terrace that is lovingly lit up at night, this restaurant is low-key, reasonably priced, family run and completely unpretentious. And the food, of course, is excellent. We are always impressed with their seasonal menu and use of high quality produce, but do pick your dishes wisely, and ask about the week's specials. Particularly recommended are the *affettati* (cold cuts and salami) and cheeses, their lovely tuna tartar, grilled octopus with arugula, the *pici* with garlic and bread crumbs done Sienese style, the excellent and slightly spicy *pici* with *baccala'* sauce, the *maltagliato* (fresh homemade pasta) with white ragu and the *tagliata*. The food menu is complemented by a similarly lengthy and tempting wine list. You may not find the most expensive brands here, but you will discover that the shelves that hold their bottles, and take up two whole walls of the restaurant's interior, are filled with popular bottles that most Italians enjoy drinking on a regular basis.

Il Campano ★★★★
Via Cavalca 19.
Tel: 050-580-585,
www.ilcampano.com
HOURS OF OPERATION:
Monday, Tuesday, Friday–Sunday, 12:30 p.m.-2.45 p.m., 7:30-10.45 p.m.; Thrusday, open for dinner only (7:30-10.45 p.m.). Wednesday closed.

¶¶ 101 | Take pleasure in the innovative dishes at the Michelin-Starred Lunasia Restaurant in Pisa

Pisa isn't short of good restaurants. Il Campano, for example (see previous tip) is a great choice for a reasonably priced and delicious lunch or dinner, while Osteria Bernardo and La Stanzina are two very good alternatives. But if it's a more innovative, modern, even experimental cuisine you're looking for, then your best option is out of town. **Lunasia** is located in Tirrenia, a beach town just 15 minutes from Pisa, mostly known as a popular venue for sun and sea loving locals, who come here in droves during the summer vacation to work on their tans. This is also where you will find the **Green Park Resort**—a wellness spa and villa, located in lush green surroundings.

The undoubted highlight of the resort is the aforementioned Michelin-starred restaurant, run by Chef Luca Landi. Laid out in a luminous, comfortable, open plan fashion, and surrounded by full-length windows looking out onto the grounds, Lunasia offers a particularly comfortable dining space. The tasting menu, which we recommend, will give you the chance to savor some of Landi's best creations. The food here is beautifully presented and the dishes are a particular treat for seafood lovers, though the cuisine may be too innovative for some people's taste. Try the *arca di noe*, a complete reinterpretation of the traditional Tuscan seafood soup (the famous *cacciuco*), the fish carbonara, and the excellent desserts. Despite the fact that this is a seaside restaurant with a vast fish menu, the meat is of excellent quality.

Prices match the quality and the ambience; expect to pay around €120 to €150 per person, including wine, making this restuarnt one of the pricier 1-Michelin-star restaurants in Tuscany. A more reasonably priced alternative to Lunasia would be the excellent Lux Lucis restaurant in Forte dei Marmi, 40 minutes north of Pisa (see tip 125).

Lunasia ★★★
Green Park ResortVia dei Tulipani 1, Calambrone (Pisa).
Tel: 050-313-5711,
www.greenparkresort.com.
OPENING TIMES:
The restaurant is open for dinner only, reservations are required. Closed off-season (January-mid-April).

102 Rent the Hugely Impressive 16th-Century Montelopio Villa, Surrounded by Stunning Views

If you can afford to stay at Villa di Montelopio, it is sure to be a time you will never forget. Five bedrooms, including one in the villa's tower, four bathrooms, three grand fireplaces, maid and chef services included in the price, and a piano in the living room, which guests may use if they please, mean that to spend a few nights here is a one-of-a-kind experience. Stunningly designed in an authentic, traditional manner, the 300 year old villa feels quaintly old-fashioned, but is equipped with all modern comforts. The recent renovation kept much of the building's original features, such as the wooden ceiling beams, but added satellite TV and an outdoor swimming pool shaded by olive trees. The outside stone courtyard catches the summer sun perfectly and is the ideal spot for an al fresco *aperitivo*.

The villa is well placed in the Pisan countryside, though you will need your own car to get to it. A location near Lajatico, a little-known area which hides some stunning views, just 30 minutes from Pisa and about an hour or so from both Lucca and Florence, makes the Villa di Montelopio a great find if you're planning on touring the whole area. This place isn't suitable, however, if you are interested in touring central and southern Tuscany. It is necessary to book a minimum stay of seven nights and the maximum number of guests is nine. The cost of one night starts at $735.

Villa di Montelopio
can be rented through agencies which specialize in luxurious vacation homes. Consult the following websites, for example, and search for "Villa di Montelopio":
www.tuscany-villas.it
www.luxuryretreats.com

103 Visit One of Italy's Best Food Markets– The International White Truffle Exhibition in San Miniato (and Hunt for Truffles Yourself!)

Every November, more than 100,000 visitors descend on San Miniato for the annual *Mostra Mercato Nazionale del Tartufo Bianco di San Miniato*. This international white truffle market and exhibition is spread over the last three weekends of November, and is a pure delight to the senses. At this time each year since 1969, San Miniato, which is known as the second most important truffle producing town in Italy (after Alba, in Piemonte), becomes packed with stands offering fresh, high-quality truffles, all adding to the intoxicating and wonderful aromas which fill the air. Apart from the truffles all types of gastronomic and cultural events take place, and there is also the opportunity to taste a whole range of traditional Tuscan cuisine. The highlight, though, must be the tent which is set up in the town's Piazza del Duomo. It is here that you will find some of the best quality fresh truffles that San Miniato has to offer.

The truth is that, although truffle hunting is a serious and skilled business, it can also be a lot of fun and there is no better way to discover this ancient art than to join a real, experienced truffle hunter and his dog on their daily exploration. For such an activity, we would recommend the tours led by **Truffle in Tuscany**. Unlike in other countries, as a rule, pigs aren't used to search for truffles in Italy. They often eat the truffles and dig the soil with such violence that they damage it and prevent future spores from growing there. Dogs, on the other hand, specifically from the *lagotto* breed, are trained from a very young age and accompany the truffle hunters on their excursions. In terms of tours, a number of options are available, including accompanying the chef, hunter, and dog on a search for truffles followed by a cooking class, lunch, or wine tasting.

Truffle in Tuscany ★★★
Tel: 366-2930-563,
www.truffleintuscany.it

🏃 104 | **Get to Know San Miniato** for Foodies

San Miniato's historical center is quaint, but lacks that spark you find in other Tuscan towns and villages. In fact, it isn't the local Duomo or the medieval center that draws visitors here—it is the food. And rightly so. San Miniato is famous not only for its white truffles, the *tuber magnatum pico*, the most prized of all edible truffles, but for the century old tradition of *norcineria* (charcuterie) in town. In fact, many restaurants across Tuscany make a point of offering San Miniato *salumi* and cured meats, known for their fine quality.

Located halfway between Florence and Pisa, San Miniato is easy to reach. The town is divided into San Miniato Alta, the historic old town, located high up on the hill, and San Miniato Bassa, the more modern part located at the bottom of the hill.

Indeed, from a gourmet lover's

point of view, San Miniato, a slow food town, is an interesting destination. Though small, you'll find at least four to five very good restaurants where you can enjoy a truffle-themed lunch or dinner. The intoxicating smell and the delicate mouth-watering flavors are something that will stay with you long after you leave. And if you are visiting Tuscany in November, you absolutely shouldn't miss the truffle festival, known as the Mostra Mercato Nazionale del Tarufo (see Tip 103 for details).

A foodie's tour of San Miniato will include a few obligatory stops. First on the list is **Macelleria Gastronomica Falaschi Sergio**, which is considered to be one of the best butcher shops in Tuscany. Just a minute from the tourist office, it is easily reachable and well-stocked. The shop is currently run by Sergio, a fourth-generation butcher, who speaks with passion and deep understanding about his produce. Here you will find fresh meat (half a veal was hanging from the ceiling when we came in last time, though none of the customers seemed to mind), cuts ready to make *bolito misto* and *osso buco*, steaks, excellent sausages (ask for their *salsiccia*), and a vast selection of *salumi* (cured cold cuts). Some of the best choices here are their Tuscan *prosciutto*, which has a soft and delicate flavor, the *spalla* and *capocollo*, and the *salame di cinta sense* (made from the locally-grown breed—the *cinta sense* pig). The brave and curious may also be tempted by some more unusual products on display, such as the *soppressata*, a traditional Tuscan cold cut, which has a very gelatinous consistency, or even the *soppressata di sangue* (a type of blood sausage). From November to January you can buy real truffles in the shop (though it's better to call in advance if you are interested), and throughout the year you can find products from neighboring farms, such as saffron, salt, butter, olive oil, and local wine.

Just across the street from the Macelleria awaits **Cosi e' se vi Piace**, the best grocery shop in town, which stocks everything from artisanal dried pasta, to traditional biscuits, cheeses and wines, to chocolates to liqueurs. In short: the makings of what some may call decadent (and we would call decent) picnic basket. If you are shopping for products to take home with you, check out the truffle pasta and the truffle-infused oils, which give a wonderfully intoxicating aroma to any dish.

For truffles, go next door to **Tartuffi Gemignani**, a tiny shop right next to the Falaschi butcher shop, which belongs to one of the prominent truffle-hunting families in the area. The Gemignani family has been selling truffles for half a century and offer an interesting array of products, from the fresh and preserved truffles themselves to infused oil, truffled honey, sauces, and more. For more places where you can buy good truffles (outside of San Miniato), see tip number 105. Naturally, those visiting the town during the annual truffle festival, will enjoy an unparalleled selection.

Meat lovers will also be interested to know that yet another well known *macelleria* (butcher shop) offers a vast array of produce as well as organized tastings (which have to be booked in advance). **Lo Scalco** is a popular local establishment and merits a visit, too. Try their V*ignaiolo*, a Tuscan salami, aged in chestnut barrels filled with grape skins, which give the meat a unique flavor; the *Avvoltino di San Miniato*, a dish invented in this delicatessen, made with spicy cuts of pork meat cooked in lard and conserved in juniper infused boxes, or *Il Cenerino*, a salami aged in ash.

Staying for lunch in town is highly recommended and, of the many restaurants which fight for the toursit's attention, we particularily like two. **Ristorante Pepnero** is an elegant and tastefully decorated restaurant, with some very good truffle-based dishes on offer (during truffle season, naturally). The *tagliatelle* with fresh truffle is our personal favorite, but the meat dishes are quite good, too. Book a place out on the terrace to enjoy the impressive vista.

Another good option is **Ristorante Papaveri e Papere**. This is one of the most popular restaurants in town, and our personal favorite.

Located outside the historical center, you'll need your car to reach it. Run by Paolo Fiaschi (the former chef of Pepenero), this simple but delicious little place offers a modern, well-executed version of local traditional dishes. Their pasta dishes are highly recommended, and the desserts (such as the *cannolo* with the almonds) are very good. The main courses, on the other hand, shine a little less.

Macelleria Sergio Falaschi ★★★★
Via Augusto Conti, 18, San Miniato,
Tel: 0571-431-90,
www.sergiofalaschi.it
HOURS OF OPERATION:
Monday-Tuesday and Thursday-Saturday, 8 a.m.-1 p.m., 4:00-8:00 p.m.
Sunday, 8 a.m.-1 p.m. (though not always, on Sunday the shop is often closed, better to call first). Wednesday closed.

Gemignani s.r.l.-Truffle and Mushrooms ★★★
Via Conti 22, Tel: 0571-419-470,
e-mail: commerciale@filippogemignani.it

Lo Scalco ★★★
Via Tosco Romagnola Est 633 and553, Tel: 0571.418727,
www.loscalco.it,
www.lacalvana.it

Ristorante Pepenero ★★★
Via 4 Novembre 13, San Miniato.
Tel: 0571-419-523,
www.pepenerocucina.it
HOURS OF OPERATION:
Sunday-Monday, Wednesday-Friday, noon-2:30 p.m., 7:00-10:30 p.m.;
Saturday, 7:00-10:30 p.m. Tuesday closed. Hours may vary off-season.

Ristorante Papaveri e Papere ★★★★
Via Dalmazia 159D, San Miniato,
Tel: 0571-409-422,
www.papaveriepaolo.com
HOURS OF OPERATION:
open Thursday-Tuesday for dinner only, 7:30-10:30p.m. Sunday open for lunch, too. Wednesday closed. Check their website for directions on how to reach the restaurant.

105 | Buy Some Delicious Truffle-Infused Products from Selektia

Many of the truffle shops in the area surrounding San Miniato often look like they've been taken straight out of a film. Their old world designs ooze a romantic charm, while their products are often delicious. But some of our favorite products, surprisingly, come from a rather more charmless, industrial style place. **Selektia**, in Castelfiorentino, about half an hour from San Miniato, may not be an alluring setting but their goods are top notch. The company was founded by Simone Calugi, who inherited his love for truffles from his father, Renato Calugi, a well-known truffle hunter. Alongside his passion, Renato clearly also passed on a knowledge of quality to his son. The truffles are carefully picked exclusively in the surrounding areas of Colline Sanminiatesi, Balze Volteranee and in the Crete Senesi. After a rigorous selection procedure, the truffles are processed and combined with other high quality ingredients to make some really fantastic products. Take these truffles home with you and prepare something special; the rich, seductive smell of the truffle will immediately bring back memories from your trip.

Try their range of mushroom products or their gourmet selection—we particularly like the *porcini* spread for *crostini* and the artichokes in oil. Of course, getting something from their line of truffle products is a must. The truffle cream is very good while the truffle-infused butter, or *burro tartufo*, with just a touch *of parmigiano reggiano* that adds extra flavor and texture, is excellent. Their truffle salt adds an irresistible smell to any dish. In fact, we often sprinkle a little onto fried eggs to add something a little different to a special brunch or even breakfast!

Selektia ★★★
Via Vittorio Niccoli 316,
Castelfiorentino.
Tel: 0571-582-016,
www.selektia.it
HOURS OF OPERATION:
Monday-Friday, 8:30 a.m.-12:30 p.m.,
2:30-6:30 p.m.

San Gimignano

🏃 106 | **Book a Vespa Tour** of Magical San Gimignano

The Vespa has to be the quintessential Italian means of transport. So what better way to tour one of Italy's most "Italian" towns than on one of these wonderful scooters? There are several companies offering tours.

Fun in Tuscany is a well-known tour operator offering a number of organized tours, including regional wine tours, cooking classes, and quads. They also offer fun Vespa tours through quiet and scenic roads and trails in the Chianti region. They usually cater to a younger crowd (largely students), but honestly, you can ride a Vespa at any age!

The tour takes you into the heart of Tuscany where some of the most famous Chianti wines are produced. If you don't feel comfortable enough to ride on your own, you can join one of the guides, receiving a €20 discount. The tour covers the famous medieval town of San Gimignano. The first stop in town is to the famous Dondoli Gelato to sample some award-winning ice cream. For lunch the tour stops at a local winery for some fantastic Tuscan grub, including *antipasti toscani*, *ribolita* soup, *lasagna*, and *cantuccini* for dessert. Following that is a wine tasting. The only problem you will have then is getting back on your scooter...

Another good option for Vespa tours is **Florence Town**. These tours leave from Florence, and participants are transported by minivan to Chianti, where the actual tour begins. The tour includes a visit to a cantine, and lunch (or dinner, depending on the hour). We recommend checking both websites, to make an informed decision. If you feel like going your own way, check out **Tuscany Scooter Rental**, a Vespa rental service (not an organized tour), which operates in collaboration with the Gaiole in Chianti tourist office.

Fun In Tuscany ★★★★
Via Bernardo Cennini, 6, Florence,
Cell: 338-592-2682 or 392- 633-9101,
http://www.funintuscany.com
NOTE: You need a driving license to participate (not necessarily a motorcycle license). Book at least a week in advance. Since the tour includes wine tasting and a light lunch, inform the staff in advance if you are vegetarian or suffer from any allergies. Pick up service from your hotel can be organized for a fee. Tours leave daily at 9:30 a.m. Service may not be availble off-season.

Florence Town ★★★
Via de' Lamberti 1, Florence,
Tel: 055-0123994. Number for emergencies: 346-152-5515. www.florencetown.com. Book well in advance. Tours leave March-October, daily, at 9:30 a.m. May-September, tours leave twice a day, 9:30 a.m. and 2:30 p.m.

Tuscany Scooter Rental ★★★
Via Bettino Ricassoli 50, Gaiole in chianti, Tel: or 055- 941-747, Cell: 338- 979-6038, www.tuscanyscooterrental.com

107 See Tuscany from a Unique Perspective
–From a Hot Air Balloon!

Tuscany is renowned as one of the most photogenic parts of Europe, if not the world. It goes without saying that the views on offer in this scenic part of Italy are memorable, but for a truly unforgettable experience, why not appreciate the view from the unique perspective of a hot air balloon? How better to commemorate a romantic getaway or a special occasion than with a hot air balloon ride over the Tuscan fields, vineyards, and hill towns, looking down over San Gimignano, the Val d'Orcia and the Chianti region?

One recommended company for rides is **Banda Balloons** who offer outstanding, although expensive trips. They also offer photography classes from the air, while you are in the balloon; which means you'll have souvenirs to remember your ride long after it's done. Their balloons leave from Montaione, 25 minutes north of San Gimignano. The flight lasts for 50 to 70 minutes and they usually leave early in the morning or late in the afternoon. Prices start from 500 euro. Book at least a week in advance.

Another good option is **Balloon Tuscany**. Prices are similar, though you can also book a ride with other participants, so the price goes down to the more affordable level of about 250 euro per person. They also offer the choice of a number of different launch sites, giving you the choice between an aerial view of Siena, Lucca, Florence, Chianti, and more. When you land they'll also hand you a celebratory glass of champagne—now that's service!

Banda Balloons ★★★★
Cell: 320-853-8998 (Nicola), or 335-765-6200 (Massi).
www.bandaballoons.com

Balloon Team Italia ★★★★
Cell: 348-404-4117, www.ballonteamitalia.it

♨ 108 | Enjoy a Tasty Dinner and the View
over San Gimignano from Le Vecchie Mura Restaurant

San Gimignano, one of Tuscany's best-known and loved hill towns (perhaps too loved, judging by the number of tourists who roam the streets in high season), is a must-see destination. Famous for its medieval skyscrapers—the impressive towers built by local noble families competing for fame and glory—San Gimignano bursts with medieval charm, and its well-preserved streets are a joy to explore. While the town boasts a number of pretty picnic stops with views, picnics aren't the only way to enjoy an *al fresco* dining experience with a wonderful view. **Le Vecchie Mura** is one of the more popular restaurants in town, so book ahead and specifically ask for a table on the terrace. The menu here is varied—our favorites include *affettati di cinghiale* (wild boar salami and cured meat) for *antipasti*, and the *ravioli al tartufo*, the lasagne, or the *scaloppini ai funghi* for mains. (Note that in vogue with current food trends, Le Vecchie Mura also serves gluten-free pasta.) We love sitting back in the glimmer of the late afternoon sun, glass of wine in hand, and gazing out at the countryside tumbling below us.

Le Vecchie Mura Restaurant ★★★
Via Piandornella 15, San Gimignano.
Tel: 0577-940-270,
www.vecchiemura.it
HOURS OF OPERATION:
Wednesday–Monday, 6:00–10:00 p.m.
Closed Tuesday and from early November to mid March.

109 Taste San Gimignano's Delectable Vernaccia Wine

The Vernaccia is undoubtedly one of our favorite choice for a summer lunch or *aperitivo*. Prepared from *vernaccia* grapes from the area around San Gimignano, this crisp-tasting white wine immediately brings to mind scenes of open hills and gorgeous Tuscan mornings. Though not as venerated as Brunello, Nobile di Montepulciano or super-Tuscans, it is one of Italy's best loved whites, and has been produced since the early 13th century. Popular among noble families and clergy, the Vernaccia was even the thirst quencher of choice for famous gluttons such as Pope Martino IV, who was, according to Dante Alighieri, especially fond of a nice plate of Bolsena eels pickled in Verncaccia wine.

A number of vineyards en route to San Gimignano offer tastings and the chance to buy bottles to go. Here are some of our favorites:

Fontaleoni, an elite producer whose fresh and crisp-tasting Vernaccia has won numerous awards and is among the best in the area. They also have a B&B with a restaurant and wine bar on-site if you are interested in spending more time here.

La Mormoraia is another excellent choice, and a producer of award-winning wines. The location of their *tenuta*, which is also an *agriturismo* with a spa, is simply magical. With a magnificent view of San Gimignano in the distance, green and well maintained gardens, endless vineyards, and an old rustic building of brick and stone, it is quite simply the Tuscan ideal. Organized tours and tastings are also available (and recommended). Their most basic

tour includes a tasting of two wines and their olive oil. More extensive tours with tastings of three or more wines and a light lunch with cold meats and cheeses are also available. Though the standard tours are meant for groups of six or more people, personal tours can be organized, and tailored according to preferences. Booking in advance is necessary.

Last but not least is **Sovestro in Poggio,** a charming place which offers guests a beautiful vista, a feature that makes this tasting experience all the more sumptuous. Run by very friendly and informative owners who offer interesting explanations, Sovestro is a lively *agriturismo*, with wine tasting tours and a light lunch on offer, all of which must be booked in advance. The ambience is pleasant, with good wine and appetizing food, while the view of the surrounding hills is stunning, especially if you are visiting in late August or early September, before the *vendemia* (harvest). Ask to be seated outside, if they have space.

If you don't have the time to venture out of town and visit one of the estates, a perfectly enjoyable alternative is to visit one of San Gimignano's many *enotecas*, for wine tastings with some fine food. For a rustic, no-frills kind of experience, we like **Enoteca Gustavo Mescita**, a simple and friendly place, which serves up tasty snacks at a good price. It is located right on San Gimignano's main street: Via San Matteo. Order a glass (or three) of a good Vernaccia, preferably from one of the producers listed above, and some tasty *bruschette*. Or, if the fresh air has made you develop a more serious appetite, try one of Gustavo's huge *panini*, a sandwich which is simply impossible to eat with any grace or neatness. After the second glass of Vernaccia you will probably do as we do and surrender to the mess.

For a more serious tasting experience, try the **Cantina del Convento**. With a large selection of Tuscan wines, comfortable seating and a knowledgeable staff, this is a place to start off any exploration of the region's produce.

Fontaleoni ★★★★
Loc. S. Maria 39, San Gimignano.
Tel: 0577-950-193,
www.fontaleoni.com
NOTE: Tours and tasting can be organized, book a week in advance.

La Mormoraia ★★★★
Loc. Sant' Andrea, San Gimignano.
Tel: 0577- 940-096,
www.mormoraia.it

Sovestro in Poggio ★★★★
Loc. Sovestro, San Gimignano. Long: 11.0585 E (11° 3' 31" E), Lat: 43.46 N (43° 27' 36" N). Tel: 0577-907-209,
Cell: 335-482-192,
www.sovestroinpoggio.it
NOTE: Simple wine tastings don't have to be booked in advance and can be organized on the spot, during business hours (10:30 a.m.-6:30 p.m., in season). If you are interested in a full tour of the grounds, lunch and a more extensive tastings, you need to book in advance.

Enoteca Gustavo Mescita ★★★
Via San Matteo 29, San Gimignano,
Tel: 0577-940-057,
HOURS OF OPERATION:
Wednesday–Monday, 9:30 a.m.-8:00 p.m.
Hours may change off-season.

La Cantina del Convento ★★★
Via Quercecchio 2, San Gimignano.
Tel: 0577-907-132,
www.lacantinadelconvento.com
HOURS OF OPERATION:
March–October, daily, 11:30 a.m.-7:30 p.m. (Saturday until 10:00 p.m.). November–February, open on weekends only, 11:30 a.m.-7:30 p.m.

110 | **Book a Romantic Stay** at Agriturismo Guardastelle in San Gimignano

The combination of the magical views, friendly and attentive service, and charming atmosphere makes Agriturismo Guardastelle a great choice for a weekend in San Gimignano. The style and decor here are romantic, with a sense of old-world charm—wooden furniture and iron cast beds, rich colors, and beautiful linens. Outside you will find a manicured lawn with roses and other beautiful flowers, as well as a pool, perfect for a morning or afternoon dip, to escape the boiling Tuscan summer.

It is reasonably priced and you can choose between rooms or self-catering apartments. The *agriturismo* is surrounded by vineyards and olive groves, which belong to Fausto and Susanna, the owners, who produce their own excellent oil and wine (pick up a bottle when you leave). The views of the valley are very picturesque, and at night the *agriturismo* justifies its name; *guardastella* literally means "looks at the stars". You can sit outside on a hot summer night, look at the sky, and feel happy about making the decision to stay in this wonderful little corner of the world. At night, the panoramic view of San Gimignano and the beautifully lit towers is magical. The *agriturismo* is conveniently located at a short walking distance from the town itself, so take advantage of the proximity and enjoy a pleasant evening walk into town, for some dinner. As this is one of the most popular accommodation choices in the area, we recommend booking a room well in advance.

Agriturismo Guardastelle ★★★★
Loc. Sovestro, San Gimignano. GPS Coordinates: Long: 11.0585 E (11° 3′ 31″ E), Lat: 43.46 N (43° 27′ 36″ N).
Tel: 0577-907-209,
www.guardastelle.com

Volterra and the Elsa Valley

111 | **Book a Gourmet Dinner** in Jail!

If there's one experience we are sure very few people will be able to top, it's this one: enjoy a dinner in jail, cooked by prisoners, and the chef of a leading Tuscan restaurant. Wait, it gets better...

The impressive Medici fortress can be seen from many points across the town of Volterra. It was built in the 15th century as a symbol of the family's control over the town they had conquered. The fortress serves as an impressive example of military Renaissance architecture and has been used as a political prison since its inception. Today it is one of Italy's most secure prisons, even holding a number of high-ranking mafia members. However, once a month the prison comes to life thanks to a relatively new initiative, designed to aid inmate rehabilitation; a fresh dinner is cooked and served to a few dozen lucky guests who booked well in advance.

Fresh ingredients are donated by the chain of supermarkets Coop and the wine is provided by local company Fisar. Prisoners are paid for their work and the successful project enjoys the support of the Ministry of Justice. The food, not surprisingly, is served on paper plates with plastic cutlery. There is even music provided—Bruno, a convicted murderer, plays the piano beautifully!

These dinners take place once a month, from November to June. The prisoners cook under the guidance of some of the leading chefs in Tuscany, from restaurants such as Il Santo Graal in Florence and Follonica's Oasi. Book well ahead as each visitor has to complete an advance security clearance. We recommend booking at least three months prior to your visit. For foreign nationals, special documentation is required to enter the prison, and to get clearance. Contact the agency to find out more.

Agronauta Viaggi Travel Agency
★★★★★
Tel: 055-234-5040,
www.cenegaleotte.it

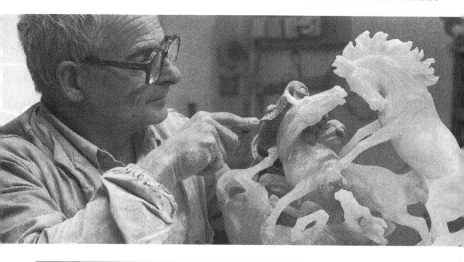

112 | **Buy Some Beautiful Alabaster Artifacts** in Volterra

Alabaster craftsmanship has been sewn into the fabric of life in Volterra for hundreds of years. Generations of families have honed the skill of sculpting with this elegant stone, and many of today's master alabaster artisans still use traditional techniques. The items they create are some of the best souvenirs you will find in Tuscany.

There is a wide selection of alabaster workshops in Volterra, catering to different budgets. If you are looking for something special, skip the run-of-the-mill items in the touristy shops, and head to the **Artieri**, a large store with an impressive and varied collection of alabaster and agate items, all made by the 33 artists who own the cooperative. Another recommendation for artisanal items, is **the Alabastri Lavorati Italiani** shop, better known simply as Ali, situated right next to Piazza Martiri della Liberta.

A smaller, more specialized store is **Romano Bianchi**. This shop is renowned for its intricate chess sets, as well as its elegant statues.

To get a closer look behind the scenes try visiting **Alabarte**, a workshop and a store, that offers a peak into the processes and techniques used by the artists. Alabarte, as well as most other shops in Volterra, can also personalize orders and will ship around the world.

Ali

Piazza Martiri della Liberta' 5, Volterra.
Tel: 0588-860-78,
www.alialabastro.it
HOURS OF OPERATION:
Daily, 10:00 a.m.–7:00 p.m.

Artieri ★★★★

Piazza dei Priori, 5, Volterra.
Tel: 0588-87590,
www.artierialabastro.it
(They also have a much smaller shop in Pisa, near the Leaning Tower, in Via Santa Maria 12). Hours of operation: September–June, daily, 10:00 a.m.–1:00 p.m., 3:00-7:00 p.m.; August, open daily 10:00 a.m.–8:00 p.m.

Alabarte ★★★

Workshop: Via Orti di Sant'Agostino 28, Volterra. Shop: Via Don Minzoni, 18, Volterra,
Tel: 0588-879-68,
www.alabarte.com
HOURS OF OPERATION:
Monday-Friday, 10:00 a.m.–12:30 p.m., 3:00-6:30 p.m. March–September, also open on Saturday. August, open on Sunday, too.

Romano Bianchi ★★★

SR 68, Km. 37,200 (right outside Volterra),
Tel: 0588 87237,
www.romanobianchi.com
Hours of operation tend to change, especially off-season. Usually open Mondat-Friday, 10:00 a.m.–1:00 p.m., 3:30-6:30 p.m. May be open for longer hours in summer.

113 | Try Some Excellent Artisanal Cheeses from Farms around Volterra

The area around Volterra is filled with little farms each offering its own individual interpretation of pecorino cheeses. Of course, much of this cheese is very good but at the same time, not every farm deserves a visit. A few producers rise high above the others thanks to the quality of their products. **Fattoria Lischeto,** located six kilometers from Volterra, is one of these. The pecorino made by Giovanni Cannas on his beautiful farm really stands out among the competition. Their forte, in our opinion, is the more delicate pecorino cheeses, where the freshness and creaminess really come across. Try, for example, the Pecorino degli Sposi, made with pasteurized sheep milk, a subtle, smooth pecorino that is aged for about a month and goes perfectly with a nice bottle of Vermentino or San Gimignano Vernaccia. For a stronger flavor, try the Pecorino Balze Volterrane, aged for at least two months and made with vegetable based rennet (making it perfect for vegetarians). Their *ricotta* cheese is another recommended choice. It is only produced when fresh sheep's milk is available. A soft delicacy, this cheese is excellent on its own or with a light drizzle of honey. This farm, which is also an active *agriturismo* with comfortable, inviting rooms and apartments for rent, also produces organic cosmetics, and a light, yet full-bodied, olive oil.

Lischeto Farm and Agriturismo
★★★
Strada Provinciale del Monte Volterrano, Volterra (check the detailed explanations and map on their website),
GPS coordinates 43.420385, 10.813465.
Tel: 0588:30414 / 30403,
Cell: 348.3327570 / 393.9036970,
www.agrilischeto.com
HOURS OF OPERATION:
Daily, 9:00 a.m.–5:30 p.m. Hours of operation may change off-season. In the summer, the agriturismo's shop is often open later than 6:00 p.m.

 114 | **Discover the Charms of Colle Val d'Elsa**
and Buy Some Stunning Crystal Artifacts

Souvenirs can be a tricky business. What seems like a sane purchase when traveling becomes an unnecessary—and sometimes embarrassing—extravagance when back at home. But thoughtfully purchased souvenirs can and do serve as happy reminders long after our travels have finished.

With our past mistakes informing our future decisions, we have identified two rules for souvenir shopping. Firstly, we only buy souvenirs that we can actually use. Second, the items must represent the essence of the place we've visited rather than the Disneyland-esque version.

A case in point is a set of six hand-made crystal wine glasses we bought a few years ago at a small shop called La Grotta del Cristallo, hidden in an alley in Colle val d'Elsa's historical center. Every time we sip wine from

them, we are fondly transported back to that fresh winter morning we spent in town.

Despite its small size, the town of Colle val d'Elsa is responsible for over 95% of the authentic crystal production Italy, and even hosts a small museum dedicated entirely to the history of crystal production.

The town may not be as lovely as nearby San Gimignano or Monteriggioni, but it has a special kind of atmosphere to it and is worth a stop. If you plan on purchasing any housewares or other souvenirs, note that while there is a reasonable selection of shops to choose from inside the historical center, the best artisans are located outside the walls, in the industrial area about 10 minutes from town. Colle Val d'Elsa's (tiny) local culinary scene is thriving, too—consider stopping in at the excellent Michelin-starred Arnolfo restaurant (see tip number 115) or at the lively Officina Popolare (see tip number 116).

Among the multitude, a few crystal shops stand out from the others:

Franco Cucini has been making quality crystal items for over 40 years. To get a better idea of his style, and admire the delicate artifacts he makes, check his website before your tour of the town.

Mezzetti Cristalerie is another good choice. We especially admire their Da Vinci collection, which mostly consists of bottles and carafes.

Duccio di Segna has an interesting show room and some beautiful pieces worth exploring.

La grotta del Cristallo and **Cristalleria Moleria** both have beautiful collections and are located within Colle Val d'Elsa's historic center. We especially like La Grotta's glasses, and Moleria's selection of gorgeous masculine bottles and tableware.

Franco cucini ★★★
Zona industriale, Ingresso 5, number 36, Colle di Val d'Elsa.
Tel: 0577-931-890,
www.formesulcristallo.it
HOURS OF OPERATION:
Monday-Friday 8:15 a.m.-1:00 p.m., 3:00-8:00 p.m. Saturday 8:15-noon. Groups interested in guided visits should book about 4-5 days in advance.

Mezzetti Cristalerie ★★★★
Via Guglielmo Oberdan 13, Colle di Val d'Elsa. Tel: 0577-920-395,
www.cristalleriemezzetti.com
HOURS OF OPERATION:
Monday 3:30-7:30 p.m. Tuesday-Saturday 9:00 a.m.-1:00 p.m., 3:30-7:30 p.m. Sunday closed.

Duccio di Segna ★★★
Loc. Pian dell'Olmino 42, Colle val d'Elsa.
Tel: 0577-929-656,
www.ducciodisegna.com
HOURS OF OPERATION (SHOWROOM AND SHOP):
Monday-Friday 9:00 a.m.-12:30 p.m., 2:30-7:30 p.m. Guided visits to the workshop should be booked in advance, and can be organized Monday-Saturday 9:00 a.m.-noon.

La Grotta del Cristallo ★★★
Via del Murolungo 20, Colle di Val d'Elsa, G.P.S : 43°25'22" Nord - 11°07'24" Est.
Tel: 0577. 924676,
www.lagrottadelcristallo.it
HOURS OF OPERATION:
April-November, daily, 10:00 a.m.-7:00 p.m. December-March, 10:00 a.m.-1:00 p.m., 2:30-7:00 p.m.

Cristalleria La Moleria Show Room-outlet ★★★
Via delle Romite 26-28, Colle di Val d'Elsa.
Tel: 0577.920163,
www.lamoleriagelli.com
HOURS OF OPERATION:
Monday-Saturday 9:30 a.m.-12:30 p.m., 2:00-6:00 p.m.

🍴 115 | **Dine at Arnolfo–**One of Tuscany's Best Restaurants

It is difficult to enter **Arnolfo's** and not be immediately enchanted. The two-star-Michelin restaurant is set just above the town of Colle Val d'Elsa in a 15th-century palace. There are just 28 seats in this place, and combined with the candlelit tables and the subtle, smart décor, Arnolfo's exudes a feeling of intimate romance. Run by Gaetano Trovato, the chef, and Giovanni Trovato, the sommelier and manager, these are two brothers who are passionate about food, wine, and hospitality.

The food is, as you would imagine, exceptional. In fact, we prefer it to the three-Michelin-starred *Enoteca Pincchiori* in Florence, or to the two-starred *Da Caino* in Montemerano.

Chef Gaetano Trovato is renowned for blending innovation and tradition. The beautiful presentation (every plate resembles a little work of art) and the combination of contradicting yet complementary tastes are a trademark of this restaurant. Try sumptuous dishes such as *fois gras* with strawberries, *ravioli* filled with *scampi* and the delicious pigeon in coffee sauce. The tasting menu is probably the best way to go (a vegetarian menu is also available). To complete the experience, visitors enjoy an extensive wine list. For such a small restaurant it barely needs to be mentioned that booking well in advance is essential.

Arnolfo ★★★★★
Via 20 Settembre 50-52, Colle Val d'Elsa.
Tel: 0577-920-549,
www.arnolfo.com
HOURS OF OPERATION:
mid-March-late Janurary, Thursday-Monday, 8:00-10:00 p.m. Closed Tuesday-Wednesday, closed for winter break (usually February-mid-March).

116 | **Have a Wonderfully Authentic Meal**
at L'Officinia della Cucina Popolare

L'Officina della Cucina Popolare is a place for locals. While Arnolfo's (see the previous tip) holds the honor of being Colle val d'Elsa's most famous restaurant, Officina is our favorite everyday option. This little side street restaurant is the perfect place to grab a light, tasty local dish. The restaurant's owners rigorously stick to seasonal cuisine, utilizing regional produce and suppliers. Wine is sourced from small local wineries and meticulously paired with the food. The menus and wine lists change on a monthly basis and the Officina even lists its suppliers on the website, so if you are feeling inspired you will know where to go to buy some produce to take back home with you. The Officina is a real treat for anyone who enjoys slow food, great wine, and people-watching. Be sure to book a place in advance, especially in summer, as this restaurant is rarely empty.

L'Officina della Cucina Popolare
★★★★
Via Gracco del Secco 86, Colle di Val d'Elsa.
Tel: 0577-921-796, Cell: 338-411-9803,
www.cucina-popolare.com
HOURS OF OPERATION:
Monday, Tuesday and Thursday 7:30-10:30 p.m. Friday–Sunday 12:30-2:30 p.m., 7:30-10:30 p.m. Wednesday closed. Opening hours may vary off-season.

 117 | **Visit Casole d'elsa,** Catch a Jazz Concert, and Stop by Caseificio Carai, a Charming Artisanal Cheese Maker

Here's our idea of a perfect and alternative day: spend the morning in Volterra, exploring its charming streets, the Duomo, the Etruscan museum, the Roman Theater, and, of course, the town's wonderful array of alabaster shops (see tip number 112). Then, drive south to Casole d'Elsa (not to be confused with Colle Val d'Elsa).

Located in the middle of the Elsa Valley this is a relatively unknown town with a small but beautiful center and some truly spectacular views. On the way, we will make sure to stop off at the excellent Caseificio Carai, to nibble on some mouth-watering artisanal cheeses.

Parting from Volterra, drive along the scenic SR68 towards Casole. After about 16-kilometers, turn right (still directed towards Casole), and get on the SP52. After about one kilometer, you will see Caseificio Carai. Watch

out as it's easy to miss, the only marker is a tiny sign on your right.

This *caseficio* really is a tiny establishment, and the setting is extremely simple. If you feel like you're in someone's back yard, you're not wrong; this is actually the owner's house. The Carai family have produced multiple award-winning cheeses and the business dates back to the early 1900s in Sardinia. In the 1950s the family moved its herd and its home to Tuscany, and today the operation is headed by Giuseppe Carai, a man with a unique personality, or a *personaggio*, as one might say in Italian. The family has a small herd, no more than 1200 sheep, but they manage to produce some really excellent cheeses. A strong emphasis is placed on organic ingredients. Beware that like most cheeses in Tuscany, the milk used is raw. Nothing here is pasteurized or chemically altered, it's just pure and simple naturally delicious cheese. Don't miss Il Bandito, a flavorsome, aged, sharp-tasting cheese, the cervellone, which is more delicate but still rich and intense, the barricato, aged in marc, and the fresh ricotta, when available.

From here continue towards Casole. Park in the car park on your right as soon as you enter Casole and look up—you'll see an elevator attached to the back of the mountain. This is a system which will bring you directly to the center though you can of course walk up if you prefer. Once you exit the second elevator, you will see two benches; take a seat, relax, and enjoy one of the best views in all of Tuscany. Alternatively you can soak it all in while having a walk around the town walls. Casole occupied an important defensive position in Renaissance times and because of this, her walls were frequently refortified, a fact that today makes it an impressive site to visit. Other interesting buildings to visit are the Rocca, which today houses the town's city hall, and a pair of Romanesque parishes.

Once finished touring Casole itself, stop at **Caffe Casolani**, a unique place which oozes charisma. Based in a charming row of terraced red brick stores Caffe Casolani has a

novel way of serving its food. You pay beforehand for a set menu of four courses without knowing what you are going to be served. Don't worry—you shouldn't be in for any nasty surprises, the food here is not only appetizing but authentically Tuscan. A rotating wine list also ensures you can try different but equally palatable wines every time you visit. The owner is very knowledgeable about wine, and can recommend a bottle to buy and take home with you, from his large collection. This place prides itself on quality, so you will find some of the top Tuscan names here—chocolate from Amedei in Pontederra, pasta from Martelli in Lari, Chianti from Castello d'Ama, and much more. Jazz shows and other events take place in the summer months so if you are visiting around then be sure to check their website before you go to see if there's something on.

Caffe Casolani ★★★★
Via Casolani 41, Casole d'Elsa.
Tel: 0577-948-733
www.caffecasolani.com

Caseificio Carai
Località Montemiccioli, Casole d'Elsa.
Tel: 0588 35006, Cell. 339 5975830 ,
www.formaggicarai.it.
HOURS OF OPERATION:
Daily, 8:00 a.m.-1:00 p.m., 3:30-8:00 p.m.

118 | **Dine at the Smart** Il Colombaio Restaurant in Casole d'Elsa

Despite its petite size, the town of Casole d'Elsa holds a small but surprising array of treasures from which to choose, starting with the striking view overlooking the valley. As you ramble through its medieval streets, you will encounter a number of restaurants competing for the tourists attention, but in our opinion the best choice is clear—Il Colombaio. And while the delightful Caffe' Casolani (see previous tip), with its summer jazz concerts and fun menu, is the perfect place for an *aperitivo* or a relaxed dinner, for a more serious dining experience, Il Colombaio is the place to go. An extensive wine list along with a varied food menu, both in terms of price and the dishes on offer, means this Michelin-starred restaurant is accessible to everyone (though the full tasting menu here is far from cheap, at around 80 euro per person). Inside the décor is a little outdated, but the building itself is lovely in its rural simplicity. The narrow terrace overlooking the view is the perfect place for an intimate dinner on a sweet summer night.

Il Colombaio ★★★★
Loc. Colombiao, Casole d'Elsa.
Tel: 0577-949-002,
www.ilcolombaio.it
HOURS OF OPERATION:
Wednesday–Sunday, 12:30-3 p.m., 7:30-10p.m. Tuesday open for dinner only (7:30-10 p.m.). Monday closed.

119 Book a Lesson with the First Lady of Cooking

Judy Witts Francini has been living in Italy for over 30 years, and her cooking classes, which emphasize traditional cooking and the use of fresh local seasonal produce, are interesting, informative, and delicious. Witts Francini offers a range of classes lasting in length from a day to a week. We recommend her Friday market class which combines a day's cooking lesson with a visit to source regional produce in the market of Colle Val d'Elsa, a town located near to both Monteriggioni and San Gimignano. Her prices are higher than other courses—the market course, for example, will cost you $300 (217 euro) whereas the standard four-hour cooking class in other places around Florence normally works out at around 100 euro. However, Witts Francini is a real professional, whose cooking is renowned both regionally and internationally. Log on to her website to find out more.

Judy Witts Francini
www.divinacucina.com

Lucca

¶| 120 | Stop for a Perfect Little Lunch or Dinner in the Heart of Lucca

Not only tourists come to dine in Lucca's many restaurants but many locals, too; which means there are several interesting culinary options in town. When we are in the mood for a homely, simple meal, we like going to **Gigi's Trattoria**. The food isn't exactly high cuisine, but it is hearty and authentic. They make good *ravioli Luccesi* (the traditional local version of ravioli, filled with either meat or potatoes, and served with a meaty sauce), and the place itself is fun —a real Italian family eatery. For a more serious culinary experience, we like **Paris Boheme**. This French–Italian *osteria* is tasty and inviting, and personally we find the menu to be more inspired than that of other local establishments.

Our favorite spot in town, however, is **L'Imbuto**. Be warned that this is not your typical Tuscan tavern,

but more of a modern, sometimes experimental kitchen, run by Cristiano Tomei, a passionate local chef who enjoys twisting tradition and playing it off in interesting ways. Tomei offers a reasonably priced quick lunch (for 20 euro) and more elaborate dinner menus (the 6-course tasting menu costs 60 euro, the 9-course menu costs 90 euro). If you enjoy seafood, and are looking for a bit of an unusual experience, this is definitely the place to try.

Lastly, we cannot end this tip without recommending a good, cheap but delicious place where you can grab something to eat on the go. **Pizzeria Pellegrini,** in Piazza San Michele, looks anything but special, but their food is surprisingly tasty. The pizza (sold by the slice) isn't bad at all, their sandwiches are tasty; but what stands out is their *cecina* (a flat, oily dish, made of ground chickpea flour. Very popular in Tuscany). And if you visit around autumn or early winter, you must try their *neci*: a satisfyingly chubby pancake made from chestnut flour filled with ricotta cheese.

Trattoria Gigi ★★★
Piazza del Carmine 7, Lucca.
Tel: 0583-467-266.
HOURS OF OPERATION:
Daily, noon-2:30 p.m., 7:30-10:30 p.m.

Paris Boheme ★★★★
Piazza Cittadella 6, Lucca.
Tel: 338 930 5275.
www.parisbohemelucca.com
HOURS OF OPERATION:
Wednesday-Monday, 12:30-2:30 pm, 7:30-10:00 p.m (hours may vary off-season).
Tuesday closed.

Pizzeria Pellegrini ★★★
Piazza San Michele 25, Lucca.
Tel: 0583-467-891.
HOURS OF OPERATION:
Monday-Saturday, 8:30 a.m.-9:00 p.m.

Il Ristorante L'Imbuto, (located inside the Lucca Center of Contemporary Art) ★★★★
Via della Fratta 36, Lucca.
Tel: 0583-491-280,
www.limbuto.it
HOURS OF OPERATION:
Tuesday-Sunday, 12:30-2:30 p.m., 7:30-10:30 p.m. Closed on Monday.

121 | Get Some Serious Shopping Done
in Lucca

Lucca is known among tourists as a delightful little town to visit, and rightfully so. It is easy to fall in love with its perfectly preserved, romantic streets, and *piazze*; and it is impossible not to enjoy a walk along its beautiful Reniassance ramparts, especially at sunset. However, what many visitors miss is the fact that Lucca is also a great place to get some shopping done. The town's main street, Via Fillungo, is a shopper's small paradise. Fun, compact, and varied, Via Fillungo is lined with shop after shop of leading mid-range brands, from Sephora to Guess, from Patrizia Pepe to Motivi. This continues into the adjacent streets, too; many of these streets are worth touring if you are looking for some swanky Italian fashion, shoes, bags, or jewelry. Because the historical center is so small, it is actually easier to get some of your shopping done here than in Florence. But other, lesser-known corners of Lucca, offer their fair share of surprises, too. If you are looking for something slightly different than the usual popular stops, try one of the recommendations listed below.

When you feel the blood sugar dropping (or the shameless hedonist level rising), visit the **Laduree** shop. The famous Parisian shop has recently opened a small branch in town, and their macaroons are nothing short of wonderful. You will also find several high-end products, from fashionable bags to scents and perfumes and even books. We would choose one of Laduree's vanilla macaroons over any other sweet treat; but if it is chocolate that you want, then **Taddeucci**, centrally located in Piazza San Michele, is a local historic institution, and has been serving pastries and sweets to various noble guests, from Prince Charles and the King of Thailand to just about every noble Tuscan family since 1881.

Easy to miss but well worth a visit is **Barsanti**, in via San Paolino (just off Piazza San Michele). This little neighborhood shop, serving mostly a local clientele, doesn't look particularly interesting from the outside, but they do have a great selection of copper serving dishes and other interesting cooking utensils in the back. If you are a fan of the rustic country chic or if you like to collect special kitchenware during your travels, this shop may hold some surprises for you. Sometimes you find nothing, sometimes you hit the jackpot. For more modern and professional kitchen utensils, don't forget to visit Penelope, in Piazza San Frediano, right across the street from the San Frediano church.

All that spending will surely build up a thirst—for wine, that is. Luckily, Lucca's graceful *piazze* and alleys are the perfect setting for a fun *aperitivo*. There are many options in town, but we just love **Il Baccanale**. Hiding in a small street off Via Fillungo, Il Baccanale is located in a converted shoemaker's shop, and has a young vibe. Cramming inside with the jovial locals is half the fun! If you don't particularly enjoy vivacious locals invading your personal space, choose **Vinarkia** instead. A centrally-located, old world bar with a nice wine list (the food isn't as good), this is the place to relax with a glass of a good Tuscan Red.

If you are interested in purchasing or bottle or two, the best *enoteca* in town is without a doubt **Enoteca Marsili**, in Piazza San Michele. Their selection is excellent, with everything from a Poggio di Sotto Brunello to a nice Tignanello, from Solaia and Guado al Tasso to Sassicaia and Peppoli wines.

Laduree ★★★
Piazza dei Mercanti, Lucca.
Tel: 0583-491-344.
HOURS OF OPERATION:
May-late September, Monday-Friday, 10:00 a.m.-7:30p.m. Saturday, 10:00 a.m.-8:00 p.m. Sunday 3:30-8:00 p.m.; 10:00 a.m.-1:00 p.m., 3:30-8:00 p.m. Sunday 3:30-8:00 p.m.

Tadeucci ★★★
Piazza San Michele 34, Lucca.
Tel: 0583-494-933,
www.tadeucci.com
HOURS OF OPERATION:
Daily 8:30 a.m.-7:30 p.m.

Barsanti ★★★
Via San Paolino, 88, Lucca.
Tel: 0583-55-962.
HOURS OF OPERATION:
Monday-Saturday, 8:30 a.m.-12:30 p.m., 3:00-7:00 p.m.

Penelope kitchen supplies ★★★
Piazza San Frediano 11, Lucca.
Tel: 0583-495-042.
HOURS OF OPERATION:
Tuesday-Saturday, 9:00 a.m.-1:00 p.m., 3:30-7:30 p.m. Monday: 3:30-7:30 p.m.
Third Sunday of every month, 3:30-7:30 p.m.

Il Baccanale ★★★
Via S. Andrea 14, Lucca.
Tel: 0583-080-743.
Tuesday-Sunday, 11:30 a.m.-3:00 p.m., 6:00 p.m.-midnight. Monday closed.

Vinarkia ★★★
Via Fillungo 188, Lucca.
Tel: 0583-495-336.
HOURS OF OPERATION:
Daily, 11:00 a.m.-1:00 a.m.

Enoteca Marsili ★★★★
Piazza San Michele 38, Lucca
Tel: 0583-491-751. Hours of operation:
Monday-Saturday, 11:00 a.m.-7:30 p.m.

122 | **Hunt for Antiques** in Lucca's Hidden Alleys

Antique lovers will find Lucca bubbling with interesting finds. Among our favorite shops is **Daniele Squaglia**, where you can find some beautiful antiques at reasonable prices, everything from 18th-century frames and prints to pictures and sculptures. A bronze Napoleonic statue, which dates back to the early 19th century, will cost around 750 euro, but there are much more affordable, classical pieces to discover. **Be Mi Tempi** is another shop worth stopping at, and, of course, don't miss the monthly antiques festival (see tip number 138). You may very well discover a small treasure in the rough. **Via del Battistero**, a small street connecting the Duomo with Piazza Napoleone, is filled with small and delightful antique shops and shouldn't be missed. Here you will find the beautiful **Galleria Kraag, Raffaela Manfredini's**, a small shop which focuses on antique globes and ancient prints, **Galleria Vanucci**, which holds some beautiful artwork, and **Antiqua**, owned by collector Gabriella di Gregorio.

Daniele Squaglia ★★★
Via Cenami 21, Lucca.
Tel: 0583-492-140,
www.danielesquaglia.it
HOURS OF OPERATION:
Tuesday-Saturday, 10 a.m.-1 p.m.,
3:30-7:30p.m.

Be Mi Tempi Antiques ★★★
Via del Gallo 24, Lucca.
Tel: 0583-462-575,
www.bemitempi.it
HOURS OF OPERATION:
Tuesday-Saturday, 10:30 a.m.-7p.m.

Galleria Kraag ★★★
Via del Battistero 17,Lucca.
Tel: 0583-496-074.
HOURS OF OPERATION:
Tuesday-Saturday, 10:30 a.m.-7:00 p.m.
Hours of operation may vary.

Raffaela Manfredini ★★★
Via del Battistero 46, Lucca.
Tel: 0583-487-59, Cell: 328-5396-334.
HOURS OF OPERATION:
Monday-Saturday, 9:30 a.m.-1:00 p.m.,
4:00-8:00 p.m. Open on the third Sunday of every month, 9:30 a.m.-8:00 p.m. (off-season hours of operation may change).

Galleria Vannuci ★★★
Via del Battistero 50, Lucca.
Tel: 0583-955-815, Cell: 349-808-5564.
HOURS OF OPERATION:
Monday, 3:30-7:00 p.m. Tuesday-Saturday, 9:30 a.m.-1:00 p.m., 3:30-7:00 p.m. Open on the third Sunday every month, same hours.

Antiqua ★★★
Via del Battistero 28, Lucca.
Tel: 0583-495-364, Cell: 388-569-1161.
HOURS OF OPERATION:
Monday-Wednesday, 3:00-6:30 p.m.,
Thursday-Saturday 10:00 a.m.-7:00 p.m.

123 Enjoy a Puccini Concert in the San Giovanni Church in Lucca

San Giovanni is one of the most beautiful churches in Lucca. Though it doesn't have the crowd-gathering art of the Duomo, which hosts Tintoretto's *L'ultima Cena* (Last Supper), or San Michele's church, with its Filippino Lippi's *Pala Magrini*, San Giovanni does boast two very special attractions.

The first is the underground tour. This ancient church which, until the 8th century, served as Lucca's main cathedral and residency for the town's bishop, was built on a Roman temple, as so often happened. Though most of the decorations of the church itself did not survive the Napoleonic invasion (except for the exquisite wooden ceiling—look up!), the Roman excavations, which include ancient mosaic floors and pre-Roman and Roman relics, remained intact and can still be visited.

The second attraction is the concert program—the church regularly hosts concerts and arias by Puccini. The location is no coincidence—this was the church where Giacomo Puccini (or, to be exact, Giacomo Antonio Domenico Michele Secondo Maria Puccini) was baptized. This means that if you love opera, and aren't visiting Tuscany during the annual Puccini festival, you can still enjoy a fun concert. Find out the monthly program, and make a free booking for a very special night, on their website.

Chiesa di San Giovanni ★★★★
Piazza San Giovanni, Lucca.
www.puccinielasualucca.com
The church is open daily,
10:00 a.m.–6:00 p.m.

124 | Stay in One of the Best Hotels
in Lucca

Choosing a place to stay in Lucca is easy. Depending on your tastes and preferences, there are some excellent choices in town.

For a homely, easy going, B&B experience, try **Villa Agnes.** Simple, tranquil, unassuming, and romantic, this B&B has its fair share of fans. As soon as you walk up the marble white staircase and enter the 19th-century villa, you feel welcome. The décor is unpretentious yet elegant, the staff is friendly and pleasant, and the free parking and the air conditioning in the rooms (not a given in many Italian B&B!) are added bonuses; which more than make up for any disadvantages this B&B may have. The villa even offers guests free bikes for rent, to tour the historical center, and ride along Lucca's famous ramparts.

San Lucca Palace Hotel offers a more luxurious stay. Hailed by many as the best accommodation in town, this perfectly positioned four-star hotel is definitely an option worth examining before booking your stay. This 16th-century former hospital, which once sheltered the town's sick and weak, has been beautifully restored and the rooms are elegant and spacious. The rich buffet breakfast, friendly and

professional staff, and air conditioning in the rooms, as well as a small parking lot for guests (useful, since the hotel borders on the ZTL) are just some of the strong points of this hotel.

Finally, **Palazzo Rocchi** is one of our favorite choices in Lucca. The hotel's lobby is absolutely beautiful, and looks like the main dining room in a noble family's town mansion. Many of the rooms, which are still filled with historical decorations and paintings, are quite impressive. The rooms facing the inner courtyard are much quieter (the rooms facing Piazza san Michele, one of Lucca's busiest *piazze*, naturally suffer more from noise); and if you prefer to do your own cooking, there is an apartment to rent on the top floor.

B&B Villa Agnese ★★★
Viale Agostino Marti 177, Lucca.
Cell: 348-731-2588,
www.bbvillaagneselucca.it

San Lucca Palace Hotel ★★★★
Via San Paolino 103, Lucca.
Tel: 0583-317-446
www.sanlucapalace.com

Palazzo Rocchi★★★★
Piazza San Michele 30, Lucca.
Tel: 0583-393297, Cell: 338-207-0261,
www.palazzorocchi.it

Forte dei Marmi
and The Tuscan Riviera

🍴 125 Indulge yourself with an Aperitivo with a View, Followed by a Splendid Dinner, at the Principe Hotel

The 67 Sky Lounge Bar in the Principe Hotel in Forte del Marmi is relaxed luxury at its most inviting. Situated near the beach we can't imagine a better place to unwind and chill out with a cocktail or a glass of champagne in your hand, while snacking on some of their fusion finger food. After a day of sightseeing in Pisa or in Lucca, Come here to breathe in the fresh salty air and the perfumes of summer and take in the tranquil view of the sea in one direction and the serenity of the mountains in the other direction. To drink here can be a little pricey (a glass of vermentino will cost about 10 euro, a cocktail 16), but that is to be expected in such a fashionable hotel bar.

For dinner, we would highly recommend the hotel's very own **Lux Lucis** restaurant, run by one of

the most up-and-coming star chefs of the region—Valentino Cassanelli. Their innovative five- or nine-course tasting menus are well worth your time, and we suspect this restaurant will soon become one of the leading spots on the Tuscan Riviera and will earn its first Michelin star. Cassanelli's distinctive and delicious menu combines haute cuisine techniques that, quite frankly, are

rarely found in Tuscan restuaurants, with the freshest procuce. Dishes such as Ravioli filled with anchovies and served with chicory and burrata cheese, or Sea Bass covered in Mediterranean herbs are especially delicious.

Alternatively, if you prefer to dine al fresco, take a pleasant half-mile walk from the hotel to the **Orsa Maggiore Restaurant.** Chef Alessandro Lucchinelli's fresh, modern kitchen offers a rather short menu but makes up for it with great ingredients and fine recipes, most of which, naturally, are fish and seafood dishes. Dine in the simply designed, white painted interior or, better yet, outside, right on the beach, looking out over the sea and sitting under the stars. Booking a place in advance is highly recommended, as they are almost always full.

Sky Bar Lounge and Lux Lucis Restaurant - Hotel Principe Forte dei Marmi ★★★★★
Viale Amm. Morin 67, Forte dei Marmi, Tel: 0584-783-636,
www.principefortedeimarmi.it
Hours of operation: the Sky Lounge: open daily, after 6:00 p.m. Lux Lucis Restaurant: Summer months, daily, 8:30-10 p.m.; Off-season, Wednesday-Sunday, 8:00-10:00 p.m. Monday-Tuesday closed.

Ristorante l'Orsa Maggiore ★★★★
Via Arenile 29, Forte dei Marmi.
Tel: 0584-882-19,
www.ristorantelorsamaggiore.com
HOURS OF OPERATION:
June-mid September, daily, 12:45-3:00 p.m., 7:30-10:30 p.m. Mid September-late May, Friday-Tuesday, 12:25-3:00 p.m., 7:30-10:30 p.m. Advanced reserverations recommended, opening hours may change.

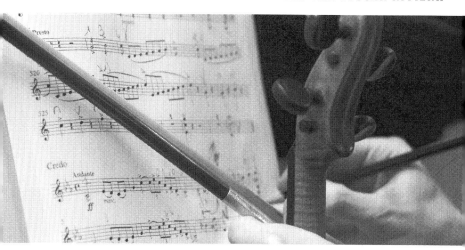

 ## 126 Book Tickets for the Puccini Festival in Torre del Lago and Visit the Composer's Graceful Villa

The Giacomo Puccini opera festival is a veritable feast for opera lovers. One of Tuscany's best known events, it is the only festival in the world exclusively dedicated to the composer who wrote such beautiful pieces as La Bohème, Madam Butterfly, and Turandot; works that anyone, opera lover or not, can hum. The location itself is quite charming: set in an open air theater in Torre del Lago, a historic resort town, situated just 15 minutes from Lucca. Every year, the four or five full productions of Puccini's work draw a crowd of tens of thousands of spectators. The annual program can be found online. If you are thinking about seeing one of the performances make sure to book a ticket in advance.

Nearby is Puccini's villa, a fascinating site not only for music lovers and fans of the composer's work but anyone with an interest in history. Sitting on the shores of Lake Massaciuccoli, this small but beautifully decorated historic mansion was Puccini's home for thirty years, from 1891 to 1921, until pollution from the lake forced him to move. Visitors can see various antiques and mementos, including Puccini's piano, an assortment of photos and paintings, music sheets, and much more. After his death, his son, Antonio Puccini, turned the house into a museum and converted the drawing room into a mausoleum, where Puccini is buried. The villa can be toured with a guide only, and the tour, which is available in English, too, is interesting and detailed. In fact, we would recommend a visit here above Puccini's home in Lucca. Though that site has also recently been converted into a museum, too, it is far less interesting to explore.

If you are looking for a place to eat that's easy to reach either before or after a concert or a tour of the villa, and you don't mind a short drive to Pietrasanta, the next town along the beach from Torro del Lago, then we would recommend **Il Circo**. A very good restaurant, this place is simply and neatly designed. The dining area and staff are small but this ensures a very personable standard of service. The cuisine here is modern; a change from the traditional type of Tuscan restaurant so commonly found in these areas. The best dishes are usually seafood-based and a good, affordable option is to try their *menu degustazione*, the tasting menu. You'll surely be pleased by the price at 35 euro per person, as well as the dishes, which include couquille Saint Jacques served on a pea cream, salmon with saffron and more. For a more sophisticated dining experience, try the Michelin-starred **Lorenzo** in Forte dei Marmi (see tip 128).

Festival Puccini (held in the Gran Teatro all'Aperto Giacomo Puccini)
★★★★★
Via delle Torbiere, Torre del Lago.
Tel: 0584-359-322,
www.puccinidestival.it
Tickets: ticketoffice@puccinifestival.it

Villa pucini ★★★★
Viale G. Puccini 266, Torre del Lago.
Tel: 0584-341-445.
The villa can be visited with a guided tour only. Tours leave Tuesday-Sunday, every 40 minutes. Monday morning closed. November 30-January 31, tours leave at: 10:00 a.m., 10:40 a.m., 11:20 a.m., noon, 2:00 p.m., 2:40 p.m., 3:20 p.m., 4:00 p.m., 4:40 p.m.; February 1-March 31, tours leave at 10:00 a.m., 10:40 a.m., 11:20 a.m., noon, 2:30 p.m., 3:10 p.m., 3:50 p.m., 4:30 p.m., 5:10 p.m.; April 1-November 1, tours leave at: 10:00 a.m., 10:40 a.m., 11:20 a.m., noon, 3:00 p.m., 3:40 p.m., 4:20 p.m., 5:00 p.m., 5:40 p.m.; July-August (during the Puccini Festival), tours leave at: 10:00 a.m., 10:40 a.m., 11:20 a.m., noon, 4:00 p.m., 4:40 p.m., 5:20 p.m., 6:00 p.m., 6:40 p.m., 7:20 p.m., 8:00 p.m.

Ristorante il Circo ★★★
Vicolo San Biagio 28, Pietrasanta.
Tel: 0584-704-36, Cell: 348-803-9628,
www.ristoranteilcirco.it

127 | Tear the Floor at the Best Clubs
in Forte dei Marmi and the Area

During the summertime, The Tuscan Riviera (commonly known as Versilia) offers the liveliest night scene in Tuscany; and the undoubted queen is Forte dei Marmi, a glitzy town that has been serving as playground for Italy's rich and famous for many decades. Today, expect to find here a sometimes weird but always entertaining combination of trash, glam, and chic, as well as a mixed crowd: from fun-loving locals to wealthy Russian tourists, businessmen, and showgirls to students and veteran dancers; they all come here to party.

To see and be seen in one of Forte dei Marmi's leading lounge bars and discoteques, head to **Costes**. Come here for an *aperitivo*, dinner or for some after hours fun. This place caters to the well dressed, well-heeled champagne drinkers, out for a good time. Order a plate of seafood and champagne-based cocktail and join the fun!

If you want to dance the night away surrounded by 20- and 30-something fashionable Italians, then **La Bussola**, or **La Capannina**, two of the best known discotheques on the Tuscan beach, are your safest bet. The music is fun (just don't expect anything alternative, Italians like their music very poppy, with the occasional streak of nostalgia). The night is hot, the people are beautiful, the girls dance carelessly, defying gravity on their 6-inch heels, the boys sport the classic Italian swagger, and passion is in the air. La Bussola caters to a slightly younger crowd, while La Capannina is also a restaurant, comfortably located right on the beach, and offers entertainment for those over 30, as well. A night here can start with a fun *aperitivo*, continue with a tasty seafood dinner, and end with dancing on the floor. Whichever place you choose, just make sure you dress the part. Italians frown upon those who dress poorly and nowhere will this matter more than at the entry door to a trendy club.

For the best gay parties in the area, the **Mamamia** club is your obvious choice. A Tuscan institution, the Mamamia is hardly what it used to be, but from time to time it still manages to throw some of the craziest summer parties in the region. Another popular venue is **Stupid!A**, a LGBT disco club in Torre del Lago, which organizes regular drag shows. You can also find some good parties organized by **Krisco Club**, mostly in different venues around Florence (log on to their website to find out if anything special is planned during your stay).

Costes,
Via Achilli Franceschi 6 Lungomare Forte dei Marmi.
www.costes-fortedeimarmi.it

La Bussola
Viale Roma 44, Marina di Pietrasanta.
Cell: 347-477-4772,
www.bussolaversilia.info

La Capannina
Viale della Repubblica 16, Forte dei Marmi.
Tel: 0584- 801-69,
www.lacapanninadifranceschi.com

Mamamia
Torre del Lago.
Cell: 393.2239322,
www.mamamia.tv

Stupid!A
Viale Europa 5, Torre Del Lago.
Cell: 393- 223-9322,
www.stupida.tv

Krisco club
www.criscoclub.com/

128 Savor the High Cuisine at Lorenzo,
One of Tuscany's Best Seafood Restaurants

A Tuscan institute and symbol, Lorenzo is a restaurnat rivalled by very few. Some critics claim that it has lost some of its charm in recent years, but even the most stringent guests cannot deny that this is still one of Tuscany's leading venues. Stylish, smart and always tasty, Lorenzo offers something for everyone. The menu is seasonal, so ask for your waiter's recommendation. We greatly enjoyed dishes such as delicioius Royal red Prawns, cooked in vegetable stock and flavoured with a dash of dry vermouth, ravioli stuffed with white fish, pan roasted scallops, and creamy, rich champagne spiced risotto, dotted with shelfish. Those who do not shy away from raw delicacies, will surly enjoy the *antipasto crudo*. The wine list is incredible, and there is a very good selection of both Italian and foreign bottles (though prices tend to be too high). If you play your cards right, you may be invited to visit the cantine.

Lorenzo ★★★★★
Via Giosuè Carducci 61, Forte dei Marmi.
Tel: 0584-896-71,
www.ristorantelorenzo.com
HOURS OF OPERATIONS:
September 16-December 15, and March 1 to June 15, the restaurant is open Wednesday-Sunday, 12:30-2:30 p.m., 8:00-10:00 p.m. Monday closed. Tuesday open for dinner only. June 15-September 15, open for dinner only. December 15-Feburary 1, closed for winter break.

Pescia, Pistoia, and Motecatini Terme

🏃 | 129 | Spoil your senses with an Exclusive Dip in the Monsummano Terme Thermal Pool and Caves

At first glance, the **Giusti Hotel and Spa** seems like your average Tuscan 4-star hotel; golf course, spa, elegantly converted rooms overlooking the town of Monsummano Terme. But look (quite literally) a little deeper and it becomes clear that Giusti has some secrets. Below the hotel and set deep into the Tuscan hills is an enchanting grotto spa. The labyrinthine cave system, which experiences 100% humidity and temperatures between 31°C and 34°C, has been converted into a full-service thermal spa. Stalactites loom overhead across three steamy zones delectably named Paradise, Purgatory, and Hell, each of which offers luxurious treatments and therapies, including mud packs and chocolate treatments for ultimate pampering and relaxation.

Diving excursions through the depths of the cave system can be organized for the more adventurous. Alternatively, the view of the Tuscan countryside from the thermal swimming pool is the perfect way to relax, and a cheeky cocktail will surely contribute to your overall condition.

After your visit to Giusti, don't forget to stop by **Slitti**, a renowned local chocolatier, in the nearby town of Monsummano Terme. This little place was World Champion in a chocolate competition held in London in 2012. Try the excellent *espresso*-flavored chocolates (for a start).

Grotta Giusti Resort ★★★★★
Golf & Spa, Via Grottagiusti 1411, Monsummano terme.
Tel: 0572-907-71,
www.grottagiustispa.com

Slitti ★★★
Via Francesca Sud 1268, Monsummano Terme. Tel: 0572-640-240,
www.slitti.it
HOURS OF OPERATION:
Monday–Saturday, 7:00 a.m.–1:00 p.m., 3:00–8:00 p.m. The shop is closed in August.

🍴 | 130 | **Visit the Magnificent Garzoni Gardens**
and Stop for a Sophisticated Meal at the
Michelin-Starred Atman Restaurant in Pescia

Pescia isn't a particularly touristy destination in Tuscany. Located amidst the Apuan Alps in the province of Prato, this hilly area draws in a much smaller crowd. However, Pescia is also only 20 km west of the popular thermal resort towns of Montecatini Terme and Monsumano Terme (see previous tip), and 40 km south of Bagni di Lucca, making it an easy stop to work into your tour of northern Tuscany. And while it is a bit gloomy off-season, during the spring and summer months this area bursts with color. Near Pescia you will find Collodi Park, named after Carlo Collodi, the author of the world famous book "The Adventures of Pinocchio". This attraction is both rundown and geared towards families and can therefore be skipped. Instead, make a stop at the historical **Garzoni Garden** and the Collodi butterfly

house. Built by the Garzoni family on a dramatic slope, the gardens are truly beautiful and a perfect example of 17th-century Italian landscape design. They have also been chosen as one of the most beautiful gardens in Italy. The grand staircase connects the different terraces of the manicured lawns and makes for a great place to spend a couple of hours in the afternoon (even if the price of the entry ticket is entirely too high, and the butterfly house, located at the base of the garden and included in the admission price, is in poor condition). The gardens are especially worth visiting during the months of June and July, when nocturnal live concerts are organized under the stars. To find out more, contact the garden's secretary directly: 0572 427314.

To end your day in style, visit Atman restaurant in Pescia. Run by award-winning Chef Igles Coreli, **Atman Restaurant** specializes in turning seasonal (sometimes organic) produce into exquisite dishes. Their menu often changes, so choose carefully and ask your waiter if there are any special dishes of the day. We especially recommend the tagliolini all'uovo (thin, hand made pasta) served with vegetables and shrimp, the salmon tartar, and the tuna steak. In any case, don't miss the desserts!

Atman Restaurant ★★★★
Via Roma 4, Pescia.
Tel: 0572-190-3678,
www.ristoranteatman.it
HOURS OF OPERATION:
Wednesday-Monday, 8:00-10:30 p.m.;
On weekends the restaurant is also open for lunch, from noon-2:30 p.m.; Closed on Tuesday.

Garzoni gardens ★★★★
Piazza della Vittoria, Collodi (PT).
Tel: 0572-427-314
www.pinocchio.it
HOURS OF OPERATION:
March 1-November 3, open daily, 8:30 a.m.-sunset; November 3-February 28, Weekends and Holidays only, 10:00 a.m.-sunset.

🏃 131 | Book a Fun and Delicious Wine Tasting and Cooking Class at the Capezzana Estate

When it comes to historic Italian wine estates the **Capezzana Estate** in Carmignano stands out. The earliest written document noting the wine production at Capezzana dates back to 804 and in 1716 the Medici family designated the area a top class wine-producer. The current owners, the Bonacossi family, purchased the estate in the 1920s and, opened the doors of this magnificent place to the public in the 1980s.

The 100-hectare farm produces Carmignano DOC wine and olive oil. At 100 to 200 meters above sea level, the estate has fresh night breezes and warms days, a delicious climate if you decide to stay some nights here. A visit to the estate can include a tour of the wine cellar, tastings, and cooking classes. The cookery classes are taught by the friendly and exuberant Chef Patrick and are available Monday to Friday. Each participant receives a bottle of olive oil and a bottle of wine from the estate plus an apron.

For us this is a country estate at its best—historic and of high quality, yet still rustic, authentic, and familial. The area around Capezzana is quite different from the familiar hills of Chianti and the Val d'Orcia. This is a more rural, hilly, remote area that goes about life at its own pace. Naturally, don't leave without tasting a bottle of this famous producer's Carmignano wine. The Barco Reale and the Trebbiano are quite good, too.

Tenuta di Capezzana ★★★★
Via Capezzana 100, Carmignano.
Tel: 055-870-6005,
www.capezzana.it
NOTE: All tours and cooking lessons must be booked in advance. No cooking lessons are held in August.

🏃 132 | **Discover Delicious Surprises** in Pistoia for Foodies

Pistoia is the perfect destination for half a day spent idly roaming old streets and dipping into lovely little eateries and boutiques. A well-off town about thirty minutes from Florence, Pistoia is often skipped by tourists. And to be perfectly honest, it's their loss. Pistoia may lack monuments on the scale of Pisa or Lucca, but that is precisely the town's main advantage, as it offers a break from tightly-packed sightseeing schedules. If you are a foodie looking for a bit of a change of pace and a place to relax for the afternoon, Pistoia is a good choice. We would also add that the town's historical center is not absent of charm. Surrounded by its original 14th-century walls you can also find a number of impressive medieval and Renaissance palazzi and churches here, mostly based around the central Piazza Del Duomo.

Make **Pastificio Gastronomia Il Raviolo**, just a couple of minutes away from the Duomo, your first stop. Here, in a tiny non-descript pasta shop, located on the oval-shaped Piazza Da Vinci, hides the best fresh pasta of any shop we've tried in Tuscany. This may be a dramatic statement, but we stand by it. Once you try their potato ravioli, or the salmon gnudi, we know you will agree. Il Raviolo, as it's known among locals, also offers a small selection of other dishes and produce which change daily. We highly recommend their fantastic *treccia mozzarella*, a mouth-watering mozzarella in the form of a braid. It's difficult to go wrong here as Gabriele and Giulio, the team that runs Il Raviolo, have a magic touch. Everything they make is delicious. All their products aren't always available but just about anything, even dishes that aren't on the menu, can be made especially for you if you call and order in advance. They have a website in English, too, but for whatever reason, the photos on it don't do the food justice

When you leave Il Raviolo, turn right onto Via Carratica, and walk towards the town center. **Da Romolo**, perhaps the most famous butcher in town, will immediately come into view on your left. Charcuterie fans will adore this place. If you like Tuscan *prosciutto* then ask for theirs, it's lovely. If you prefer a milder version, they also stock the renowned Prosciutto San Daniele and Parma. Fans of the rustic Tuscan traditional flavors will find a wide selection of salamis, a very good *finnocchiona* and much more. English isn't their strong suit, but with short sentences and a lot of pointing everything should go smoothly enough.

Pistoia's historical center (the *centro storico*) houses a number of popular artisanal produce shops. Specifically, don't miss **Fiordilatte**, a traditional *caseificio*, or cheese producer, run by Fabrizio Nerucci. Their oven-baked ricotta is excellent, as is their fresh mozzarella filled with ricotta or gorgonzola. Also recommended is the *burrata*, a mozzarella filled with cream, though be warned: it's as heavy as it sounds! You will also find homemade butter, perfect to make

a butter and sage sauce to go along with the fresh pasta of Il Raviolo. The many shops in **Piazza della Sala**, as well as the small produce market set up daily at the center of the piazza, are the perfect places to pick up some more cheeses, bread, roasted meats, wine, wonderfully fresh vegetables and fruit, and other delicacies.

Alternatively, if you are out looking for a place for a real Italian *aperitivo* or dinner, Pistoia offers a small but deligfhtful selection of places to choose from. We prefer to meet up with friends for a pre-dinner *aperitivo* in **Gargantua**, in Piazzetta dell'Ortaggio, just off the well-known Piazza della Sala. This is a funky little place, with a fun, laid-back vibe. Do as the locals do, and lunch here on a hot day to enjoy light food and good music in a relaxed atmosphere. This isn't, however, the place for a serious dinner. Another popular place for an *aperitivo* is **Voronoi.** Small but intimate, we often enjoy a glass of wine here while debating where to eat dinner. Do as the locals do, and grab a table outside and do some people-watching.

For a more serious culinary experience, try **La Bottegaia**. The friendly owners, Alessandro and Carlo, offer a fine choice of regional dishes, prepared with quality ingredients. Some dishes may be a little too rustic, but for the most part, the chefs here do a good job of providing a delicious menu which updates traditional dishes in interesting ways.

Alternatively, great local beers and wines, attentive service, and delectable hamburgers and sandwiches can be found in the intimate confines of the eternally popular **Vineria Number 4**. For a simple dinner on a hot summer day, this is definitely a place to try. If you are interested in buying some unique jams, why not try those prepared by in the **Ancient Apothecary**, by nuns from the Bendectine Order? The nuns grow and harvest the fruit themselves, within the monastery, and prepare all their products according to ancient recipes. Try their bitter orange marmalade or their secret herbal tea.

Lastly, Pistoia offers the ardent shopper quite a few surprises. The entire historic center is filled with interesting little shops and boutiques. Via Porta Carratica, Via Cavour, Via Buozzi, Piazza Roma, Via Curtatone e Montanara, Via dei Fabri and the entire area around the Duomo are worth exploring. Some of our favorite shops here are **Doligosi** (in via dei Fabri 14), **La Soffitta delle Idee** (Via Porta Carratica 30), **Michele Fabbricatore**'s beautiful ceramics studio (Via Pacini 40), the antique prints and books in **Taberna Libraria** (Via della Rosa 38), Fagni (Via Curtatone e Montanara 6), and the various fashion boutiques surrounding the Duomo.

Il Raviolo ★★★★★
Piazza Leonardo Da Vinci 6, Pistoia.
Tel: 0573-247-38,
www.ilraviolopistoia.com
HOURS OF OPERATION:
Tuesday–Sunday, 8:00 a.m.–1:00 p.m.,
4:30–7:30p.m. Wednesday and Sunday closed in the afternoon. Monday closed all day.

Da Romolo ★★★★
Via Porta Carratica 84, Pistoia. Tel: 0573-213-97. Open Monday–Saturday, 9:00 a.m.–1:00 p.m., 4:30–7:30 p.m.

Fiordilate ★★★
Via Orafi 35, Pistoia.
Tel: 0573-452-216,
www.caseificiofiordilattepistoia.com.
HOURS OF OPERATION:
Monday–Saturday, 9:00 a.m.–1:00 p.m.,
4:30–7:30 p.m. 3 stars

Gargantua ★★★
Piazzetta dell'ortaggio 11, Pistoia. Tel: 0573-23-330, www.tavernagargantua.com, Hours of operation: Daily, noon–midnight.

Vornoi ★★★
Piazzetta dell'Ortaggio, 14, Pistoia.
Tel: 0573-197-1214. www.ristocaffetteriavoronoi.it, Hours of operation: Daily, 11:00 a.m.–midnight

La Bottegaia ★★★
Via del Lastrone 17, Pistoia. Tel: 0573-365-602, www.labottegaia.it. Hours of operation: Tuesday–Sunday, noon–3:00 p.m., 7:00–11:00 p.m. Closed Monday.

Vineria number 4 ★★★
Via del lastrone 4, Pistoia.
Tel: 0573-977-338,
www.vinerian4.it
HOURS OF OPERATION:
Daily 12:30–2:30 p.m., 7:30–10:30 p.m.

The Ancient Apothecary of the Benedctine Nuns ★★★
Vicolo S. Michele 8, Pistoia,
Tel: 0573-227-95, Cell: 320-425-0364,
www.spezieriabenedettinepistoia.com
Call ahead to order and to buy directly from the nuns.

The Garfagnana and Northern Tuscany

🏃 133 Discover Michelangelo's Marble Quarries
and the Ancient Fosdinovo Castle in Garfagnana

The Garfagnana, an area in Northwest Tuscany, is often overlooked by tourists, who are more interested in the picture postcard views of the Chianti region, Florence, and Siena. But if you are looking for a change of pace and to get away from the crowds, this area offers quite a lot.

The Garfagnana is backed by the Apuan Alps and dominated by forests of chestnut trees, which were once the main source of income for poor local farmers who would build their homes from chestnut wood and grind the fruit into chestnut flour, to this day a popular dish in this rural area.

For nature lovers the Garfagnana is a dream: beautiful hiking trails crisscross the entire region and biking, canoeing, quad riding, canyoning, and cave exploring are all popular sports here (find out more at the local tourist offices). Of the many highlights this rustic but charming area has to offer, two stand out as particularly interesting. One is the world famous marble quarry near Carrara and the other is the charming Fosdinovo castle.

The Marble Quarry (or perhaps quarries, plural, as there are several in the area towering above Carrara) supplied one of the greatest artists in human history: Michelangelo. The famous artist sourced his marble from the quarry, as it was known to be some of the highest quality in the world. In fact, Carrara marble could be found in the homes of noble families and the rich for hundreds of years.

Today, the only way to visit the quarry is with a tour—just as well as it is also the most interesting method of discovering this attraction. The **Marmo Tour**, which is the most basic option, allows you full access and lasts for 30 minutes, leading you deep into the mountain and into huge, cavernous rooms. It's

fascinating to learn about the full extraction process. However, if you are serious about experiencing the quarries and the local scenery, we recommend the **Cave di Marmo Tours**, which include an exciting (albeit bumpy) jeep ride up into the mountains and into the quarries. The guide and driver take you to some beautiful panoramic points, 900 meters high, with gorgeous views of the marble mountains and exclusive entry right into the paths used by the workers themselves. You also make a stop at the nearby village of Colonnata, to pick up the world famous *lardo di colonnata* (a northern Tuscan delicacy—aged lard). Ideally, book this tour on a weekday, so that a visit to a working quarry can be included in your itinerary, to see how the experts extract the marble.

Another unmissable spot is **Castello Malaspina di Fosdinovo,** better known simply as **Fosdinovo Castle.** Built in the second half of the 12th century, this medieval fortress and mansion is one of Tuscany's best-preserved castles and today hosts a museum and an arts center.

The museum is open daily (except for Tuesdays), and all tours are guided. You will learn of the sad and sometimes frightening story of the noble family which once lived here and have the chance to peruse the many rooms, including the arms room, the main bedrooms, the ramparts and the panoramic terrace. If you are a group, you may book a special "costume tour", during which the tour leader will dress in medieval costume. Alternatively, join a spooky night tour of the castle (on Fridays, at 10:00 p.m.; it depends on the number of people who have booked the tour and may not be available year round). On Halloween and New Year's Eve, the Fosdinovo castle hosts some of the best parties in Tuscany!

For foodies, a visit to the Garfagngna area can't be complete without a stop in Colonnata, the town famous in all of Italy (and abroad) for its "*lardo di colonnata.*" **Lardo di Colonnata** is a lard seasoned with salt and a mix of ground herbs and aged to give it a distinct and rich taste and smell. In Tuscany, they love spreading it on toast as *antipasti,*

Just about every bar and restaurant in the tiny village of Colonnata, up in the Apuan Alps above Massa-Carrara, carries a sign saying "we sell Colonnata". If you've come all the way up here, the best place to taste it is **Ristorante Venanzio**, comfortably located in the town's main piazza. They serve the creamy *lardo* on just about anything, and if you are lucky enough to be visiting during truffle season (late autumn–early winter) you can try some very tasty dishes with the fragrant truffles.

Carrara Marble Quarry ★★★
Piazzale Fantiscritti 84, Miseglia (near Carrara). Cell: 339-765-7470,
www.marmotour.com
OPERATING HOURS:
A pril 12–November 2, daily, 11:00 a.m.–5:00 p.m. (until 6:30 p.m on weekends and holidays); May–August, daily, 11:00 a.m.–6:30 p.m.

Quarry Jeep Tours ★★★★★
Tel: 0585-857-288, Cell: 333-419-6688,
www.cavedimarmotours.com

Fosdinovo castle ★★★★
Via Papiriana 2, Fosdinovo.
Tel: 0187-680-013,
www.castellodifosdinovo.it.
OPERATING HOURS:
May–September, Wednesday–Monday, tours start at 11:00 a.m., noon, 3:30, 4:30, 5:30, and 6:30 p.m.; October–April, Wednesday–Monday, tours start at 11:00 a.m., noon, 4:00, and 5:00 p.m. Closed year-round on Tuesdays. Note that tour hours here tend to change, call before you leave.

Ristorante Venanzio ★★★
Piazza Palestro 3, Colonnata (MS). GPS coordinates: Latitude: 44.086189, Longitude: 10:155794.
Tel: 0585-758-033.
www.ristorantevenanzio.com.
OPERATING HOURS:
Monday–Wenesday and Friday–Saturday, noon–3:00 p.m., 7:00–10:30 p.m.; Sunday, noon–3:00 p.m. Thursday closed.

or adding it to bean dishes or even to pasta to enrich the flavor. The base of the spices is ground black pepper, rosemary, salt, and garlic; but depending on the family and their traditional recipe of choice, other herbs may be added. The delicacy is only prepared from September to May, like in ancient times.

The lard is seasoned and then aged in boxes made of Colonnata marble, which is considered one of the best marbles in the world. Today the Lardo di Colonnata is marked with a symbol of quality—IGP. The symbol indicates a certain product came from a certified geographic location in Italy—a *lardo* made in Florence, for example, will never be a Lardo di Colonnata IGP.

🏃 134 | **Visit Villa Pescigola** during the Colorful Daffodil and Tulip Festival

The landscape of Northern Tuscany is dominated by forests which begin to appear in the middle peaks of the Apuan Alps. High in this resilient yet inviting landscape is Villa Pescigola. At over 600 years, its faded peach walls and green shuttered windows emit an aura of austere, romantic beauty.

The villa is closed to the public for much of the year, but once annually the gates are opened as the villa hosts a wonderful daffodil festival (though the numerous tulips which fills the villa's gardens are every bit as impressive as the daffodils). The grounds fill with vibrant colours, enchanting yellow, red, orange and pibk, as over 200,000 flowers of 400 varieties are on view.

Villa La Pescigola ★★★★
Località Pescigola, Fivizzano.
Cell: 329-82505512,
www.villapescigola.com
NOTE: The exact date of the festival changes yearly, but it's always around late March or early April. Check the villa's website to see the exact date. The garden also occasionally opens on weekends during May and June.

Throughout Tuscany

🏃 135 | Visit One of the Top Ten Festivals
in Tuscany

The full list of music concerts, farmer's markets, exhibitions, competitions, food, opera, and medieval festivals on offer in Tuscany is almost inconceivably varied and numerous. In truth, these events would require a guide of their own to fully do them justice. Until we get around to writing such a guide, we have done our best to highlight some exceptional events as tips for this publication—ten top festivals you shouldn't miss if you happen to be visiting when they are on; information on others can be found online. Regardless, we always recommend checking with the local tourist office to see if any interesting events are taking place while you are visiting the region. The busiest time of year, naturally, is during the summer months in the height of the tourist season, from May to October.

1. **The Luminara** ★★★ lights up Pisa on June 16th. On Piazza Garibaldi and the streets which stretch along the river, which are referred to as the "Lungarni di Pisa", an incredible 70,000 candles are lit, filling the town with a yellow and orange glow. A magical atmosphere takes over the city as the streets become filled with locals, tourists, and vendors enjoying the many concerts and cultural events organized for the night. Alternatively, visit Pisa during the Gioco del Ponte–a colorful and lively medieval procession crosses through the town, accompanied by music and people dressed in period attire. The "Gioco del Ponte", or Battle on the Bridge, then takes place as groups of men from various neighborhoods in Pisa have a faux battle dressed in elaborate 16th-century costumes for the glory of their district. Find out more here: www.giugnopisano.com

2. **Palio di San Paolino** ★★★★ also known as Palio della Balestra, is an animated medieval feast in Lucca which has taken place since the 15th century. Replete with fantastic Renaissance outfits and ages old contests, this event is dedicated to the ancient art of crossbow shooting. Enjoy the banquet, accompanied by medieval processions and music, on July 12th at Piazza San Martino. For more information, go to www.Luccaturismo.it

3 If you are in the area toward the end of August, don't miss
Volterra A.D. 1398 ★★★★
Medieval Volterra comes to life with the whole town dressed as fearless knights, noblemen and ladies, artisans, merchants, peasants, flag-wavers, crossbowmen, musicians, and jesters from the year 1398. Re-enactments take place to transport people back to how life was lived more than 600 years ago. Each year's event revolves around a different theme which ensures that no one festival is the same as the previous. The celebration kicks off around the *centro storico* on the third and fourth Sundays of every August.

4. It is worth the drive out to the lovely borgo of **Monteriggioni,** ★★★★★ south of Siena, for this town's medieval festivals that take place every July. Artists, vendors, and performers fill the main piazza while stalls are set up selling medieval wares. Processions of men and women in costume dance through the streets to music of the time to create a fun and festive atmosphere. The main events usually take place during the first two weeks of July. Find out more and check for the exact dates each year at www.Monteriggionimedievale.com

5. **The Tuscan Sun Festival ★★★★** is a popular local festival which takes place all over Cortona during July and August. Often attracting world-renowned artists this event plays host to numerous concerts, dances, theatrical and cultural events. Many of these are suitable for children and can provide the opportunity for an enjoyable family day out. Check the festival's website to see if any of the events might be suitable for your family: www.tuscansunfestival.com

6. **La Giostra del Saracino ★★★★★** is a festival which dates back to the 13th century. It is based on the historic jousting matches that took place in piazze during the medieval and Renaissance times and is Arezzo's most renowned event. Jousts are held twice a year, one in June and one in September. On each of these days the whole town comes to life with colorful processions and men and women in medieval clothes descending on the town's Piazza Grande. Other colorful events are usually organized during the week preceding the giostra, too. For more information, visit the website: www.giostradelsaracino.arezzo.it Equally impressive is the **Giostra di Simone,** in the delightful village Montisi in southern Tuscany. Read more here: www.giostradisimone.it

7. A pleasant destination on its own, the town of **Massa Marittima ★★★★★** is especially popular for the duration of the Balestro del Girofalco, one of the greatest medieval feasts in Tuscany. At this time, the town becomes awash with medieval processions, colorful flags, and wonderful decorations. The highlight of the entire festival has to be the arrow-shooting contest held between the ancient quarters of the town, during which arrows are spectacularly shot from a huge wooden instrument. The Balestro del Girofalco is celebrated twice a year; on the fourth Sunday of May and the second Sunday of August. The events take place in the piazza in front of the Duomo. Find out more here: www.massamarittima.info/folklore/balestro.htm

8. **The Bravio delle Botti ★★★★** is Montepulciano's main summer event. A slightly insane contest between the various contrada (neighborhoods) of the town, the aim of this competition is to see who can roll an 80-kg barrel fastest two kilometers uphill. The event, which dates back to 1373, was once celebrated to honor the town's patron, Saint John the Baptist. How exactly such a challenge commemorates the saint is anyone's guess. This is another ideal day out as a medieval court complete with decorations, music, and flags accompany the event. This takes place on the last Sunday of August; arrive early to catch a place near Piazza delle Erbe or Piazza Grande or along the Corso. Find out more at www.braviodellebotti.com

9. A real treat for music lovers, **the Pistoia Blues Festival ★★★★** annually attracts artists of a high caliber, along with many international names. One of the main music festivals in Tuscany, Pistoia Blues sees a large stage erected in a fabulous Piazza in the heart of the lovely town of Pistoia, making a beautiful temporary venue to accompany some great music. It beats getting stuck in the mud at Glastonbury, anyway! The yearly program and ticket prices can be viewed here: www.pistoiablues.com

10. **The Lucca Summer Festival ★★★★** is the best rock show in town, a month filled with concerts by world famous artists, from Alicia Keys and Elton John to Lenny Kravitz and Leonard Cohen, in the town's Piazza Napoleone. Every year since 1998, this festival has provided a special experience for music lovers. As long as you don't mind the crowds and having to stand outside in the heat, as there is no seating available, then these concerts, and the atmosphere around the town, are great. Find out more here: www.summer-festival.com

136 Book a Hike in the Beautiful Tuscan Countryside, Led by a Professional Guide

Think about exploring the hills of Chianti on foot, following the hidden trails of the Val d'Orcia, or wandering along the ancient roads traveled by pilgrims on the way to Rome. Imagine discovering the Maremma on unknown paths once controlled by the Etruscan population. Or think about a more adventurous trek into the heart of the Orrido di Botri Canyon in Northern Tuscany. Can there be a better, more intimate way to discover the beauty of the land? To learn its secrets, to take in the smells, the sounds and the wonderful sights Tuscany has to offer?

Tuscany may not be the first place that comes to mind when thinking about hiking and trekking, but the region actually has a truly wonderful variety of walks. Approaching maps and navigation can be intimidating, but don't let your sense of direction (or lack thereof) deter you from discovering the charm of the countryside. There are several tour companies and professional guides who will build a custom-made hike, based on your interests, time, budget, and physical abilities. Everything from a light, two-hour walk in a reserve to a challenging Alpine hike can be arranged.

Terre di Mare is a group of licensed guides which offers several tours into hidden, charming corners of Tuscany, as well as kayak and bike tours, jeep-led excursions, and Nordic walking.

If you are looking to discover Florence and its province from a different angle and perspective, book a walking tour with **Italian Footprints**, a company lead by two women: Angelica Turi (Italian) and Elizabeth Namack (American).

For those wishing to discover the wild beauty of the Maremma, in southern Tuscany, we recommend looking into one of the tours lead by **Le Orme**. Whether you are interested in discovering the treasures of the archaeological park in Sorano, the Etruscan paths near Pitigliano, or the natural res erves of the Maremma, they will be able to offer a suitable tour. Activities are available for all fitness levels, including tailor-made tours for handicapped people.

Terre di Mare ★★★
www.terredimare.org

Italian Footprints ★★★
www.italianfootprints.com

Le Orme ★★★
www.leorme.com

🏃 | 137 | Enjoy the View from One of Our Top Ten Favorite Spots

Choosing the best view in Tuscany is an impossible task. There are simply too many options to choose from. Writing this list, we couldn't stop debating; should we focus on the famous options, like the view from the dome of the Duomo in Florence? Or should we concentrate on those pleasant surprises you encounter when driving along a country road; those beautiful views which reveal themselves when you take a turn and suddenly there it is—an immense and striking vista you won't soon forget?

After intense discussion, we decided to simply make a list of our personal favorites, a mix of panoramic spots and spectacular drives that left us bewildered by their beauty. Some places are well known, while others you probably won't find in a guide book. All ten places are special, and we daresay none of these will disappoint. Note that the view does change with the seasons, and some of the recommendations are specifically intended for a certain time of the year. As a rule of thumb, don't waste your time climbing to top panoramic spots on foggy, rainy days. The vista will be very limited and disappointing.

1. **The view from the top of the tower of Palazzo Vecchio ★★★★**
   From here you can get a bird's eye view of all of Florence, including the Duomo, and survey all the little roofs and buildings that make up this sublime city. It also happens to be in a great location on Piazza della Signoria, the beating heart of Florence. The Uffizi Gallery is on one side, the Arno River and Ponte Vecchio are on the other, while the Duomo is only a few minutes away, making it a logical pit stop as you tour the city's main sights. It's best to visit in the summertime, on a clear and sunny day, to fully enjoy the view (the tower is closed to visitors on rainy days).

2. **The view from Piazzale Michelangelo** ★★★★★ Okay, so it's swarming with tourists, but still, what a way to see the entire city! The best time to come is at sunset when the dying sun fills the sky with a warm pink and orange glow, but the monuments of Florence can still be easily recognized from a distance. Once the dark sets in, the lights of Florence come on shining brightly along the river and lighting up its many churches and winding streets. To say the scene is special barely does it justice.

3. **The view from the Torre Grossa in San Gimignano** ★★★★ This is one view that has to be earned. After a tough climb up a fair amount of stairs you will be rewarded with the perfect viewing point for this gorgeous area. The fairy tale medieval town itself is a pleasure to look down upon while the beautiful countryside, filled with vineyards and hills and dotted with little houses, is enchanting.

4. **The view from the bench in Casole d'Elsa** ★★★ Right next to the exit of the lift that takes you from the town's main car park to its center some very smart architect placed a couple of benches facing the view. And what a view! A tapestry of colors, endless fields, and hills which serenely rise and fall far off into the distance. Sit here with someone special, and stare out in silent wonder. The autumn is probably the best moment to enjoy this luscious view (which spreads around the town, too–take a walk along the panoramic ancient walls of Casole).

5. **The view surrounding the Teatro del Silenzio in Lajatico** ★★★★★ Visiting here in summer doesn't do it justice as this sight is at its best after it has rained for a while. If you are visiting Tuscany off-season, in late autumn or early spring, you really must come here for a picnic or even as a quick stop on your way to Volterra. This little corner of Tuscany is spectacular. Even from mid-November to early-December there are still many cold, clear winter days in Tuscany during which you can take in the lush green landscape that stretches out before you. The experience is peaceful, almost meditative, and the fact that it's off-season means it's very unlikely there will be other people around to distract from the amazing outlook.

6. **The view from the Torre del Mangia in Siena** ★★★★★ Much has been written about Piazza del Campo in Siena, Italy's most unique piazza, and the beauty of the Palazzo Publico which stands at the piazza's narrow base. If you have entered the palazzo pubblico, take the opportunity to climb the 290-foot tower, too. It not only affords a wonderful view of the architectural ingenuity of the piazza below, but you will also enjoy a bird's eye view of the entire historical center.

7. **The view from behind the Duomo in Pienza** ★★★★★ This is another area that shows its true beauty off-season, either in May, or on a clear day in winter, when the fields are lush, green, and wild. From here, the views of the famous Val d'Orcia are simply amazing. Combine both with a drive around the stunning Val d'Orcia (ideally, the road from Montalcino to Pienza) to complete a breathtaking experience.

8. **The drive up to Pitigliano** ★★★★ There is a moment as you approach Pitigliano, a splendidly ancient looking town in the Maremma, also known as Little Jerusalem, when the town is suddenly revealed from between the hills. Here, you can see its old buildings towering impressively above the gorge below. It's impossible to resist the urge to stop the car and take a photo. Luckily, there is a small parking lot and a pizzeria on the roadside where you can stop for a quick snap of the quaint, visually imposing town.

9. **The drive from Carrara to Miseglia or Codena** ★★★★ When you drive to Carrara you can already enjoy the spectacular view of the mountains where the white and blue-grey marble quarries are. However if you leave the town and head further up north, to the tiny villages of Miseglia, Codena, Torano or Colonnata (the latter village is also famous for its unique seasoned lard, see tip 133) you are in for a truly magnificent view. White veins crisscross the dark black rock of the mountains while the brilliantly white quarries themselves seem to cascade out of the mountainside. Of course make sure you go on a clear day. Don't go up in bad weather or fog as it's dangerous and you won't see anything anyway. Avoid private roads, which are only meant for service cars, and if you do decide to drive all the way up into the mountains, make sure your car is up for the challenge. A tiny smart or a cinquecento probably won't be powerful enough. To make the best of your day, combine your drive with a tour of the quarries themselves (see tip 133). Cave di Marmo (cavedimarmotours.com), for example, offer three-hour tours in a 4X4 jeep, driving right into the quarries.

10. **The drive from Gaiole in Chianti to Castelnuovo Berardenga** ★★★★
This journey offers the ideal Tuscan scenery. Endless vineyards and rolling hills, small villages and lonesome farmhouses, all sat under the beautiful glowing sun. On a warm summer's day, this is just inspiring.

Torre di Palazzo Vecchio
Piazza della Signoria, Florence. Tel: 055-276-8325, www.museicivicifiorentini.comune.fi.it/palazzovecchio. Open April–September, Friday–Tuesday, 10:00 a.m.–9:00 p.m. and Thursday, 10:00 a.m.–2:00 p.m. Last entry one hour before closing time.

Torre Grossa, Piazza Duomo
2, San Gimignano. Tel: 0577-990-312. Open April 1–September 30, daily, 9:30 a.m.–7:00 p.m.; October–March 31, 11:00 a.m.–5:00 p.m.

Torre del Mangia
Piazza del Campo 1, Siena. Tel: 0577-292-342.Open daily, year round, 10:00 a.m.–7:00 p.m. Last entry: 6:15 p.m. (If visiting off-season, call to make sure the tower doesn't close early, at 4:00 p.m.) Note that the tower closes down in case of rain, regardless of the season.

138 | Visit One of Tuscany's Fun
Antique Markets

For antiques enthusiasts, Tuscany offers great variety. Both casual buyers and more experienced antique hunters can find everything from mid-century silver cutlery and exquisite tea sets to 19th-century lamps, knickknacks and handicrafts, furniture, and even swords (though getting them back through customs might be challenging!).

Florence is a good place to get your first taste of Tuscan antique markets. As the capital of the region, Florence has a nice variety. Piazza Ciompi, for example, hosts a daily antiques market. Though vibrant and popular with plenty of souvenirs to be had, we do find this place to be too touristy. For something more prestigious, head out to the Fortezza Antiquaria market, which is held every third weekend in the garden of Fortezza da Basso, ten minutes' walk from the SMN train station. With just over 120 stands, the market is small but more authentic. Sellers come from all over Italy and antiques are unique and varied, if a little pricey! A third option is the Mercatino dell'Artigianato e del Piccolo Antiquariato, a small market held once a month in Piazza Santo Spirito, where you will find a combination of antiques, knickknacks, and artists selling their handicrafts.

For an ample selection, head towards Arezzo. This off-the-beaten-track beautiful town, located just an hour southwest of Florence, hosts one of the biggest markets in all of Italy. **Arezzo** comes to life once a month when over 500 stalls spread through the historical center—a visit here is a must for curious buyers.

Moving north from Florence, antique lovers and keen buyers will find satisfaction in charming **Lucca**. Though the town is quite small, it boasts a market with over 200 stands—twice the size of Florence's equivalent. Lucca is worth a visit in itself, but we recommended making the special effort to come on market day. To complete your visit, explore some of the town's fantastic little antique shops (see tip 122), where you can interact with experienced antique dealers and hunt for hidden treasures.

Lastly, **Pisa** and **Siena** also have their own markets. In Pisa, the second weekend of every month, there is an interesting little market on Piazza Cavalieri and the surrounding streets. Buyers can pick up ancient books, delicate china, hats, antique furniture, jewelry, and much more. The few but interesting antique shops dotted across Pisa (see tip number 99) will fulfill the needs of more serious buyers. Smaller **Siena** also has a monthly antiques market with about 100 stands in Piazza del Mercato, just behind the Palazzo Publico in Piazza del Campo.

Arezzo ★★★★ Piazza della Republica and the adjacent streets, the first weekend of every month, 9:00 a.m.-6:00 p.m. (may close earlier during the winter months).

Lucca ★★★ In the area around Via del Battistero, Piazza San Martino, Piazza San Giusto, etc., the third weekend of every month, 8:30 a.m.-7:00 p.m. The market usually closes down from January to March

Florence ★★★ Mercato di Piazza Ciompi, open Monday-Saturday, 9:00 a.m.-1:30 p.m.; Fortezza Antiquaria, third weekend of the month, closed in July and August; Mercatino dell'Artigianato e del Piccolo Antiquariaro, Piazza Santo Spirtio, second Sunday of the month, closed in July and August.

Pisa ★★★ Piazza Cavallieri, second weekend of the month, including July and August. The market may not take place off season.

Siena ★★★Piazza del Mercato, third Sunday of the month, usually closed in August.

Index by subject

Wine Tastings and Tours

GUIDED TOURS

NOBILE DI MONTEPULCIANO ESTATES

CHIANTI ESTATES

SUPER-TUSCAN ESTATES

VERNACCIA ESTATES

BRUNELLO ESTATES

OTHER

Artisanal Produce

Cooking Classes

Brunch, Aperitivo & Nightlife

Attractions & Activities

Shopping

Events and Markets

Spas & Thermal Pools

Page 7, Francesco R. Iacomino/Shutterstock.com; Page 10, JeniFoto/Shutterstock.com; Page 14, FooTToo/Shutterstock.com; Page 15, Malgorzata Kistryn/Shutterstock.com; Page 17, Maxim Blinkov/Shutterstock.com; Page 22, Peter Bernik/Shutterstock.com; Page 25, ilolab/Shutterstock.com; Page 28, Goodluz/Shutterstock.com; Page 33, The Royal Suite Living Room at the Four Seasons, photographer: Barbara Kraft, photo courtesy of the Four Seasons Hotel Firenze; Pages 34&35, Terazza Brunelleschi and Sala Pano, photo courtesy of Grand Hotel Baglioni; Page 36, The Panoramic Restaurant at the Westin Excelsior Hotel, Florence. Photo courtesy of the Westin Excelsior Hotel, Florence; Page 37, photos courtesy of Il Santo Bevitore Restaurant; Page 38, Caminoel/Shutterstock.com; Page 39, Scenes from the opera, photos courtesy of St. Mark's Opera Florence; Page 40, niepo/Shutterstock.com; Page 42, photo courtesy of Florence with a view apartments; Page 43, photos courtesy of Vestri ice cream shop; Page 46, top photo: TixXio/Shutterstock.com, bottom photo: Naten/Shutterstock.com ; Page 48 , martiapunts/Shutterstock.com; Page 49, Kzenon/Shutterstock.com; Page 50, photo courtesy of Pistocchi; Page 51, photos courtesy of Soulspace Spa; Page 53, Denis and Yulia Pogostins/Shutterstock.com; page 54, Subbotina Anna/Shutterstock.com; Page 55, fotocociredef73/Shutterstock.com; Page 57, samarttiw/Shutterstock; Page 60, top photo: Il Palagio Restaurant, photographer: Peter Vitale, bottom photo: The Royal Suite Living Room at the Four Seasons Hotel, Florence, photographer: Barbara kraft. Both photos are courtesy of the Four Season Hotel Firenze. Page 61, the Four Seasons Hotel Spa, photographer: Peter Vitale, photo courtesy on the Four Seasons Hotel Firenze; Page 62, top photo courtesy of the Santo Graal Restaurant, bottom photo: Ariela Bankier; Page 64, photos courtesy of the Magnani Feroni Hotel; Page 65, photographer: Ariela Bankier; Page 66: Baloncici/Shutterstock.com; Page 67, Warren Price Photography/Shutterstock.com; Page 68, top photo: photo courtesy of Flo concept store, Florence. Bottom photo: courtesy of Il Fiorentino, Florence; page 70, top photo: courtesy of the Genten Firenze, bottom photo: courtesy of the Scuola del Cuoio, Firenze; Page 72, photo courtesy of Madova gloves; Page 73&74, photographer: Ariela Bankier; Page 75, photographer: Ariela Bankier; Page 77, top photo: courtesy of Bartolini. Bottom photo, Ariela Bankier. Page 78: Ariela Bankier; Page 79, photo courtesy of Sartoria Rossi; Page 80, photo courtesy of Loretta Caponi; Page 81, photo courtesy of Gonnelli 1585; Page 82, Villa Petraia, Malgorzata Kistryn/Shutterstock.com; Page 84, photo courtesy of The Mall; Page 86, photos courtesy of Gonnelli 1585; Page 87, top photo: 4Max/Shutterstock.com. Bottom photo: photo courtesy of Castello Poppiano; Page 89, photo courtesy of Castello Spaltenna; Page 90, photo of THE LABYRINTH by Jeff Saward - photo courtesy of the Chianti Sculpture Park; Page 91, Polifoto/Shutterstock.com; Page 92, photo of Castello di Ama and the art work on the estate, all rights reserved to Alessandro Moggi (www.alessandromoggi.com); Page 93, MARCELODLT/Shutterstock.com; Page 94&95, photos of Badia a Coltibuono, all rights reserved to Nedo Baglioni; Page 96, photo of Dario Cecchini –Antica Macelleria, photograpger: Tommaso Iorio; Page 98 & 99, photos of the Antinori Cantine, courtesy of Marchesi Antinori; Page 100, top photo: Malgorzata Kistryn/Shutterstock.com, bottom photo: all rights reserved to Alessandro Moggi (www.alessandromoggi.com); Page 101, all rights reserved to Alessandro Moggi (www.alessandromoggi.com); Page 103, Alessandro Colle/Shutterstock.com; Page 104, photos courtesy of Castello Fonterutoli ; Page 107, photo of Brolio castle, bonzodog/Shutterstock.com; Page 109, photo courtesy of Castello di Spaltenna; Page 110, photo courtesy of La Bottega di Giovannino; Page 111, photo courtesy of Lamole Restaurant; Page 112, photos courtesy of the Borgo San Felice Resort; Page 113, photo courtesy of La Bottega del 30 Restaurant; Page 114, photo courtesy of Le Fonatanelle Hotel; Page 116, photos courtesy of Podere Fornaci; Page 117 & 118, photos courtesy of Campo Regio Relais, Siena;

NOTES

Made in the USA
San Bernardino, CA
22 November 2015